FOOD LOVERS'
GUIDE TO
BALTIMORE

The Best Restaurants, Markets & Local Culinary Offerings

1st Edition

Kathy Wielech Patterson & Neal Patterson

Guilford, Connecticut

To buy books in quantity for corporate use
or incentives, call **(800) 962-0973**
or e-mail **premiums@GlobePequot.com**.

Editor: Kevin Sirois
Project Editor: Lauren Brancato
Layout Artist: Mary Ballachino
Text Design: Sheryl Kober
Illustrations by Jill Butler with additional art by Carleen Moira Powell and MaryAnn Dubé
Maps: Melissa Baker © Morris Book Publishing, LLC

ISBN 978-0-7627-8109-6

Printed in the United States of America
10 9 8 7 6 5 4 3 2 1

All the information in this guidebook is subject to change. We recommend that you call ahead to obtain current information before traveling.

Contents

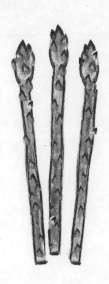

Recipes, 301

Appendices, 330

About the Authors

Back in the mid-1970s, on a trip to London and Paris with her family, **Kathy Wielech Patterson** started her first food blog, only back then it was called a diary. While there were entries about fun stuff like the multiple visits she made to Harrods' toy department, there were more notes about food than anything. These days Kathy would rather poke around in jewelry stores or the beauty floor at Bergdorf's than shop for Barbies, but she's still obsessed with food. She started the blog Minxeats.com in 2005, roping in her husband, Neal, as an accomplice, and has ever since shared their adventures both in restaurants and their own kitchen with the world. They also write the blog AllTopChef.com. Kathy is a graphic designer and avid blogger who has written for *Sniffapalooza* and *Baltimore* magazines. She and Neal live in Baltimore with their cat, Julie, and dog, Milo.

Neal Patterson spent several years in public relations and later worked as a financial writer for a major investment firm. It was during this time that he formed a small independent publishing company with a friend, first producing a pulp-style fiction magazine titled *Nemo,* then moving on to comic books with the action comic

Iron Angel and the all-ages fantasy yarn *Forty Winks*. Yearning to break free of the corporate world, Neal ventured into the murky waters of freelance writing. Since then he has written horror fiction for the anthology *The Dead Walk!*, contributed to websites as diverse as Hey Kids, Comics! and *Sniffapalooza Magazine,* and coauthors the blogs Minxeats.com and AllTopChef.com with his wife, Kathy. Neal lives and eats in Baltimore.

Acknowledgments

I got into food blogging for two reasons: I like to write and I like to eat. I also like to write about eating. So after six years of doing both on the blog Minxeats.com—and enjoying it immensely—I was thrilled to get the opportunity to put together an actual book on the subject.

I want to start by thanking my dad, Dennis Wielech, who instilled in me an adventurous palate. While he denies anything to do with my passion for calamari, sushi, or okra, without his introductions to Szechuan, Japanese, and Indian foods, I'd probably still be eating Spam and Velveeta. (OK, no, I wouldn't.) My late mom, Teresa, and grandmother, Katarzyna, were also big influences on my eating habits, particularly my peculiar enjoyment of chicken cartilage and random pig parts. I hope that they would be proud of me. And *dzieki* too to my brother David, fellow adventurous eater, who has long been one of my dining partners in crime. And he loves me enough to have preordered this book from Amazon.com way back in May of 2012, while we were still writing it.

Grazie mille to all of the Baltimore-area foodies and bloggers who offered up their favorite restaurants and otherwise cheered us on with this project, especially *HowChow*'s Brent Mitchell and *Mango & Ginger*'s Kit Pollard. We particularly would like to thank Dara Bunjon, the ladies at PRofiles Inc. (especially Marianne Ortiz,

Jamie Watt Arnold, and Amy Burke Friedman), Shelby Goldman of Bullfrog & Baum, Sergio Vitale, and David Derewicz for their time, generosity, and general assistance with this project.

And let's not forget a big *gracias* to our editor, Kevin Sirois, who had the fine judgment to hire us to write this book and made it seem rather easy.

I owe the most gratitude to my dining partner for life, Neal Patterson, who has eaten my occasionally experimental cooking for over a dozen years now without complaint. He's encouraged my writing and was happy to take this project on as my co-writer. Without him, I would not even be here. (Literally, he saved my life once . . . I'll spare you the long, gross story.)

—*Kathy Wielech Patterson*

I've wanted to be a writer from the time I learned how to string words into sentences. The foodie thing started much later. So I must first thank my late father, George Patterson, for encouraging my literary aspirations by buying me every comic book, magazine, and book I ever asked for without question; reading every fledgling bit of prose I presented to him; and offering me words of encouragement and criticism as needed. I am also tremendously grateful to my mother, Florence, for all her love, support, and encouragement in both my literary and foodie pursuits. After all, if she hadn't taught me how to make spaghetti and meatballs as a child, I don't know if I would have had any interest in food at all. And special thanks to my brother Craig for joining Kathy and me on our culinary adventures and providing his own gastronomic insights.

Regarding this book, I wish to thank all the waiters, waitresses, store clerks, and baristas who provided us with valuable information about their respective establishments and the culinary goodies they serve. We're equally grateful to the chefs who were gracious enough to share their favorite recipes with us. A big thank-you to our editor, Kevin Sirois, who gave us this opportunity to tell the world about our city and guided us through the process.

Most of all, I have to thank Kathy Wielech Patterson for bringing out the inner foodie in me. While I always enjoyed experimenting in the kitchen, Kathy showed me why certain flavors work together, how to balance flavors and textures, and generally how to cook well. For opening the whole amazing world of food to me, and for a million other reasons, I will always be her grateful and willing sous chef.

—*Neal Patterson*

Introduction

When most people think about Baltimore cuisine, one thought usually jumps to mind: the blue crab. While this may seem like a stereotype, it is not a notion to be underestimated. Sitting at the top of the Chesapeake Bay, Baltimore has long benefited from the seafood treasures swimming and crawling in the waters at its doorstep. Just as Maine is known for lobster, Maryland is known for blue crab. Baltimoreans love to sit around a picnic table on a hot summer night with pitchers of beer, ripping into a dozen or more crabs. And if one is repulsed by the idea of having a pile of steaming crustaceans dumped on the dining table to be attacked with a mallet, there's always the more user-friendly crab cake. A sublime combination of sweet crabmeat and spicy Old Bay seasoning formed into a convenient patty, the crab cake alone should win Baltimore culinary immortality.

As with anything, however, there's more to the story, and Baltimore certainly has more to offer than seafood. Historically, the city's food scene was influenced by the diverse ethnic groups who immigrated to our neighborhoods, starting with the Germans

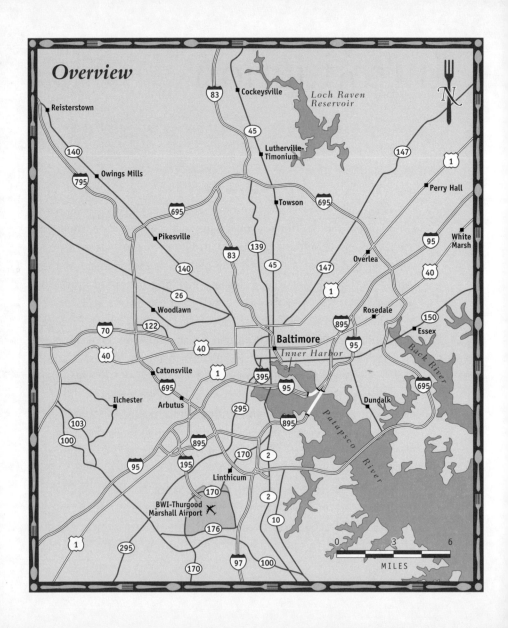

Overview

Reisterstown

Cockeysville

Loch Raven Reservoir

140

Owings Mills

795

Lutherville-Timonium

45

83

147

1

Perry Hall

695

Towson

695

Pikesville

95

White Marsh

83

139

140

45

147

Overlea

40

26

1

Woodlawn

Rosedale

70

895

122

40

150

Essex

Baltimore

Back River

40

Inner Harbor

95

Catonsville

1

695

395

695

Ilchester

Arbutus

95

Dundalk

103

295

895

Patapsco River

100

895

170

2

95

195

Linthicum

170

2

BWI-Thurgood Marshall Airport ✈

10

176

1

295

170

97

100

0   3   6

MILES

in the 1800s and followed by the Italians, Poles, and Greeks. More recently, growing Latino and Indian communities have widened the food spectrum. Today the city's restaurants and markets offer a taste of virtually every cuisine in the world. Whether you're craving moussaka, *carne asada,* pad thai, or lamb *saag,* you will find it in Baltimore.

Growing up in Baltimore in the 1970s, the fine-dining scene was dominated by what our parents called "continental cuisine." Haussner's in Highlandtown featured as many items on their menu as the number of paintings that filled every square inch of its walls. Diners could enjoy elk steak, lobster dainties, or chicken croquettes, and their strawberry pie was legend. Danny's on Charles Street served Caesar salad tableside, the waiter assembling each element with care. Sadly, those fine landmark restaurants are long gone, but Baltimore has a new generation of chefs who are creating the next landmark restaurants, reflecting current trends and sensibilities.

Living in the shadow of our nation's capital 40 miles to the south, Baltimore has often suffered a bit of an inferiority complex, and that is no more true than in its dining scene. While the city cannot boast of having as many celebrity chefs or nationally acclaimed restaurants, there remains an underdog mentality that spurs on the ever-growing gastronomic experience. The development in recent years of Harbor East, with its myriad dining choices, speaks to the city's indomitable foodie spirit. We hope a little bit of that spirit is reflected in these pages.

How to Use This Book

As with most old cities, Baltimore City is a collection of neighborhoods. The restaurants are listed according to their respective neighborhoods. Baltimore County wraps around the city like a shawl, with the southern end more or less occupied by the Patapsco River. Therefore, we have divided the county into three basic regions: North, East, and West. Within these categories, the restaurants are listed alphabetically under:

Foodie Faves

These are the restaurants we feel are well worth your time to visit. Some are new, while some have been around for years, but all offer great food.

Landmarks

The restaurants in this section have stood the test of time and are generally known as the best at their respective cuisines. If you ask a Baltimorean for dining recommendations, these are most likely the restaurants he or she will mention.

Specialty Stores, Markets & Producers

Helping you navigate the array of bakeries, specialty stores, and markets in the area, this section will guide you to the best pastries or those hard-to-find ingredients.

Recipes

At the back of the book, local chefs offer some of their favorite recipes for you to try at home.

Price Code

Each listing provides an easy price code indicating the average cost of a single entree.

$	**Less than $10**
$$	**$10 to $20**
$$$	**$20 to $30**
$$$$	**$30 or more**

Keeping Up with Food News

Baltimore **magazine,** baltimoremagazine.net. For decades, *Baltimore* magazine has been covering city life from all its myriad aspects. The "Best of Baltimore" issues are received with particular anticipation to see what they think are the best places in Baltimore. Each spring their "Best Restaurants in Baltimore" issue draws interest from foodies, who argue over the magazine's appraisals. *Baltimore* magazine's food blog, *In Good Taste* (baltimoremagazine.net/ingoodtaste), written by food editor Suzanne Loudermilk, provides up-to-date information on Baltimore's food scene.

Baltimore Dining Examiner, examiner.com/dining-in-balti more/dara-bunjon. Examiner.com is an online source for information about the community, with articles written by local contributors. Dara Bunjon, who runs her own public relations business called Dara Does It—Creative Solutions for the Food Industry, writes the *Dining in Baltimore* blog. Her broad background and insider connections provide her with a unique perspective on all things food related. Also check out her other blog, *Dining Dish,* at diningdish.net.

The Baltimore Sun, baltimoresun.com. As the only major daily newspaper in Baltimore, the *Sun* covers all things Baltimore, including food. Richard Gorelick provides restaurant reviews in both the print and online versions of the paper, while his online blog, *Baltimore Diner,* covers the latest news and events in the Baltimore dining scene. You can also sign up for their weekly *Food and Drink Newsletter,* which is e-mailed to subscribers every Thursday.

City Paper, citypaper.com. For decades, Wednesday's free weekly has offered the hip, alternative perspective on Baltimore life. Our favorite section of the *City Paper* is the one on food, which includes columns like "Free Range" and "Cheap Eats" (restaurant reviews) in the print edition and lots more online. Their blog, *Feedbag,* is a potpourri of foodie news. Articles from other blogs, such as BrokeAssGourmet.com, are also featured in the Eats section of the online edition.

DonRockwell.com, donrockwell.com. This chatboard for Baltimore and DC foodies sports many food-knowledgeable members who are always happy to share information on local restaurants and food events.

Downtown Diane, downtowndiane.net. If you want the lowdown on Baltimore's restaurants, attractions, and events, Downtown Diane's website will fill you in. She also writes a column on the local CBS website (baltimore.cbslocal.com/tag/dishin-with-downtown-diane).

Style **magazine,** baltimorestyle.com/index .php/style/dining/front. A bimonthly lifestyle magazine, *Style* covers all aspects of Baltimore life with vibrant photography and sharp writing. Their Food & Dining section provides restaurant reviews, wine advice, recipes, and articles related to food and entertaining.

Bloggers

Adventures in Baltimore Restaurants, adventuresbaltimore.com. Blogger Jessica Lemmo updates her blog regularly with news on Baltimore-area food events, restaurant openings, and special deals, and she occasionally posts a dining review.

Baltimore Pizza Club, baltimorepizzaclub.blogspot.com. The group who writes this blog are completely obsessed with pizza. Not only do they review all the pizza restaurants in the Baltimore area, they provide pizza news, reviews of frozen pizza, and any odd tidbits of pizza-related business they can find. Reading it will make you crave pizza in a big way.

Baltimore Restaurant Reviews by Bob Ganoosh, bobganoosh .blogspot.com. Shawn Eccleston (aka Bob Ganoosh) heads a group of foodies who provide reviews of area restaurants from the point of view of young professionals. This means the reviews lean toward places that serve hearty comfort food and spirit-lifting beverages. Good food at low prices is also emphasized. This is a great resource if you are looking for local haunts with soul-satisfying cuisine.

The Baltimore Snacker, baltimoresnacker.blogspot.com. The Baltimore *City Paper*'s Best Local Blog for 2010 is always an entertaining read. In addition to offering his opinion on recent dining experiences, John Donohue is cooking his way through every state in the union. An older—and entertaining—series on his blog titled Snackin' Around the Beltway details his foodie finds near the exits on I-695.

Black Coffee and a Donut, blackcoffeeandadonut .blogspot.com. The Podolny sisters, Xani and Erin, write about their dining experiences in an infectious manner that makes readers want to be there with them. They're avid home cooks as well. This one is always an entertaining read.

Always More to Blog About

There are oodles of food bloggers in the Baltimore metro area. Those that talk about the local restaurant scene are outlined in the introduction, but we feel it's important also to mention the bloggers who concentrate mostly on home cooking. After all, we can't eat in restaurants every day. Here are some of our very favorites:

Angry Asian Creations (angryasiancreations.com)
Coconut & Lime (coconutandlime.com)
Grace Before Meals (gracebeforemeals.com/soul)
LoveFeast Table (lovefeasttable.com/blog)
My Morning Chocolate (mymorningchocolate.com)
990 Square (990square.com)
Pleasant Living (blahabakes.com)
Savory Simple (savorysimple.net)
Tasty Trix (tastytrix.blogspot.com)

The City That Feeds, citythatfeeds.com. With an acerbic, irreverent style, the City That Breeds takes a look at the quirkier side of Baltimore. While the posts cover many topics, a good portion of the site is devoted to area restaurants and food. If you like a little bite to your humor, it's a fun blog to peruse.

Crab Cake Review, crabcakereview.com. Want to know if the crab cakes at X restaurant are worth a try? Check out *Crab Cake*

Review first for an honest opinion on the subject. If the restaurant in question isn't on the blog, you can submit your own review.

Disco Files, discosaturday.blogspot.com. Disco Files touches on various subjects, but its take on local food, particularly sandwiches, is extremely entertaining, detailed, and well thought-out.

Food, Wine, Beer, Culture, foodandwineblog .com. Although based in Baltimore, this blog covers wine, beer, culture, and fine dining in New York, New England, and other parts of the world. The Baltimore/ DC section provides a helpful directory of restaurants, farmers' markets, wine bars, and wine shops, along with tips on the best happy-hour deals and wine dinners.

HowChow, howchow.blogspot.com. An indispensable source for those interested in the Howard County dining scene, Brent Mitchell's blog gives readers the lowdown on openings, closings, and what's worth eating in HoCo and environs.

Mango & Ginger, mangoandginger.blogspot.com. Kit Pollard, who also does restaurant reviews for the *Baltimore Sun,* is a detail-oriented writer. Whether it's a restaurant review or a new recipe she's just tried out, Kit brings you into the story so you can practically taste the food. While Mango & Ginger touches on a variety of topics in the world of pop culture and design, much of it is food related. We particularly enjoy her adventures in cooking and new foodie finds.

Strawberries in Paris, strawberriesinparis.com. Elizabeth Maria is an environmental chemist with a love for strawberries and Paris. Although her posts cover many areas of interest, she devotes a good part of the blog to baking and cooking recipes. It's quirky, warm, and fun.

Taste of Baltimore, tasteofbaltimore.blogspot.com. Nakiya Vasi Schurman has frequent obsessions, most of which revolve around food. Her blog presents her favorite recipes along with restaurant reviews and foodie news.

This Is Gonna Be Good, thisisgonnabegood.blogspot.com. With a conversational writing style and excellent photography, *This Is Gonna Be Good* covers restaurants from all over the country but focuses primarily on the Baltimore food scene. If you are a Baltimorean who travels around a bit, this blog can give you some eating tips when you're out of town.

Unique Culinary Adventures, uniqueculinaryadventures .blogspot.com. When Jake Slagle is not pursuing his interest in mineralogy, he is looking for exotic food experiences. From raccoon stew to fried duck tongues, Jake will go where most foodies have never gone before. It's great fun to read about the culinary road less traveled.

Festivals & Events

February

Health Care for the Homeless Chocolate Affair, Baltimore Waterfront Marriott Hotel, chocolateaffair.org. This charity event brings together some of Baltimore's best restaurants, caterers, and chocolatiers for an extravagant evening of hors d'oeuvres, a chocolate-inspired dinner, and desserts.

March

Beer, Bourbon, and BBQ Festival, Timonium Fairgrounds, beerandbourbon.com/maryland/show-info. As they say on their website, the festival is "a great day of beer sippin', bourbon tastin', music listenin', cigar smokin', and barbeque eatin'." Your admission to one of *Baltimore* magazine's Best Festivals entitles you to a sampling glass so you can taste as many of the 40 bourbons and 60 beers as you like. The barbecue covers the gamut from pulled pork to ribs to chicken and sausages. Live rock, blues, and bluegrass provide the background music to your day of decadence. ***Note:*** The scheduling of this event can change from year to year.

Lunch with the Elephants, Lexington Market, lexingtonmarket .com/annual. While not exactly a foodie event for humans, the peckish pachyderms from Ringling Bros. and Barnum & Bailey Circus enjoy their annual vegetarian buffet lunch at the Lexington Market each March when the circus arrives in town. While performing at Baltimore's 1st Mariner Arena, the ele-phants take a walk up Eutaw Street to the market for an abundant buffet of 1,100 oranges, 1,000 apples, 500 heads of lettuce, 700 bananas, 400 pears, and 500 carrots. The curious spectators are entertained by live music and circus clowns.

April

City Paper Brew Fest Fells Point, weekly.citypaper.com. This annual festival, held rain or shine at the Broadway Square, celebrates the best in local, national, and international brews by tapping dozens of kegs for your drinking pleasure. You can sample from more than 80 beers, meet and mingle with beer enthusiasts, and enjoy music and karaoke.

June

Great Grapes Wine, Arts & Food Festival, Oregon Ridge Park, uncorkthefun.com/hunt-valley-maryland/site-info. With more than 200 wines from 20 local wineries, this festival is a must for those who want to learn more about Maryland's wine industry. In addition to wine, special pavilions focus on other culinary experiences such as cheese, grilling, seafood, spices, and olive oil. Cooking competitions and demonstrations complement the musical entertainment.

Latinofest, Patterson Park, latinofest.org. Since 1980, this celebration of Hispanic culture has entertained Baltimoreans with its Latin music, colorful costumes, and cuisine from the Caribbean and the Americas.

St. Nicholas Greek Folk Festival, St. Nicholas Greek Orthodox Church, greekfolkfestival.org. The Showcase of Nations Ethnic Festival season kicks off with this event begun in the mid-1970s, voted by *Baltimore* magazine as one of Baltimore's Best Festivals in 2011. In addition to the music, dancing, and shopping, the festival is famous for its authentic Greek cuisine made entirely at home by members of the community. Visitors can dine on traditional dishes like spanakopita, souvlaki, and moussaka. You may also wish to try the St. Nicholas specialty dessert galaktoboureko, a custard-filled phyllo pastry with a light honey syrup. For those who wish to escape the heat for a while, cooking classes are held in the library.

July

African American Festival, M&T Bank Stadium Lots B and C, african americanfestival.net. A family-oriented celebration of African-American life, music, and culture, the three-day event features numerous food vendors with everything from Jamaican-style jerk chicken to more conventional festival fare like funnel cake.

Artscape, Mount Royal, artscape.org. This one is a biggie! America's largest free arts festival features three days of live concerts on three outdoor stages, opera and theater performances at nearby locations, more than 150 fine artists, fashion designers, and craftspeople either exhibiting or selling their wares, and a stunning array of food and beverages reflecting cultures from around the world. Locals have been known to refer to this festival as "Foodscape."

Caribbean Carnival Festival, Clifton Park, itsbmorecarnival .com. The biggest attractions for this festival are the carnival parade, reggae and soca music, and the dancers in colorful costumes, but you might want to stick around for the jerk chicken and Carib beer.

September

Moveable Feast's Dining Out for Life, diningout forlife.com/baltimore. For one night in September, participating restaurants in the Baltimore metropolitan area donate at least 20 percent of their proceeds to support AIDS service organizations. The annual event raises tens of thousands of dollars to help feed those in the community who suffer from HIV/AIDS or other challenging diseases like breast cancer.

October

Fells Point Fun Festival, Fells Point, preservationsociety.com. During the first weekend in October, South Ann Street, Thames Street, and Broadway are crowded with arts-and-crafts vendors, merchants of international goods, fine artists, entertainers, and food vendors offering cuisine from all over the world. For nearly half a century, this event has been a major draw in Baltimore.

Lexington Market Annual Chocolate Festival, Lexington Market, lexingtonmarket.com/annual. In mid-October Lexington Market becomes a chocolate lover's nirvana when the annual chocolate festival plays host to the best chocolatiers and bakeries in the Baltimore area. Cakes, cookies, pies, and all manner of fruits covered in chocolate are to be had. Come for the chocolate, but stay for the live music, cooking demonstrations, and the chocolate-eating contest.

Maryland Brewer's Oktoberfest, Timonium Fairgrounds, balti morebeerweek.com. As part of Baltimore Beer Week, the Brewer's Association of Maryland holds its annual Oktoberfest featuring more than 80 beers from 15 local breweries. The food is pure German with bratwurst, sauerkraut, schnitzel, potato pancakes, and pretzels. There's live oompah music and contests as well.

Russian Festival, Holy Trinity Russian Orthodox Church, russfest .org. The Showcase of Nations festival season closes with this annual celebration of all things Russian. The extensive food selections are all made by the parishioners. In addition to a wide array of homemade breads, the festival features authentic Russian dishes like kolbasa, borscht, and blinis. There's also an authentic Russian tearoom.

Taste of the Nation Baltimore, American Visionary Art Museum, strength.org/baltimore. A lavish evening of wine and fine dining provided by major area chefs. All proceeds from ticket sales go to support Share Our Strength's No Kid Hungry program.

November

Maryland Irish Festival, Maryland State Fairgrounds, irishfes tival.com. Irish Charities of Maryland, Inc. sponsors this annual event that features live music, competitive events, lectures, play areas for children, and food. Among the Irish specialties are Irish stew, fish-and-chips, ham, cabbage, and soda bread. You can wash it down with an Irish coffee, a Black & Tan, or Irish whiskey.

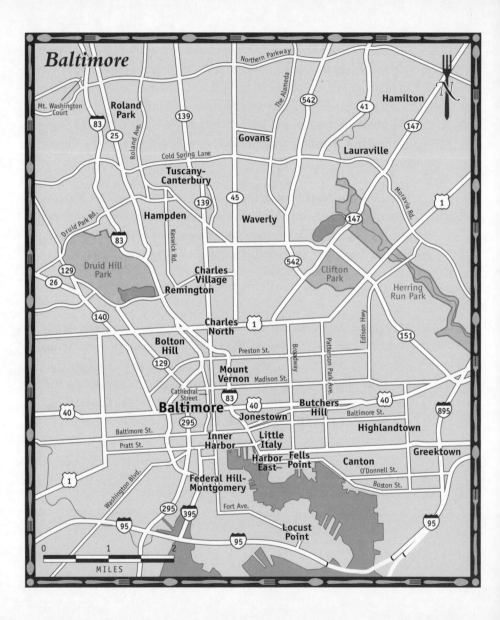

South Baltimore

The South Baltimore Peninsula provides the southern border of the Inner Harbor and is home to several neighborhoods, including Federal Hill and Locust Point. Federal Hill Park, established during the Civil War when Union soldiers trained cannons on the city to quash any Southern sympathies, is a must-see location for visitors as its high elevation allows for a perfect view of the Baltimore skyline. Federal Hill itself received its name more than 70 years earlier when a celebration was held there in honor of the ratification of the US Constitution.

One of the first neighborhoods in Baltimore to experience urban renewal, Federal Hill feels like a cozy little community with a plethora of restaurants, pubs, and shops clustered along its narrow streets. Any foodie can do some serious eating and drinking there without a whole lot of walking.

Nearby Locust Point has experienced a similar gentrification thanks in part to the Locust Point Industrial Area and sportswear manufacturer Under Armour. While the neighborhood has its share of narrow, brick row houses like Federal Hill, Locust Point is more a mix of old and new, reflecting the continuing industrial development of the area. While not exactly the same pub-crawling environment as Federal Hill, Locust Point has a wide variety of restaurants in close proximity.

Foodie Faves

The Abbey Burger Bistro, 1041 Marshall St., Federal Hill, Baltimore, MD 21230; (443) 453-9698; abbeyburgerbistro.com; Burgers; $. It seems like burger restaurants are popping up everywhere—they're the bagel shops of the early 21st century. Even famous chefs have gotten into the act, so it's no wonder that Baltimore sports at least one specialty burger restaurant. At the Abbey Burger Bistro, there's a whole barnyard worth of burgers on the menu: beef, turkey, chicken, lamb, bison, kangaroo, elk, wild boar, duck, and red elk. Toppings can be equally exotic, like peanut butter, crab dip, and pineapple. Though we don't necessarily recommend that particular combination on the same burger, at Abbey you can definitely have it your way, with any of 50 or so cheeses and toppings, your choice of bread (or lettuce, for the low-carbers), and an assortment of meat and veggie patties. If a chili-and-cheddar-topped burger isn't decadent enough for you, milkshakes seem to be the de facto accompaniment—at Abbey you can get yours spiked. But a beer from the regularly updated menu of bottles and draughts might be a better, and less-caloric, option.

Baba's Mediterranean Kitchen, 745 E. Fort Ave., Locust Point, Baltimore, MD 21230; (410) 727-7482; babaskitchen.net; Mediterranean; $. The first thing that will get your attention at Baba's is the colorful tiles that decorate the walls and counter. Painted by local designer Kinnereth Ellentuck and artist Rebecca Castle, they lend a Middle-East-meets-Maryland flair to a typical exposed-brick row-house interior. Farid Salloum's charming cafe has only a handful of tables (made from bowling alley lanes), but it does a bang-up carryout business. If you choose to dine in at this BYOB establishment, you're rewarded with no corkage fee, not to mention some yummy food. "Mediterranean" at Baba's encompasses dishes from the Middle East as well as Italy and Greece, so both a Caprese salad and superlative hummus are on the menu; the smoky eggplant dip, cleverly called "Baba's Ghannouge," is one of the best around. There's plenty for vegetarians to enjoy, and many items on the menu are gluten-free. If you can tolerate gluten, don't leave without trying the crisp pistachio-filled baklava with a cup of cardamom coffee.

Blue Agave Restaurante Y Tequileria, 1032 Light St., Federal Hill, Baltimore, MD 21230; (410) 576-3938; blueagaverestaurant .com; Mexican; $$. Blue Agave, located a stone's throw from Cross Street Market, offers authentic Mexican food and lots and lots of tequila to wash it down. While a regular margarita—on the rocks with salt—is always an option, we're partial to the spicy Guavarita, which adds chilis, guava, and pineapple juice to the classic tequila-and-lime combo. As for the food, while you'll be tempted to fill up on the addictive tortilla chips and trio of salsas that come to the table while you peruse the menu, save room for the fresh guacamole, the simple yet delicious tequila-lime shrimp quesadilla, and tender slow-roasted pork carnitas. For something a little different, try the portobello relleno, which is stuffed with goat cheese and the unusual fungus known as huitlacoche and topped with a nutty mole Chatino.

Bluegrass Tavern, 1500 S. Hanover St.; Federal Hill, Baltimore, MD 21230; (410) 244-5101; bluegrasstavern.com; Modern American; $$$. Don't let Bluegrass Tavern's casual atmosphere belie the fine-dining nature of their cuisine. Sure, it's called a tavern, but it's a tavern that serves boudin made with pheasant and black cod served with sea beans and saffron-poached mussels. The kitchen really has a way with proteins, be they familiar, like a rib eye, or something more exotic, like venison, but it also turns out some mean crawfish hush puppies and macaroni and cheese. Food like this begs for a nice glass of wine or a well-matched beer, and bar manager Kelli Kulnich and wine director Christopher Coker make it easy for you by listing both wine and beer recommendations for each dish on the menu. Should you want something harder, the staff would be happy to help you select one of the nearly 30 brands of bourbon available.

Harborque, 1421 Lawrence St., Locust Point, Baltimore, MD 21230; (410) 685-7675; harborque.com; Barbecue; $$. This little joint isn't much to look at, but you'll be too busy shoving pork into your mouth to really notice. Smoked over hickory for more than half a day, their pulled pork is a moist and vinegary Carolina-style preparation piled high on a bun with your choice of sauce (or not). You can also get it piled atop nachos or french fries. There's plenty more meat on the menu, including tender pit beef, ham, and smoked turkey and brisket. If you're looking for something more messy to tackle, try the Combo for a King—half a smoked chicken with half a rack of smoked baby backs. With two sides, it's less than $20 and big enough to feed a king, queen, and maybe a prince too.

Hersh's Pizza & Drinks, 1843-45 Light St., Federal Hill, Baltimore, MD 21230; (443) 438-4948; hershspizza.com; Pizza; $$. Chef/Co-Owner Josh Hershkovitz has worked at two of the best restaurants in town, Charleston and Petit Louis, so you know he has some kitchen chops. He opened Hersh's with his sister, Stephanie, to, as they put it so nobly, "feed people and liquor 'em up." Their two-story restaurant, decorated with amazing murals and trompe l'oeil wood paneling by artist Kerry Cesen, is a fine place to imbibe, whether it be wine, beer, or a cocktail like the amusingly named Ape & Rooster (Aperol, grapefruit juice, lime, Cava). Food choices include a couple of pastas, one a silky homemade tagliatelle with asparagus, mint, chèvre, and pistachios, and a selection of Italian-inspired small plates. There is also, of course, pizza, which is baked in a wood oven and has a Neapolitan-style thin and crispy crust.

Toppings are inspired, like kale and pistachios, or clam with garlic and lemon. Additional toppings are just as interesting and include fried eggplant and mortadella.

Matsuri, 1105 S. Charles St., Federal Hill, Baltimore, MD 21230; (410) 752-8561; matsuri.us; Japanese; $$. For many years, if you asked Baltimoreans about their favorite sushi restaurant, the answer was almost invariably Matsuri. There are many more Japanese restaurants in town now, but Matsuri is still mentioned with some regularity. We've always liked this snug restaurant located across the street from the Cross Street Market. Unfortunately, that gives it the same flaw as most other restaurants in the neighborhood: Parking can be a problem. But don't let that stop you from trying (hint: eat early). Matsuri has some of the freshest fish in town, but there's plenty besides sushi on their menu, including a selection of donburi (rice bowl dishes) and robatayaki (grilled items).

Miguel's Cocina y Cantina, 1200 Steuart St., Locust Point, Baltimore, MD 21230; miguelsbaltimore.com; (443) 438-3139; Mexican; $$. Starting in childhood, Miguel's owner Michael Marx took many a trip across the border to experience the food and culture of Mexico. With that passion for food . . . and tequila . . . in his heart, he opened up Miguel's. And that's a good thing for those of us who enjoy eating mole and sipping blood-orange margaritas while sitting in a dining room festooned with items commemorating El Día de los Muertos (Day of the Dead). While the moles are tasty (we're partial to the mole negro on the chicken enchiladas and mole amarillo on the *carne asada*), so are the fluffy corn cakes topped with chipotle shrimp, the simple chile rellenos, the squash-blossom quesadillas, and the *birria Guadalajara* (braised lamb in a chile sauce). And don't miss dessert, particularly the crisp churros drizzled with goat's-milk caramel and served with local **Taharka Bros.** (p. 187) vanilla bean ice cream. All of the above is good reason for *Baltimore* magazine to select Miguel's as Best Mexican Food in 2011.

No Way Jose Cafe, 38 E. Cross St., Federal Hill, Baltimore, MD 21230; (410) 752-2837; Mexican; $. Fun and friendly No Way Jose Cafe has been dishing up cheap and tasty renditions of Tex-Mex food for quite a while now, and we hope it continues to stick around. The complimentary chips and salsa are quite addictive, but save room for the monstrous 46-ounce margaritas! And then of course, you'll need something to absorb all of that tequila. All of the menu's offerings are pretty uniformly tasty and cheesy. Quesadillas come with your choice of myriad stuffings, as do burritos, nachos, and soft tacos. Everything is filling and everything is cheap. This is true especially on Fajita Night (Wed), when fajitas for two and a pitcher-full of alcoholic libations is $25. There's brunch on weekends too, with $15 pitchers of Bloody Marys or mimosas.

Ryleigh's Oyster, 36 E. Cross St., Federal Hill, Baltimore, MD 21230; (410) 539-2093; ryleighs.com; Seafood; $$. Downtown and craving oysters? Then head to Ryleigh's, where they're serious about

FOOD TOURS OF BALTIMORE

The cuisine of any city is affected directly by the people who have lived there and the ingredients readily available to the region. Food is also intrinsically linked to the culture of the neighborhoods and its social heartbeat. For visitors who want a fully immersive foodie experience, taking a food tour of Baltimore is a great way to go.

Charm City Food Tours (baltimorefoodtours.com) combines history, architecture, culture, and cuisine in its walking tours of various Baltimore neighborhoods. Explore the culinary treasures of Fells Point, Federal Hill, Little Italy, or Mount Vernon. If you wish to construct your own tour for a special group, Charm City Food Tours will work with you to pick the types and number of restaurants you want to visit and the length of the tour. A private pub-crawl tour can also be arranged. Their extensive service won them Best of Baltimore 2011 from *Baltimore* magazine.

For a more intimate and offbeat tour, there's **Charm City Chews** (charmcitychews.com). Owner Sharon Reuter offers tours she likes to call "uniquely Baltimore." With cheeky titles like "A Little Italy, A Little Not," "North (Avenue) Meets South (Korea)," and "Once Upon a Chinatown," the tours focus on small and little-known areas of Baltimore's culinary history.

Most tours cost less than $60, which is quite reasonable considering that participants will visit three to five restaurants along the way. For the cost of one meal in a fine restaurant, you get to absorb the culture of an entire neighborhood.

bivalves, serving as many kinds of oysters as they can get their hands on. There's even a special Oyster Club that sends out biweekly updates and offers members discounts and other freebies depending on the number and variety of oysters ingested. Their oyster bar, made from blue slate, comes with chalk so you can doodle while you slurp— or leave your phone number for the cute guy or gal standing next to you. Ryleigh's isn't only about oysters, though. The menu is a mix of pub grub and more-elegant meat and seafood entrees like roasted rockfish with Thai peanut sauce, and barbecue-rubbed grilled teres major with a side of cheddar grits. The handsome space also includes a dining room that opens out onto the sidewalk in nice weather, plus a loft area with a wine bar.

Sobo Cafe, 6 W. Cross St., Federal Hill, Baltimore, MD 21230; (410) 752-1518; sobocafe.net; Cafe; $$. This longtime Federal Hill eatery got both a new owner and a makeover in late 2011. The walls in the small and sunny dining room are now painted a vivid shade of mango and are decorated with a series of quirky works of art for sale by local artists. Everything served at the cafe is made in-house, from the lovely ciabatta in the bread basket to sauces to desserts. The menu is short and sweet, offering comfort-food favorites like chicken potpie and Salisbury steak, mac and cheese, and spinach pie. Those last two are vegetarian; there are other items available for the non–meat eaters among us as well. The Sunday brunch menu also features vegetarian items, one of which is not the fluffy chocolate chip and bacon pancakes. Neither is the Back to Bed sandwich, a festival of meaty protein, including bacon, ham, and scrapple, with eggs, cheddar cheese, and bacon mayo. We'll take two, please. And a defibrillator.

Thai Arroy, 1019 Light St., Federal Hill, Baltimore, MD 21230; (410) 385-8587; thaiarroy.com; Thai; $$. As lovers of the complex cuisine of Thailand, we're pleased that most neighborhoods in Baltimore seem to have at least one Thai restaurant. In Federal Hill it's Thai Arroy. The pleasant space is decorated with large murals depicting Thai deities, some of which are pretty fearsome looking. Also fearsome is the heat in some Thai dishes, but we find the standard level of spicing in Thai Arroy's food to be just right. (It can be adjusted up or down according to your personal taste.) The menu is expansive and most dishes can be had with your choice of protein. We love the *som tum* here, a traditional salad of shredded green papaya mixed with a tart and spicy sauce containing a judicious amount of garlic and *nam pla* (fish sauce). Also worth ordering is the *gang dang* (red curry); it's rich and aromatic at Thai Arroy, not cloyingly sweet as it might be elsewhere. If you do want sweetness, a glass of Thai iced coffee hits that spot quite nicely.

The Wine Market, 921 E. Fort Ave., Locust Point, Baltimore, MD 21230; (410) 244-6166; the-wine-market.com; Wine Bar; $$$. The Wine Market was one of the original Baltimore-area restaurants-within-a-wine-shop. Located in an old warehouse, the restaurant has a hip industrial decor with exposed ceiling beams, steel, and polished concrete floors. Food is as important as the wine here, and it's pretty delicious too. There are snacky things that go great with a glass of wine or two, like the charcuterie plate with house-made pickles and *mostarda,* a cheese plate, and flatbread pizzas, but there are also substantial meals to be had. Many products are locally grown, like a Roseda beef rib eye or the Truck Patch Farms pork duo. Midweek there's a 3-course prix-fixe menu for $35, with wine flights available at $4 per glass. Being a wine shop, there are, of course, oodles of delicious vinos available to go with your meal—30 or so are available by the glass—and any of the 900 wines available in the shop can be consumed in-house for a $9 per bottle corkage fee.

Landmarks

Regi's, 1002 Light St., Federal Hill, Baltimore, MD 21230; (410) 539-7344; regisamericanbistro.com; American; $$. Regi's has been around for what seems like forever. In the restaurant world, especially in our recent economic climate, 1978 is a very, very long time ago. So kudos to Regi's for serving food that people have wanted to eat for more than 30 years now. One of those items is their moist broiled crab cake, full of sweet meaty lump crab. But don't think that the rest of the menu is living in the past. Head Chef Mike Broglio (formerly at the much-missed Brass Elephant uptown) makes sure the food is up-to-date, with trendy items (like the outrageous tater tots stuffed with brie and bacon) and dishes influenced by world cuisines (like a Korean-style barbecue pork tenderloin). The lunch menu is full of interesting sandwich combinations like a Thanksgiving sandwich with turkey, stuffing, and cranberry sauce, and the Lettuce Entertain You, which is essentially an iceberg wedge salad on Texas toast. Burgers are also notable, as they come from local grass-fed, hormone-free beef and are full of meaty flavor.

Specialty Stores, Markets & Producers

Cross Street Market, 1065 S. Charles St., Federal Hill, Baltimore, MD 21230; (410) 685-6169; bpmarkets.com/crs1.html. At the Cross Street Market, which dates back to 1846, one can still buy fresh meats at Nunnally's or Fenwick's Choice Meats, fish and crabs from Cross Street Seafood, and produce from Kwon's. Much of the market, however, is prepared food. One of our favorite stalls is Bruce Lee's Wings. Their chicken wings magically remain crunchy after being drenched in teriyaki sauce, even after refrigeration (not that leftovers make it home that often). Nick's Oyster Bar (nicksoysterbar .com) has huge (32-ounce!) cups of beer, fresh sushi, raw oysters, great crab cakes, and if you're lucky, you'll also be able to grab a place to sit. Kathy's Bakery bakes all of their sweet treats on the premises. The market also has stands featuring tacos, sandwiches, fried chicken, and fresh-baked pretzels for your dining pleasure.

Midnite Confection's Cupcakery, 1051 S. Charles St., Federal Hill, Baltimore, MD 21230; (410) 727-1010; midniteconfection .com. Please don't expect Midnite Confection's to be open at midnight—the name refers to the "a-ha" moment that started the business. Some years ago owner Sandra Reeves McNeil found her son and business partner, Aaron, baking cupcakes to feed a sweet tooth. At midnight. They shared the resulting cakelets with friends and family and soon had to open a business to keep up with demand. Now Midnite Confection's sells a selection of cupcakes for the mature palate, including some that contain liqueurs. They are probably best known for one of their signature treats, the Black Velvet, a chocolatey twist on the popular red velvet. Their cakes are very moist, and the fluffy frosting has just the right amount of sweetness. It's no wonder *Baltimore* magazine considered them one of the best cupcakeries in Baltimore in 2011.

Inner Harbor

Sitting on the northwest branch of the Patapsco River, the Inner Harbor's scenic view makes it the perfect focal point for Baltimore tourism. With its numerous hotels, shops, restaurants, and attractions, visitors can spend days taking in everything that the Inner Harbor has to offer.

This was not always the case. For two centuries the Inner Harbor served as a port for light freight and commercial shipping, and it was at one time the second-largest port for immigrants into the US. With cultural and economic changes in the 1950s, this business disappeared, leaving behind decaying warehouses and dilapidated piers. By the 1970s most of the rot had been cleared away, but the only reason to go to the Inner Harbor was to see the USS *Constellation,* the only Civil War ship still afloat, or to attend the summer ethnic festivals. Changes were in progress, however, and when the Harborplace mall opened in 1980, the renaissance of the harbor started in earnest.

Today, places like the Maryland Science Center, National Aquarium, American Visionary Art Museum, and Port Discovery keep tourists flocking to the Inner Harbor year-round. As a result, many of the dining choices trend toward familiar chain restaurants and family-friendly fare. However, there's also a diverse selection of cafes and fine dining establishments to satisfy a more discriminating palate.

Foodie Faves

Brio Tuscan Grille, 100 E. Pratt St., Baltimore, MD 21202; (410) 637-3440; brioitalian.com; Italian; $$$. When we were kids, this plum corner spot, with sidewalks more than ample enough for alfresco dining and a great view of the Inner Harbor, was a Friendly's. The space has come up in the world with its current tenant, Brio Tuscan Grille. Yes, it's also a chain, but it does a nice job of making people-pleasing eats, especially during happy hour. Tuscan Tasters, a series of small plates available at the bar, are only $3.95, and drink specials are $5. At lunch- or dinnertime if you can score a sidewalk table, share some flatbreads and bruschetta with your tablemates, maybe a pasta or two, and settle back for some interesting people-watching.

The Capital Grille, 500 E. Pratt St., Baltimore, MD 21202; (443) 703-4064; thecapitalgrille.com; Steakhouse; $$$$. This high-end steakhouse is always near the top of *Baltimore* magazine's Best Restaurants list. It's a gorgeous place, dark and masculine, the

Fan Food: Tasty Temptations at Oriole Park at Camden Yards

In 1992 there was nothing else like it. A modern sports facility with all the amenities wrapped in a brick-and-cast-iron structure that was reminiscent of the Bambino and Casey at the Bat. Oriole Park at Camden Yards permanently buried the old notion of playing baseball in an anonymous, multipurpose stadium, and other cities scrambled to catch up. Although it's not unique anymore, Camden Yards is still a great place to see a ball game and, more importantly, graze.

The park is structured in such a way that it is easy to wander about and enjoy the food while still feeling connected to the game. Since fans are allowed to bring snacks, soda, and water into the park, numerous vendors are parked outside, offering food at prices far cheaper than inside. Even the nearby Old Otterbein United Methodist Church sells peanuts and water outside Camden Yards to raise money for the church. Once inside, you can wander over to Eutaw Street and grab some of **Boog's Barbeque.** If Oriole legend Boog Powell happens to be working at the stand, you might even be able to grab an autograph and a photo.

walls decorated with portraits of famous Baltimoreans like Babe Ruth and Johnny Unitas. It's a place to go for pampering and to eat luscious, dry-aged steak. It's hard to pick a favorite preparation. The Kona coffee–rubbed sirloin with caramelized shallot butter is mouthwatering, but so is the 22-ounce bone-in rib eye. Sides

For its 20th anniversary, Oriole Park has added some local flair with **Gino's Burgers & Chicken** (ginosgiant.com). Named after Baltimore Colts Great Gino Marchetti, the chain is making a comeback after a 30-year absence and, for Orioles fans, they've introduced a park exclusive called the Camden Giant Burger: a crab cake and a cheeseburger between a bun. Fells Point favorite **Stuggy's Old Fashioned Hot Dogs and Sausages** (stuggys.com) offers a Crab Mac N' Cheese Dog that has become a new favorite. Both can be enjoyed while you relax on the new rooftop deck in center field (long ago the site for Ruth's Cafe, owned by Babe Ruth's father).

Over in the warehouse is **Dempsey's Brew Pub and Restaurant** (dempseysbaltimore.com). Named after beloved Orioles' catcher Rick Dempsey, Dempsey's serves upscale pub grub like beer-steamed mussels and sliders, along with a wide selection of beers, including ones they brew on the premises. This is a seven-day-a-week restaurant that's open year-round, not just for home games.

Even if you are not a baseball fan, Oriole Park at Camden Yards is well worth a visit just to mill about, have some great food, and enjoy the casual vibe of the place.

include steakhouse classics like creamed spinach, but we love the creamed corn with applewood smoked bacon. Of course, one can also dine quite happily (and somewhat less expensively) at the Capital Grille at lunchtime; the chopped sirloin burger earns raves, and so does their version of a crab cake, dressed up with chunks of lobster. The wine list is huge and the knowledgeable staff is happy to guide diners through it. And if their wine list doesn't suit your needs, there are leasable wine lockers on-premises to house a personal collection.

Edo Sushi, 201 E. Pratt St., Ste. 2075, Baltimore, MD 21202; (410) 843-9804; edosushimd.com/innerharbor.htm; Japanese; $$. Overlooking the Inner Harbor, Edo Sushi probably has the best view of any sushi restaurant in town. The fish is always fresh, and diners can choose between white or brown  rice for their nigiri and maki. The lunch specials are a real deal, and the bento boxes are a nice option for the indecisive: They include six different menu items, which can include maki rolls, shumai, teriyaki, or tempura, with a different set of items every day of the week. Edo Sushi has three other locations in the Baltimore metro area at 53 E. Padonia Rd., Timonium, MD 21093, (410) 667-9200; 10347 Reisterstown Rd., Owings Mills, MD 21117, (410) 363-7720; and 10995 Owings Mills Blvd., Owings Mills, MD 21117, (410) 356-6818.

Fogo de Chão, 600 E. Pratt St., Baltimore, MD 21202; (410) 528-9292; fogodechao.com; Latin; $$$$. This restaurant should come with a warning label: *Caution! May lead to meat hangovers.* What? If you're laughing, you've obviously never overindulged at a *churrascaria* (Brazilian steakhouse). Take it from us, it's a thing, and it feels an awful lot like a booze hangover. In order to avoid this painful condition, make sure to fill a plate with goodies from the salad bar, like hearts of palm and asparagus, and indulge in some of the warm cheese bread and garlic mashed potatoes. In other words, eat something in addition to meat. Selections like beef top sirloin, rib eye, lamb, chicken, pork ribs, and linguica sausage make that a hard thing to do, especially when you can watch the meat traveling around the room on giant skewers and anticipate their arrival at your table. Light eaters may be able to save room for dessert, but we're usually content to end our meal with the sweet caramelized bananas that come as a side dish.

Kona Grill, 1 E. Pratt St., Baltimore, MD 21202; (410) 244-8994; konagrill.com; Asian Fusion; $$$. If you're in the mood for sushi or perhaps something Asian-inspired, then Kona Grill may be for you. Step past the large aquariums full of colorful tropical fish (avoid making jokes about how small sushi seems to be these days), and sit either in the main dining room or the indoor/outdoor patio area that opens onto the sidewalk in the summer. The sleek restaurant is usually hopping at happy hour, when specials abound. If you're there for lunch or dinner rather than to partake of the demon rum (vodka, gin, etc.), take a few minutes to peruse the ample menu, which offers salads, sandwiches, flatbreads, large-scale entrees, and lots of sushi. There are only a few varieties of nigiri and sashimi available, but there are tons of maki, both traditional and specialty. Dieters will find a lot to like at Kona Grill. Not only are there menu items that are low cal and low carb (hello, sashimi!), there are also cocktails that won't supply (too many) empty calories.

La Tasca, 201 E. Pratt St., Baltimore, MD 21202; (410) 209-2562; latascausa.com; Small Plates; $. La Tasca is a small chain, with locations in DC and northern Virginia as well as this pretty two-story space in Baltimore's Harborplace. The view is terrific, so sit outside if you can and start your meal with one of about a dozen different sangrias (there's even a version made with nonalcoholic wine), and start those small plates coming! The menu is divided into breads and starters, cured meats and cheeses, and all manner of salad, meat, seafood, and vegetable tapas. If you're a little overwhelmed by the sheer quantity of dishes, there are three helpful tasting menus, each with eight or nine of the restaurant's most popular tapas selections. There are also half a dozen or so paellas that feed 2 to 3 each. Even better is the special all-you-can-eat tapas menu available for lunch and dinner Mon through Wed.

Miss Shirley's Cafe, 750 E. Pratt St., Baltimore, MD 21202; (410) 528-5373; missshirleys.com; Cafe; $$. Father-and-son team Eddie and David Dopkin named Miss Shirley's after the late and obviously beloved Shirley McDowell, longtime cook for another Dopkin family business, Classic Catering People. The restaurant honoring Miss McDowell has done very well over the years, accruing accolades like *Baltimore* magazine's Readers' Poll Best Brunch and Best Breakfast in 2011, and Best Breakfast in Maryland from *Food Network Magazine,* among others. The big draw, of course, is breakfast, and

Miss Shirley's pulls out all the stops. One of the house specialties is a decadent dish called "Shirley's Affair with Oscar," made with two 2-ounce beef fillets, asparagus, crabmeat, hollandaise, fried green tomatoes, and bacon grits. If you're not quite that hungry, order the fresh-blueberry pancakes or waffles. Miss Shirley's lunch has its fans too. Try the lunch sliders for a taste of crab cake, pork barbecue, and fried chicken, or the Summer Strawberry Grilled Cheese. Miss Shirley's has two other locations: 513 W. Cold Spring Ln., Baltimore, MD 21210, (410) 889-5272; and 1 Park Place, Annapolis, MD 21401, (410) 268-5171. There's also a **Miss Shirley's food truck** (p. 286).

Mr. Rain's Fun House, 800 Key Hwy., Baltimore, MD 21230; (443) 524-7379; mrrainsfunhouse.com; Modern American; $$$. We're not sure what's more fun, the American Visionary Art Museum or its top-floor restaurant, Mr. Rain's Fun House. The museum is full of fascinating works of contemporary folk art, and the restaurant is decorated in a similarly whimsical manner. The food is as amusing to the palate as the decor is to the eyes. Mr. Rain's chef, William Buszinski (who owns the place with his wife, Maria, and beverage director Perez Klebahn), prepares food that uses as much local produce as possible; of course, it's seasonal as well. A recent menu was the picture of spring and included both fiddlehead ferns and ramps. Adventurous diners will appreciate the global touches like the spicy kimchee on a burger or lunchtime hot dog, and the Filipino spring rolls known as *lumpia*. House cocktails are inventive, and for the "noncommitters," they are available in a flight of three tasting portions.

Ruth's Chris Steak House, 600 Water St., Baltimore, MD 21202; (410) 783-0033; ruthschris.com; Steakhouse; $$$$. There are a number of steakhouses in the Baltimore area, and one that gets mentioned frequently is Ruth's Chris. They are justifiably famous for their steaks, which are cooked at 1,800 degrees and topped with butter, so they sizzle invitingly on their way to the table. Non–steak eaters might be happier with the lamb chops, stuffed chicken breast, or a huge fresh lobster. Make sure to leave room for dessert—their moist and custardy bread pudding is a nod to the restaurant's New Orleans heritage, and the chocolate sin cake is indeed quite sinful. There are seven locations in the Baltimore-Washington area, with two others in Baltimore: nearby at the Pier V Hotel, 711 Eastern Ave., (410) 230-0033; and Western Baltimore County, 1777 Reisterstown Rd., Pikesville, MD 21208, (410) 837-0033.

Tatu, 614 Water St., Baltimore, MD 21202; (410) 244-7385; tatu asianrestaurant.com; Asian Fusion; $$$. Stylish Tatu is decorated in dramatic shades of red, with myriad paper lanterns, plush banquettes, and fabulous-looking patrons draped on the furniture and perched at the bar, a vibe found more often in Miami or Vegas than in good-old Baltimore. It's a place to see and be seen, if you don't mind being seen while shoving giant sushi rolls in your perfectly lipsticked kisser. The menu at *Baltimore* magazine readers' choice for best new restaurant of 2011 is an Americanized mash-up of Japanese and Chinese cuisine, with lots of familiar choices like crab rangoon, spicy tuna rolls, and crispy orange beef. The crispy whole fish, arranged upright on a bed of fried noodles as if swimming upstream, is quite tasty, with moist flesh and crispy skin. Portions are large, all the better for sharing with that handsome someone on your left.

Tir Na Nog, 201 E. Pratt St., Baltimore, MD 21201; (410) 483-8968; tirnanogbaltimore.com; Irish; $$. Tir Na Nog, with other locations in Philly and New York, bills itself as a New American restaurant with Celtic flair. While the pan-roasted salmon fillet includes truffle essence, and there are a few Maryland-style favorites available, the menu is full of Irish pub favorites like Irish ale–battered fish-and-chips, shepherd's pie, corned beef and cabbage, and bangers and mash. We can't help but notice that they all go remarkably well with a draught or three. Tir Na Nog has a nice international beer menu with Irish favorites like Guinness, Smithwick's, and Kilkenny Irish Cream Ale on tap, as well as Belgian Hoegaarden, Italian Peroni, and local Heavy Seas Marzen. If beer's not your thing—heaven forfend—then you can wash down your burger with a signature martini.

Watertable Restaurant & Lounge, Renaissance Baltimore Harborplace Hotel, 202 E. Pratt St., Baltimore, MD 21202; (410) 685-8439; watertablerestaurant.com; American; $$$. Yes, Watertable is a hotel restaurant. Yes, it offers breakfast, lunch, and dinner for hotel patrons. But it also has one of the best views of the Inner Harbor, which alone might be reason enough to find the place. It's on the fifth floor of the Renaissance Hotel, so it's not one of those restaurants that will lure people in off the street; you have to know it's there. In addition to great views, Watertable serves up a menu of Maryland-inflected American cuisine, and not just crab cakes and rockfish (though they have those). They also offer Roseda beef, Cherry Glen Farm chèvre, Marvesta shrimp, and other organic and sustainable products from local growers. Try the triple-local-threat of Gunpowder Farms bison carpaccio served with Springfield Farm apple salad and Dragonfly Farms vinegar.

Landmarks

Phillips Seafood, 601 E. Pratt St., Baltimore, MD 21202; (410) 685-6600; phillipsseafood.com/menus-and-locations/baltimore; Seafood; $$$. After more than 30 years of serving up crab cakes in Harborplace's Light Street Pavilion, Phillips made a huge change and relocated to the historic Power Plant building down the street. The new interior is much handsomer than the old one, with lots of wood, stained glass, and a sparkling stainless-steel open kitchen. In the

ANATOMY OF A CRAB CAKE

There are many places in and around Baltimore that claim to serve the best crab cake in the area, but how exactly is that determined? Much of it is a matter of personal preference, but there are certain factors that should be taken into account. There are four major components to any cake: filler, binder, seasoning, and, most importantly, meat. For a proper Maryland crab cake, the meat should come from the Atlantic blue crab, *Callinectes sapidus,* which is found near the Carolinas and in the Gulf of Mexico as well as in the Chesapeake Bay. The Latin name means "savory beautiful swimmer"; and the word *savory* is the key here, as the meat of the blue crab is naturally both salty and sweet. It also has a moist texture, and the coveted "lumps" tend to be of a flattish shape, especially those from the backfin area.

Crabmeat can't just adhere to itself with sheer force of will—it needs some sort of spackle, if you will, to hold it into the customary spherical shape. This is where filler and binder come into play. The best filler is made from finely ground bread or cracker crumbs, which adhere to the meat with the help of a mayo-based binder.

Finally, there is the matter of seasoning. Some folks are happy with the blend of cayenne, celery salt, paprika, and other spices in Old Bay, while others prefer something completely different. We say there's no real right or wrong here, as long as the cakes are flavorful and not too salty.

Then there's the cooking. Deep-frying and broiling have their fans, but pan-frying is really the best way to go, as crispy shards of crabmeat are dee-licious, and it's easiest to control overall browning that way.

summer months, a crab deck with a full bar is open for alfresco dining right on Pier 4. The menu still boasts a plethora of classic seafood dishes, like oysters on the half shell, peel-and-eat steamed shrimp, and their famous crab cakes, but there are also some more modern touches, like the crab-and-artichoke flatbread; the crispy shrimp salad with dried cranberries, Gorgonzola, and pecans; and a trio of ceviches. We're fans of the garlicky steamed mojito clams, especially with a basket of bread with which to mop up the delicious juices.

Rusty Scupper, 402 Key Hwy., Baltimore, MD 21230; (410) 727-3678; www.selectrestaurants.com/rusty; Seafood; $$$$. Some folks might consider this now 30-year-old restaurant to be in the Federal Hill neighborhood, and while yes, it is at the base of that historic park, the Rusty Scupper clearly belongs to the Inner Harbor and vice versa. The restaurant has a panoramic—and quite glorious—view of the area, from Domino Sugar on the East side, clear over to Light Street on the West, and everything in between. Within the structure the dining room has a rustic, timbered ceiling that makes us feel like we're dining in an ark, but the crisp white tablecloths and tinkling piano near the bar give the room a touch of elegance. The menu is full of classic seafood dishes like stuffed shrimp, crab cakes, and fried oysters, with a couple of steaks and pastas for good measure. Try the rich cream of crab soup. The coconut fried shrimp, topped with a coating of panko and coconut and a spicy Asian-style dipping sauce, is also tasty. And don't skip dessert—the upside-down apple pie is scrumptious. See the Rusty Scupper's recipe for **Cream of Crab Soup** on p. 302.

Harbor East

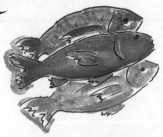

Also known as Inner Harbor East, this waterfront development is a relatively new creation. Started in the 1980s as a way to improve the industrial no-man's land just east of the tourist-friendly Inner Harbor, Harbor East was initially conceived to have a promenade that would allow visitors the opportunity to experience an unfettered view of the waterfront as they walked from the Inner Harbor to nearby neighborhoods like Little Italy and Fells Point.

Despite the impressive view, commercial development was slow in coming. At the turn of the 21st century, the Marriott Hotel, with adjacent restaurants Roy's and Fleming's Steakhouse, stood alone next to the National Katyn Memorial, while Charleston anchored the eastern side. Then a burst of activity occurred when investment firm Legg Mason chose to build a new high-rise on the waterfront, triggering growth almost overnight. While the harbor view is mostly obscured by the new buildings, the area now boasts a multiplex movie theater, numerous high-end stores, a Whole Foods Market, and, of course, restaurants.

The diversity of dining options is staggering for such a small area. From pizza to prix-fixe tasting menus, from sushi to *shak-shouky*, there's something for every appetite and pocketbook. If we're especially hungry, we enjoy grazing through Harbor East, having drinks and some appetizers in one place, a slice of pizza in another, and maybe dessert in still another. For a foodie, this is pretty near paradise.

Foodie Faves

Bagby Pizza Company, 1006 Fleet St., Baltimore, MD 21202; (410) 605-0444; bagbypizza.com; Pizza; $$. Bagby's, named after its location in the historic Bagby Furniture building, is a low-key kinda place with no frills and great pizza. Peruse the limited menu, order at the counter, and then find a table in the brick-walled dining area to wait for your order to be brought out. As the name implies, pizza is the specialty of the house, and there are a mind-boggling 8,000 varieties to be had if you mix and match sauces and toppings. To make it easy on you, the menu also lists several prechosen combinations. We like the Sweet and Spicy, with spicy tomato sauce, spinach, roasted red peppers, red onion, applewood bacon, Asiago and goat cheeses, and balsamic glaze, all on Bagby's thin, crisp, and cracker-like crust. Since the crust won't weigh you down, try a sandwich or pasta too, and don't forget the greens: Bagby's won Best Chopped Salad from the Baltimore *City Paper* in 2011.

Charleston, 1000 Lancaster St., Baltimore, MD 21202; (410) 332-7373; charlestonrestaurant.com; Modern American; $$$$. To say that Charleston, the crown jewel of the restaurant empire belonging to Cindy Wolf and Tony Foreman, has been highly regarded since it opened its doors in 1997, is putting it mildly. The restaurant's reputation is nationwide, with regular mentions in respected publications like the *Wine Enthusiast* and the *New York Times*. Executive Chef Wolf, a James Beard nominee finalist for Best Chef Mid-Atlantic in 2006 and 2008, has designed a menu that allows guests to choose from 3- to 6-course tasting menus. While her cuisine is rooted in the low-country cooking of South Carolina, it is also sophisticated, seasonal, and visually elegant. The menu includes wine pairings, but diners should feel free to choose from any of the more than 800 wines available on the award-winning wine list compiled by Foreman. In addition to amazing food, service at Charleston is outstanding—the combination leaves any guest feeling pampered.

Chazz: A Bronx Original, 1415 Aliceanna St., Baltimore, MD 21231; (410) 522-5511; chazzbronxoriginal.com; Italian; $$. Actor Chazz Palminteri is most famous for his work in films such as *The Usual Suspects* and *Bullets Over Broadway* and his one-man show, *A Bronx Tale,* but here in Baltimore, mention his name and folks think "pizza." At least we do. In particular, we think of a crispy, thin-crust, Bronx-style, coal-oven pizza topped with tomato sauce, mozzarella, and slices of veal meatball. Or wild mushrooms and goat cheese. Or swiss chard and feta. We also think about burrata, an outrageous concoction of fresh mozzarella stuffed with cream and more mozzarella that is so decadent, so luscious, we think it would be lovely to soak in a tub full of it. At Chazz the burrata comes with sweet local tomatoes and a balsamic drizzle. Also on our mind is Chazz's house-made Spaghettoni All'Amatriciana, toothsome extra-thick spaghetti topped with a spicy tomato sauce flavored with *guanciale* (unsmoked Italian bacon made from pig jowls). And last but not least, we think about the house-made cannoli stuffed with a rich ricotta and heavy cream filling. See Chazz's recipe for **Spaghettoni all'Amatriciana** on p. 314.

Cinghiale, 822 Lancaster St., Baltimore, MD 21202; (410) 547-8282; cgeno.com; Italian; $$$. Cinghiale, which means "wild boar" in Italian, is another restaurant in the Wolf/Foreman empire that emphasizes wine as much as food. The restaurant has two parts, the casual Enoteca, or wine bar (which includes a *salumeria,* featuring Italian charcuterie and cheeses), and the more formal Osteria, or dining room. Both areas share the menu, which offers a 4-course *prezzo fisso* (prix fixe, or fixed price, in Italian) option, or 3 courses with homier selections that they call *la cucina della nonna* (grand-mother's kitchen). But if you're just interested in some hand-cut tagliatelle with oxtail ragu and an *affogato* for dessert, everything is also available a la carte. As befitting the restaurant's cuisine, the wine list is entirely Italian and features selections from all of the great winemaking areas of the country.

Fleming's Prime Steakhouse & Wine Bar, 720 Aliceanna St., Baltimore, MD 21202; (410) 332-1666; flemingssteakhouse.com; Steakhouse; $$$$. If you're looking for a nice juicy steak and you happen to be on the east end of the Inner Harbor, look no further than Fleming's. Yes, it's part of a national chain, but it's hard to beat the quality and service that Fleming's dishes up. The interior of the restaurant is dim and somewhat clubby, except for the bar area, which features a flat-screen television. Over there, you can grab a prime burger (before 7 p.m. it's a real steal at $6) and a beer. At a quieter table, order up a NY strip, fillet, or rib eye, all perfectly cooked to order, and add a side of the decadent chipotle cheddar mac and cheese. Non–steak eaters can feast on salmon or lobster tails. No matter what you choose, the staff will make sure you're pleased with your order, and they're more than happy to help you choose something from their absolutely huge wine list.

James Joyce Irish Pub & Restaurant, 616 President St., Baltimore, MD 21202; (410) 727-5107; thejamesjoycepub.com; Irish; $$. The James Joyce, believe it or not, is a bona fide Irish pub, built in Ireland, shipped over to the US, and fitted into the existing structure. While the building itself is authentic, the food strays a bit. Sure, there's corned beef and cabbage, Irish stew, and fish-and-chips, but there are also US bar staples like burgers, wings, and the very Baltimorese crab cake. There's also the surprise of a cigar bar, where one can enjoy an Arturo Fuente and a quaff of Bushmills 21-year Irish whiskey. The restaurant also offers brunch on weekends.

Lamill Coffee, 200 International Dr., Baltimore, MD 21202; (410) 576-5800; fourseasons.com/baltimore/dining/restaurants/ lamill_coffee; Coffeehouse; $. *Bon Appetit* magazine named the Los Angeles outpost of Lamill Coffee one of the best boutique coffee shops around. For the Baltimore version, Lamill's Craig Min and **Wit & Wisdom**'s (p. 58) Michael Mina have joined forces. Mina's corporate pastry chef, Lincoln Carson, has developed the coffeehouse's menu, inspired by European cafes and patisseries but with an American twist. It includes hand-cut beignets with a salted caramel dipping sauce and Lamill "Pop" pies, which might be considered an upscale version of every child's favorite toaster pastry . . . if they included blue crab and Old Bay. And let's not forget the coffee, which in addition to espresso drinks and fashionable extractions, comes in signature drinks like Milk and Cookies, which also includes Valrhona chocolate cookies. Mmm.

Lebanese Taverna, 719 S. President St., Baltimore, MD 21202; (410) 244-5533; lebanesetaverna.com; Middle Eastern; $$. Lebanese Taverna is part of a local chain, with 6 full-service restaurants and

4 cafes in Maryland, DC, and Virginia. The Harbor East branch is a lovely high-ceilinged space, done up in shades of white and brown with exotic touches like a tiled wall and beaded curtains. We always feel a bit posh when we eat at Lebanese Taverna but always very comfortable. And the service is great; they're very patient with customers who have a hard time deciding. As you peruse the menu, snack on piping-hot, still-puffy pita breads and a bowl of olive oil flavored with a blend of herbs called zaatar. While it's tempting to fill up on the pitas, don't, because there are a lot of tasty items on the menu. Even eggplant haters will go wild over the *shakshouky*, a fresh and garlicky salad, and we always order the football-shaped meatballs called kibbe. The menu seems pretty meat-happy—kebabs, kofta, lamb, and more lamb—which will please any carnivore, but there's also an amazing selection of vegetarian dishes beyond spinach pie and falafel (though they have those too).

Oceanaire Seafood Room, 801 Aliceanna St., Baltimore, MD 21202; (443) 872-0000; theoceanaire.com; Seafood; $$$$. Oceanaire, like so many high-end restaurants these days, is a chain with 12 locations around the country. However, Oceanaire's nautical theme makes this restaurant very appropriate for the Baltimore area. Indeed, the dining room looks like the interior of a cruise ship, and the polished service and quality food makes us feel like we're on the *Queen Mary*. One can go the Baltimore-centric route and order crab soup and crab cakes, but there's so much more available, from classic clams casino and oysters Rockefeller to modern preparations like sea scallops with duck confit or kona kampachi with Thai red-curry coconut broth. All depending on market availability, of course! Oceanaire tends to be a bit on the spendy side, but one can still dine there on a budget. The $36.95 4-course prix fixe is a real deal and includes salad, soup, entree, and dessert.

Pabu, 725 Aliceanna St., Baltimore, MD 21202; (410) 223-1460; michaelmina.net/restaurants/locations/pabu.php; Japanese; $$. For his second Baltimore-area restaurant, superstar chef-restaurateur Michael Mina teamed up with Sonoma County sushi-master Ken Tominaga to create Pabu, a modern take on a Japanese *izakaya*. This restaurant in the Four Seasons Baltimore is bright and spacious, with an uncluttered Japanese aesthetic. An izakaya is generally a bar that serves food, and at Pabu the sake and the sushi hold equal weight. The fish is super-fresh, some of it flown in from Japan's famous Tsukiji Market, and served in delicate, jewel-like portions. The live scallop needs only a squeeze of lemon to bring out its creamy perfection, and the "happy spoon" (oyster, uni, salmon caviar, and ponzu crème fraîche) is a briny mouthful of joy. We also like the Maryland crab *okonomiyaki,* and the juicy *tsukune* (chicken meatballs) skewers. To complement these delicious morsels, sample one or more kinds of sake—Pabu's selection is unmatched in the area, and a sake sommelier is on hand to help you make a decision. Leave room for dessert: The *omakase* makes a perfect, fragrant ending to your meal.

Pazo, 1425 Aliceanna St., Baltimore, MD 21231; (410) 534-7296; pazorestaurant.com; Small Plates; $$. When we eat at Pazo, we like to imagine we've left Baltimore for a short time and ended up someplace, well, sexier. The two-story space is cavernous, yet somehow very cozy, with dark tones and low lighting, and we love to dine at a table tucked away in the upstairs balcony. This Mediterranean restaurant by powerhouse Baltimore restaurateurs Cindy Wolf and Tony Foreman specializes in the lively dishes of the Spanish coast and Italy, with an emphasis on tapas. Diners can certainly make an alluring meal out of these small plates that include Iberico ham, smoky wood-grilled mushrooms, and braised pork cheeks, or one or more of 5 Neapolitan-style pizzas, but Pazo also offers a 3-course prix fixe that can include any of 3 varieties of paella. With Tony Foreman in charge, you know the wine list is incredible, and indeed it offers reasonably priced selections by the glass or bottle. There are also a number of fun cocktails that can be enjoyed in the stylish lounge area at the front that gets livelier as the evening goes on.

RA Sushi, 1390 Lancaster St., Baltimore, MD 21231; (410) 522-3200; rasushi.com/baltimore; Japanese; $$. The Baltimore branch of this national chain is hip and boisterous, with lively music and even more lively patrons. The menu features inventive maki rolls with names like "gojira" and the "crazy monkey," but there's also plenty of more traditional nigiri and sashimi to choose from. There's also a full menu of kitchen items, like the yummy lobster with garlic sugar snap peas, and a nutty grilled-chicken-breast salad. Our favorite time to hit RA Sushi is during their fabulous happy hour—named one of the town's five best by *Baltimore* magazine—when we can grab cheap and delicious $5 saketinis and nosh on discounted sushi, apps, and tapas like shishito peppers, spicy sesame chicken wings, calamari tempura, and tuna tataki.

Roy's, 720 B Aliceanna St., Baltimore, MD 21202; (410) 659-0099; roysrestaurant.com; Hawaiian; $$$. The Baltimore branch of Roy Yamaguchi's chain of Hawaiian-fusion restaurants has long been a favorite of ours. It's our default special-occasion joint, and we've always emerged quite happy from its sunny yellow interior, whether we've had a "normal" dinner, celebrated a holiday with a prix fixe, or attended one of the lively wine dinners. While Chef Patrick "Opie" Crooks and his crew specialize in seafood dishes like misoyaki butterfish and local rockfish with lump crab risotto, we've always found the meat dishes to be just as strong. Roy's also offers a separate gluten-free menu for those with sensitivities. The staff at Roy's is friendly and hardworking and will happily divulge their favorites in any category, as well as assist you with wine selections. But try one of the cocktails first, like the pineapple-laced Hawaiian martini or the knockout mai tai.

Talara, 615 President St., Baltimore, MD 21202; (410) 528-9883; talarabaltimore.com; Latin; $$. Football fans will wonder how Baltimore let a restaurant that has roots in Pittsburgh sneak into our fair city, but once they try the food, they'll understand. Talara is a hip place that offers not only Latin cuisine but also Latin dance on Monday nights. The food is colorful, fun, and inventive. For instance, one of the several varieties of Baltimore's best seviche (according to *Baltimore* magazine) available is called Fire and Ice. The "fire" is provided by the habanero peppers that season your choice of raw or cooked seafood; the "ice" comes from a hot-pink prickly pear granita. Taken together, it's a perfect balance. We're also fond of the crabmeat chile rellenos, the mini-tostadas, and any of the flatbreads. The drink menu is quite extensive (one of the reasons for receiving Baltimore's Best Happy Hour kudos) and includes several flavors of mojitos, specialty rums, and Latin beers for your imbibing pleasure.

Teavolve Cafe & Lounge, 1401 Aliceanna St., Baltimore, MD 21231; (410) 522-1907; teavolve.com; Cafe; $$. Sometimes, after a day spent wandering through the posh shops and boutiques in Harbor East, one wants nothing more than a comfortable, quiet spot to sip a cup of Earl Grey and nibble a cookie. Or to grab a wild-berry bubble tea latte before running out for more shopping. Or to sit at the bar and enjoy a passion fruit caipirinha while comparing purchases with girlfriends. Teavolve offers all of that and more. With 3 dozen or so teas and infusions available, plus tea-infused spirits, it's a happy place for those who like to take their relaxation in liquid form. There's food too: Teavolve is open for breakfast, lunch, and dinner, with brunch on the weekends. We like the red velvet pancakes, the shrimp and grits, and the "adult grilled cheese" with feta and goat's cheese, washed down with a pitcher of rooibos-infused red sangria.

Ten Ten, 1010 Fleet St., Baltimore, MD 21202; (410) 244-6867; bagbys1010.com; Modern American; $$$. Ten Ten, the Bagby Group's second restaurant after the popular **Bagby Pizza Company** (p. 46), is tucked into the courtyard area of the historic Bagby Building and bills itself as an American bistro. We love the serene and sophisticated decor, which uses elements of the original building, including reclaimed wood and exposed brick walls and ceiling. We also love the food. In the past we've enjoyed an appetizer of ricotta gnocchi with Boursin cream and wilted leeks, and a rich pasta dish of perfectly roasted chicken and smoked mushrooms over fusilli. The gnocchi are also on the lunch menu and would be a perfect afternoon meal with a salad on the side, as would the lamb patty melt. The bar has a pretty sweet menu of its own, featuring cocktails with adventurous names like the Disappearing Act and a carefully selected menu of beers and wines.

Townhouse Kitchen & Bar, 1350 Lancaster St., Baltimore, MD 21231; (443) 268-0323; townhousebaltimore.com; Gastropub; $$. If you can't find at least half a dozen things you want to try right now at Townhouse, then you're far too picky. And we're just talking about the drink selection. There are 40 beers available on tap— that's 40 with a 4-0—and some booths are fitted with their own table tap system. And if that doesn't turn you on, there are oodles of specialty cocktails and wines available by the glass or bottle. Townhouse is spacious and can easily accommodate large parties, so it's a great place to meet your pals for happy hour or to watch the game. You might want to eat too, and Townhouse has that covered with their menu of dishes with Asian, Latin, and Mediterranean influences. Like the kung pao shrimp tacos, for instance. Or dig into a Townhouse burger, topped with Gouda, arugula, oven-dried tomatoes, and yummy bacon jam.

Vino Rosina, 507 S. Exeter St., Baltimore, MD 21202; (410) 528-8600; vinorosina.com; Wine Bar; $$. Nestled within the historic Bagby Building, Vino Rosina is a small but chic wine bar. With 150 or so wines by the bottle, and 50 of them available by the glass, plus cocktails created with house-made infusions, one can really get his or her drink on—in a sophisticated way, of course. Try the strawberry martini, *Baltimore* magazine's Best Cocktail in 2011, made with fresh strawberry-infused Prairie organic vodka, or the amusingly named Crotchless, its vodka infused with Cerignola olives, pepperocini, cocktail onions, lemon twists, and smoked ham hocks. Drinking is always more fun when food is involved, so there is a menu of both small and large plates featuring locally sourced products. If you're merely feeling snacky, try the applewood-bacon roasted almonds or put together a custom cheese plate with any of Vino Rosina's varied selections. If you want something a bit more substantial, add a couple of the small plates, like a luscious butter-poached lobster lasagna, or go for a juicy burger. And make sure to try one or more of the inventive house-made ice creams that come in flavors like maple bacon.

Wit & Wisdom, 200 International Dr., Baltimore, MD 21202; (410) 576-5800; witandwisdombaltimore.com; Modern American; $$$. The posh Four Seasons Hotel is home to Wit & Wisdom, a modern American tavern with panoramic views of the harbor, a plush bar area, and outstanding service. The restaurant is part of the Mina Group, which operates 20 or so restaurants around the country, including the Michelin-starred Michael Mina in San Francisco. The menu at Wit & Wisdom, a creative take on Eastern Seaboard classics, is divided into several sections including hot and cold appetizers, and entrees under such headings as "grilled in cast iron skillets," and "from the rotisserie." Beautifully plated appetizers like the congee-like Carolina Gold rice porridge with duck tongues, cracklins, and a raw egg please the palate, as does the local Gunpowder bison served with caramelized sweet potatoes, green apple, and brussels sprouts. Wit & Wisdom also serves breakfast and lunch, with brunch on the weekends.

Specialty Stores, Markets & Producers

Glarus Chocolatier, 644 S. Exeter St., Baltimore, MD 21202; (410) 727-6601; glaruschocolatier.com. Jennifer and Ben Hauser started their relationship in a whirlwind of chocolate. Not long after they met, they got engaged and opened a chocolate business. Named after Ben's father's Swiss hometown, Glarus has a back-to-basics approach to candy making; everything is done by hand, in small batches, so everything is very fresh and of the highest quality. Not to mention yummy. There are truffles and assorted chocolates, bars and bark, and even drinking chocolate. We're partial

to the truffles, especially the full-bodied coffee truffle enrobed in dark Swiss chocolate and dusted with espresso, and the seasonal truffle with a lavender-infused cream center, dark chocolate, and lavender sugar.

Jonestown & Little Italy

One of the oldest neighborhoods in Baltimore, Jonestown is a 10-acre area east of the Jones Falls that is bordered by Pratt Street to the south and Orleans Street to the north. The neighborhood was established in the 1600s by David Jones as a community near his mill and soon became home to the wealthy who wished to escape the noise and smells of the harbor. Jonestown was also home to Mary Pickersgill, who sewed the eponymous flag of our national anthem (her home is now a museum), and the Phoenix Shot Tower, which was once the tallest structure in the US.

By the mid-1800s immigrants from Eastern Europe replaced the wealthy, who moved farther north; the Jewish immigrants in particular made their mark by establishing a series of delicatessens on Lombard Street known as Corned Beef Row. Although many of those delis are long gone, places like Attman's, Lenny's, and Weiss Deli continue the tradition.

The area went through a difficult period during the second half of the 20th century when flight to the suburbs allowed for the building of low-income housing in the area. Projects such as those seen in the HBO series *The Wire* were all over Jonestown, but those were torn down in the 1990s to make way for more mixed-income housing. Its close proximity to the harbor has allowed new developments like Albemarle Square to thrive with their attractive town houses.

While Jonestown has seen tremendous changes over its long history, Little Italy is about as stable and tightly knit as a community can be. Generations of Italian Americans have lived in the neighborhood just south of Jonestown, making for one of the safest neighborhoods in the city. Little Italy is also quite active, whether it's bocce ball leagues or outdoor movie nights in the summer. But it's the family-run restaurants that are a real magnet for local foodies and national celebrities alike. There's plenty of old-school red-sauce Italian dining available, but you can also find lighter, more Tuscan-inflected cuisine. Despite the strong Italian roots, places like Max's Empanadas and India Rasoi reflect the ever-changing population of Baltimore even in Little Italy.

Parking is often a challenge in Little Italy, especially on busy weekends, because it is a residential area. However, most restaurants have a valet service, Da Mimmo and Della Notte have their own lots, and there's also a garage at the corner of President and Pratt Streets.

Aldo's, 306 S. High St., Little Italy, Baltimore, MD 21202; (410) 727-0700; aldositaly.com; Italian; $$$$. Aldo's doesn't look particularly fancy from the outside. Once through the doors, however, one is transported to a villa in Italy, with walls painted a soft and complexion-flattering peachy-pink, outlined with elegant wainscoting and ornamented with panels of tapestry. This is most definitely a special-occasion restaurant, but who says a weeknight dinner can't be a reason for celebration? The impeccable service provided by the black-tie-clad staff will certainly put you in the mood for the richly delicious meal to come. The batter on the *fritto misto* is so light, it crackles in the mouth. Pastas are excellent, particularly the porcini-filled agnolotti and the fresh pappardelle in a wild-boar ragu. All desserts are made in-house. The elegantly layered tiramisu is impossibly light and creamy, and the flourless chocolate cake has intense, dark flavors, but you may just want to finish your meal with a sweet cocktail of limoncello and heavy cream. Aldo's wine list is extensive, with many impressive selections from Italy, plus several at a price that won't break the bank. See Aldo's recipe for **Wild Boar Ragu** on p. 319.

Amicci's, 231 S. High St., Little Italy, Baltimore, MD 21202; (410) 528-1096; amiccis.com; Italian; $$. Amicci's began as a venture between two guys who wanted to bring a casual joint to Little Italy, a place that would be more than just a special-occasion restaurant.

New-school rather than old-school. Twenty-plus years later, Scott Panian and Roland Keh's restaurant has expanded from 25 seats to 300, and they're still maintaining that casual vibe. A must-try is their famous *pane rotundo,* a big round loaf of Italian bread that's split, toasted, buttered up, and filled with shrimp in a creamy, garlicky sauce. Also try Jody's Gnocchi, which are sautéed in Bolognese sauce before being baked with a topping of gooey provolone. In the new-school style, the wine list isn't huge (and prices are very reasonable), but there are a number of interesting specialty cocktails, like the refreshing Lil It'ly Lemonade, made with strawberries and basil muddled with vodka and pink lemonade.

Cafe Gia, 410 S. High St., Little Italy, Baltimore, MD 21202; (410) 685-6727; cafegias.com; Italian; $$. Cafe Gia is such a fun little restaurant. Both the interior and exterior are painted with colorful murals and replicas of old Italian advertising posters—even the tabletops are decorated. When there's so much to look at, sometimes it's difficult to pay attention to the menu. But don't think that Cafe Gia offers the same thing as every other restaurant in the neighborhood—items may seem familiar, but there's often a twist. For example, most of the chicken and veal dishes are served with a side of Italian-style potatoes, not pasta, and the lovely seafood ravioli is served in a rose sauce with just a hint of curry and garnished with fried artichokes. More familiar dishes, like the linguine with clam sauce, are excellent, and the eggplant parmigiana is among the best in town.

Da Mimmo, 217 S. High St., Little Italy, Baltimore, MD 21202; (410) 727-6876; damimmo.com; Italian; $$$$. Back in the day, Baltimore was abuzz with the news that Da Mimmo was actor Tom Selleck's favorite restaurant in town. The whole city welled up with pride at the thought that such a big star would favor a place in our humble Little Italy. We don't know if Tom's been back in the past couple of decades, but we do know that Da Mimmo is still worthy of his admiration. And ours. Mary Ann Cricchio, wife of the late Mimmo for whom the restaurant is named, has kept the fires going at their restaurant, which serves cuisine from all over Italy. Recommended are the giant veal chop, the tetrazzini with lobster in a rich brandy cream sauce, and the lovely grilled rack of lamb. A couple of nice extras for those who dine at Da Mimmo: They not only have a private parking lot down the street, they also offer complimentary limo service to guests in the downtown area.

Della Notte, 801 Eastern Ave., Little Italy, Baltimore, MD 21202; (410) 837-5500; dellanotte.com; Italian; $$$. Della Notte has quite the plum spot in the neighborhood because there's no way one can miss the Doric columns and circular portico that faces busy President Street. Inside, there are more columns, leading to and flanking the main dining room; also round, its walls are decorated with murals of Venice. Not only that, there's a full-size (albeit papier-mâché) tree in the middle of it all. It's a bit over-the-top, but the food is good, solid, contemporary Italian. We've enjoyed the orecchiette with broccoli rabe and spicy sausage and the pappardelle Bolognese, and we appreciate that gluten-free penne is available for those with sensitivities. The crab cakes are generally quite good as well. There's also a bar room—rectangular this time—that serves a completely different menu from the dining room, including brick-oven pizza, and tidbits like *arancione di Bolognese* (meat and risotto fritters) and truffle fries.

Germano's Trattoria, 300 S. High St., Little Italy, Baltimore, MD 21202; (410) 752-4515; germanostrattoria.com; Italian; $$$. One thing that Germano's does to set itself apart from the many other Italian restaurants in this small neighborhood is to offer cabaret-style entertainment in their upstairs dining room 4 nights a week. Performances by local and regional artists are informal but popular, so reservations are recommended. If you're not into singing with your supper, eat in one of the rooms downstairs, which are decorated with replicas of antique advertising posters. We've always enjoyed the *crespelle,* crepes stuffed with spinach and cheese in a *besciamella* sauce, and the enormous portion of osso bucco with saffron-and-mushroom risotto. Try the BongoBongo (giant, cream-filled, chocolate-topped profiteroles) for dessert, if just to say it out loud.

India Rasoi, 411 S. High St., Little Italy, Baltimore, MD 21202; (410) 385-4900; india-rasoi.com; Indian; $$. Yes, it does seem a little odd to have an Indian restaurant in a neighborhood called Little Italy, but India Rasoi has been chugging along here since 2001. Diners come back to this quiet row-house restaurant for the friendly mom-and-pop atmosphere and some of the best Indian food around. The menu offers all of our favorite Indian dishes, like butter chicken, first cooked in the tandoor and sauced with a decadent tomato, butter, and cream sauce. There's a nice variety of vegetarian items too, including a tasty dry fry of okra called *bhindi pyaza.* Both vegetarian and meat *thalis* (a selection of curries, breads, condiments, and sometimes dessert, served on a traditional Indian tray) are also available, if you find you can't decide on just one item to try.

La Scala, 1012 Eastern Ave., Little Italy, Baltimore, MD 21202; (410) 783-9209; lascaladining.com; Italian; $$$. Many area restaurants offer an antipasto platter, but La Scala allows the customer to compose their own from a selection of several Italian cheeses and cured meats including *prosciutto di Parma, bresaola,* and speck. This feature won them the title of Baltimore's Best Salumeria from *Baltimore* magazine in 2011. The rest of the menu isn't necessarily a surprise, but what they do offer comes in generous portions at

fairly reasonable prices. The grilled Caesar salad is delish, and the carbonara is irresistible. And leave room to try one of the lemon- or hazelnut-flavored house-made cannolis for dessert. La Scala's happy hour is worth a visit; many antipasti are available at discount prices, and there are also a few unusual "Mexitalian" selections, like the Italian quesadilla with Gorgonzola and prosciutto and a vegetable burrito.

Lenny's Deli of Lombard Street, 1150 E. Lombard St., Jonestown, Baltimore, MD 21202; (410) 327-1177; lennysdeli.com; Deli; $. Maybe "Corned Beef Row" isn't the most savory neighborhood in town, but there are certainly plenty of savory items to be found through the doors of Lenny's Deli. The long glass case is full of all manner of salads, meats, and smoked fish that you can take home or eat there, but corned beef and pastrami sandwiches are the way to go. Order them piled high on rye bread with a dab of mustard and maybe some swiss cheese, with a Kosher pickle on the side. There's also breakfast, when you can get almost any combination of lox, eggs, and breakfast meats on a bagel. Big bonus: Lenny's has its own parking lot. There are two other area Lenny's, at 9107 Reisterstown Rd., Owings Mills, MD 21117, (410) 363-3353, and at Harborplace, 201 E. Pratt St., Baltimore, MD 21201, (410) 230-0222.

Max's Empanadas, 313 S. High St., Little Italy, Baltimore, MD 21202; (410) 547-7900; maxempanadas.com; Latin; $. We discovered Max's Empanadas a couple of years ago at the little farmers' market near the University of Maryland. Max's delectable little pastries, filled with any number of goodies—like chorizo and walnuts, or chicken, olives, and cheddar—became a regular Tuesday afternoon lunch. And at 2 for $5, the price is definitely right. Now Max's Argentine treats are available in their own Little Italy restaurant, along with paninis, salads, desserts, and alcoholic libations. In addition, Max's sells a few Argentine products like the caffeine-rich herb yerba mate, *dulce de leche, membrillo,* and candies. If you happen to be in the neighborhood on the last Friday of the month, Max's has a free wine tasting with selections from South America and Europe from 6 to 8 p.m.

Weiss Deli, 1127 E. Lombard St., Jonestown, Baltimore, MD 21202; (410) 276-7910; Deli; $. While not as large or well lit as its compatriots on Corned Beef Row, Weiss Deli is nevertheless a popular spot for local office workers to grab a fat hot dog or corned beef sandwich for lunch. The lean and juicy corned beef is sliced to order and piled high before your eyes. Weiss also serves a Baltimore specialty, the "poor man's crab cake," also known as the coddie. Small patties of mashed potato flavored with onion and flakes of cod, coddies were once found in nearly every sandwich shop and bar in Baltimore but are fairly scarce these days. Eat 'em like we do, between crackers with a dab of mustard.

Landmarks

Attman's, 1019 E. Lombard St., Jonestown, Baltimore, MD 21202; (410) 563-2666; attmansdeli.com; Deli; $. When we were younger, Attman's deli, on Baltimore's "Corned Beef Row," was the source of many delicious dinners. We would stop by to pick up a pound each of their delicious corned beef and beef brisket, plus a well-done kosher pickle that came out of one of the large barrels by the counter. Sometimes we'd also get a couple of meat knishes, which were, shall we say, rib-sticking, and needed a Dr. Brown's cream soda to wash them down. But our favorite Attman's treat was an all-beef kosher-style hot dog served with the works, which included a slice or two of bologna. Sounds a little redundant, but it really works! In addition to the freshly sliced meat by the pound, customers line up for hearty and interestingly named sandwiches like the Tongue Fu (beef tongue, pastrami, corned beef, and swiss, topped with spicy mustard) and the Lox o'Luck (hand-sliced lox or Nova, chive cream cheese, lettuce, tomato, and onion on a bagel). While Corned Beef Row isn't quite the same it was back in the day, Attman's is still definitely worth a visit.

Chiapparelli's, 237 S. High St., Little Italy, Baltimore, MD 21202; (410) 837-0309; chiapparellis.com; Italian; $$. Just ignore the flabby Italian bread and cold, foil-wrapped butter pats and order some fried ravioli to nibble on while you peruse the menu at Chiapparelli's. This old-school red-sauce joint—Chip's to us locals—has been around since the early 1940s and is the place to go when you need a big bowl of decadent, pesto-coated, house-made linguine or tender veal saltimbocca in a buttery Marsala wine sauce. While the majority of the menu is classic Little Italy, one can also get grilled salmon or rib eye, and, of course, since this is Baltimore, crab cakes. No matter what entree you order, you'll get Chip's famous salad, a mountain of lettuce with red onion, tomato, and pepperocini tossed in a cheesy house dressing so garlicky it's practically festive. Your breath certainly will be, too, but oh, is it worth it.

Sabatino's, 901 Fawn St., Little Italy, Baltimore, MD 21202; (410) 727-9414; sabatinos.com; Italian; $$. Sabatino's is one of the last remaining grandes dames of Baltimore's Little Italy. It's old-school all the way, from the decor to the menu, which is peppered liberally with Sicilian-style classic pasta and veal dishes. Not to be missed is their famous Bookmaker's Salad, topped with shrimp, Genoa salami, provolone, hard-boiled egg, and their extremely cheese-full house dressing. Much of their pasta is homemade, and portions are huge. Try the gnocchi (ask for it baked) or the lasagna. Also worth a try is a house specialty, shrimp Renato, made with broiled shrimp topped with mozzarella and prosciutto in a wine sauce. Sab's is open until 3 a.m. on Fri and Sat. We hear red sauce and cheese are excellent for staving off hangovers.

Specialty Stores, Markets & Producers

Pâtisserie Poupon, 820 E. Baltimore St., Jonestown, Baltimore, MD 21202; (410) 332-0390; patisseriepoupon.net. We love Pâtisserie Poupon so much, we had our wedding cake made there. It was incredible: layers of chocolate mousse, chocolate meringue, crunchy hazelnuts, and white chocolate, arranged to resemble a stack of wrapped boxes topped with a huge chocolate bow. The cake was so convincing, wedding guests thought the cake table was actually the gift table. Our families have been going to this elegant French bakery for years, indulging in the pear tartlets, financier cookies, and outstanding apple tarte tatin. And the macarons! Did we mention they sell macarons? Those light, meringue-based cookies with a buttercream filling come in just a handful of flavors at Pâtisserie Poupon, but each of them is exquisite—and less than $1 each.

Piedigrotta Bakery & Pastry Shop, 1300 Bank St., Ste. 140, Jonestown, Baltimore, MD 21202; (410) 522-6900; piedigrotta bakery.com. If you don't have an Italian *nonna* of your own, Bruna Iannaccone can fill those shoes nicely. If you let her, she can and will feed you to bursting with Italian delights both savory and sweet at the bakery and restaurant she owns with her husband, Carminantonio. Mr. Iannaccone, by the way, invented tiramisu (just ask Bruna, she'll tell you the story). Needless to say, Piedigrotta's tiramisu is a thing of beauty, redolent of Marsala, which gives the dessert a more complex flavor than the rum that's usually used. All of their sweets and breads are dynamite, from sfogliatelle to olive bread, but their savory food is also incredibly delicious. Stop in for lunch or dinner and try any or all of the assortment of calzones, ravioli, lasagna, overstuffed subs, more and still more, all of which are made in-house and with love. Just like a grandmother would make it.

Vaccaro's Italian Pastries, 222 Albemarle St., Little Italy, Baltimore, MD 21202; (410) 685-4905; vaccarospastry.com. Vaccaro's started out in a tiny storefront, selling all manner of Italian cookies and pastries as well as supplying restaurants all over Little Italy with their famous cannoli. Now it's a full-blown cafe, serving panini and chicken potpie in addition to their famous bakery items and gelato. Vaccaro's is open all day, every day, but the most popular times are evenings and weekends, when there's a line out the door. Be patient—it's worth the wait, especially if you're there for dessert. Prices might seem a bit high (and dine-in prices are higher than those for carryout), but portions are huge. The items in the *"colosseo"* section of the menu are indeed colossal, with plenty of ice cream and pastry for two or more diners. We tend to stick to the gelato—the Italian cookies and cream is a favorite—and always buy several of the pignoli cookies to take home. Vaccaro's has two other locations within Baltimore: 2919 O'Donnell St., Baltimore, MD 21224, (410) 276-4744, and 118 Shawan Rd., Cockeysville, MD 21030, (410) 785-9011.

Fells Point

If there's a nightlife mecca in Baltimore, Fells Point could very well be it. With the largest concentration of pubs and bars in the city, the waterfront community is abuzz every night. That's not to say that Fells Point doesn't have its share of fine restaurants. From tiny cafes to formal sit-down establishments, Fells Point covers the culinary gamut.

Founded in 1726 by shipbuilder William Fell, the deep waters around Fells Point provided an ideal environment for commercial shipping and related industries. The lure of plentiful work brought thousands of Polish and Irish immigrants, who soon purchased property on the point from Fell's wife and son. The area thrived until the mid–20th century when economic changes and urban decay threatened the picturesque neighborhood. In 1967 much of the area was slated for demolition to make way for federal highway I-95, but the Preservation Society of Fells Point and Canton blocked the move. Once the area was placed on the National Register of Historic Districts, Fells Point was saved from the wrecking ball permanently.

Which was all for the good, because Fells Point saw a bit of a renaissance in the subsequent decades. Back in the 1970s the blue-collar families that had formed the backbone of the community were either dying off or moving on, and the preponderance of bars made for an unsavory environment. Then upwardly mobile young people saw the potential in the quaint neighborhood and revitalized many of the homes and businesses. Water-taxi service to the Point from other parts of the city brought much-needed foot traffic to the growing array of restaurants and shops. In recent years an influx of Latino immigrants has added new energy to the community as well, making Fells Point an exciting destination.

Foodie Faves

Ale Mary's, 1939 Fleet St., Baltimore, MD 21231; (410) 276-2044; alemarys.com; Pub Food; $$. Ale Mary's has received some publicity recently, not, as one would expect, for its food and drink, but rather for its decor. As in the various liturgical items that decorate this Fells Point bar: chalices, holy water fonts, photographs of clergy. Owners Mary, Tom, and Bill Rivers think it's cool, but some are offended. To others, it's just stuff. We're going to guess 100 percent of the customers at Ale Mary's are not there to blaspheme—they're there for the convivial atmosphere and good food, like tater tots with various dips, and a salmon BLT on Texas toast. One might argue that Ale Mary's is trying to kill its patrons with their Full Monte sandwich, which they say is of "biblical" proportions. Basically it's the equivalent of four Monte Cristos, with added sausage, bacon, and egg. Anyone who finishes without keeling over gets a free Father Tom's fried ice cream sundae (after which they'll need last rites). As for drinks, Mary's serves their own American pale ale, called Mary's Heavenly Ale, as well as, perhaps appropriately, **Brewer's Art** (p. 291) Resurrection.

Alexander's Tavern, 710 S. Broadway, Baltimore, MD 21231; (410) 522-0000; alexanderstavern.com; Pub Food; $$. While Spike Gjerde has found fame and fortune with his acclaimed **Woodberry Kitchen** (p. 182), his brother and former business partner, Charlie, has been operating Alexander's Tavern since 2007 with much less fanfare. Half the Tavern is a bar and half is a restaurant, with a sound-dampening brick wall between the two. Alexander's menu is huge and has a little bit of everything, including pizzas topped with such exotica as macaroni and cheese. A specialty of the house is tater tots, which they will happily smother in crab dip. The sweet-potato tots with pulled pork, cheddar, and coleslaw are pretty incredible, and their award-winning Cubano sandwich is definitely worth a try, as are the soft pretzels. The beer menu is also pretty extensive, with 60 or so options available on tap, in bottles, or in cans. The Tavern is kid friendly and even provides an assortment of games and toys to occupy them while parental units eat. There are games and toys for the grown-ups too, like foosball and darts, in the upstairs bar.

The Black Olive, 814 S. Bond St., Baltimore, MD 21231; (410) 276-7141; theblackolive.com; Greek; $$$$. The Black Olive's white-washed walls and curving archways make diners feel like they're eating in a small restaurant on one of the Greek isles, except with a view of Bond Street instead of the Aegean. The lack of a view is a small price to pay when the food is this good. The menu is fairly limited—a small selection of *mezethes* (small plates) that includes the famous spreads of Greece, *tzatziki, melitza-nosalata,* and *taramosalata;* a few soups and salads; and lots of fresh seafood. So fresh, waiters offer guests a tour of the fish waiting for their fate on ice before leaving the diners to make a selection. We like the appetizer combination, which includes the spreads mentioned above plus a parslied version of hummus. The spreads are so fabulously rich and full-flavored that when eaten with a basket (or two) of the amazing house olive bread, they are a meal in themselves. But don't miss those fish, which are either grilled simply or sautéed, expertly filleted at tableside, and doused with a light lemon-and-olive-oil sauce.

Blue Moon Cafe, 1621 Aliceanna St., Baltimore, MD 21231; (410) 522-3940; bluemoonbaltimore.com; Cafe; $$. The Blue Moon offers breakfast, breakfast, and—you guessed it—more breakfast. Tucked away in a small row house in a block just south of Broadway, this eclectic spot with its blue-painted pressed-tin walls is extremely popular; lengthy waits on the weekend are inevitable. But Chef-Owner Sarah Simington's twists on classic breakfast dishes are well worth it, particularly the enormous, "as big as your head" cinnamon rolls, and the Captain Crunch–crusted French toast; the latter was featured on an episode of Food Network's *Diners, Drive-Ins, and Dives*. More savory breakfasts are available too, notably the huevos rancheros with homemade chile verde and chorizo, and the home-made biscuits smothered in sausage gravy. The Blue Moon's hours are limited: They're open from 7 a.m. to 3 p.m. on weekdays, and 24 hours on the weekends, except when they're not. (Call to make sure.)

Bond Street Social, 901 S. Bond St., Baltimore, MD 21231; (443) 449-6234; bondstreetsocial.com; Small Plates; $$. Food and drink are always most enjoyable when shared with good friends—this is Bond Street Social's credo. The food at this Fells Point restaurant comes tapas-style in small plates designed for splitting with a pal or two. Drinks, like sangria and the grilled-pineapple mojito, are also meant for sharing when ordered in the 80-ounce "Social Drink" size. (Honestly, you have to *share* something that big!) The vibe at Bond Street Social is hip and polished, and the space, though large, is made cozy with fireplaces and leather seating. Chef Neill Howell's globally inspired comfort food includes such tasty morsels as the Foie Gras PB&J (a combination of peanut brittle, blackberry jam, shaved pear, and crisp/tender morsels of *foie gras*), and Kobe beef "pigs" in puff pastry blankets. Desserts are shareable too, like the doll-sized brownies with salted caramel, and equally dainty ice cream sandwiches that are a perfect after-dinner mouthful.

BOP Brick Oven Pizza, 800 S. Broadway, Baltimore, MD 21231; (410) 563-1600; boppizza.com; Pizza; $$. Much of our childhoods were spent eating the boring, often undercooked, thick-crusted "fresh dough" pizzas that were all the rage in the '70s and '80s. When BOP came around, with its fancy brick oven and thin-crust pies, it was a revelation. The oven, imported from Italy, is fueled with hard oak and cooks pizzas in about 4 to 6 minutes at 750 degrees F. In just that short amount of time, the crust browns beautifully and gets a nice crisp *cornicione* (the outer lip, or what we tend to think of as the crust). Myriad toppings are available—more than 50—and include surprises like Spam, carrots, and gyro meat. There are even specialty pizzas that include the fabulous carb-on-carb action of macaroni and cheese. Kids love this one, and so do we. BOP also has soy cheese on hand, which can turn any veggie pizza into a vegan one.

Henninger's Tavern, 1812 Bank St., Baltimore, MD 21231; (410) 342-2172; henningerstavern.com; American; $$$. Tucked away on Bank Street, far from the madding crowd, Henninger's feels like a real find. Despite walls busy with bric-a-brac, the soft lighting and white tablecloths make Henninger's an ideal spot for an intimate date. Seafood abounds on the restaurant's menu, and among our favorite dishes is the pan-fried oysters with a luxurious sauce of Pernod and cream, and the steamed littleneck clams in a red curry broth with lemongrass and fresh basil. The crab cakes are also pretty good; the basil aioli accompaniment is a nice change from the usual tartar sauce, and the slaw has a welcome tang. And speaking of accompaniments, the leek-and-gruyère savory bread pudding that comes with the guinea hen entree is pretty darn delicious and should be a dish in itself.

Kali's Court, 1606 Thames St., Baltimore, MD 21231; (410) 276-4700; kaliscourt.com; Mediterranean; $$$$. Kali's Court is a lovely restaurant, from the gorgeously landscaped courtyard entrance to the wood-filled and beautifully lit dining rooms. We like the tables out on the small second-floor balcony for a romantic dinner on a balmy summer evening. The menu is a seafood-lover's paradise. While it's not huge, it offers fish that aren't on every other menu in town, like roasted skate wing or a monkfish cooked osso bucco–style. There are also fresh whole fish, like branzino and dorado, displayed with pride on a bed of crushed ice, that are simply grilled to preserve the delicate flavor and texture. Starters include a grilled trio of shrimp, calamari, and octopus, charred and smoky, and a more decadent crayfish gnocchi dish that offers flavors from New Orleans. The wine list is expansive and the staff is happy to help with recommendations.

Kali's Mezze, 1606 Thames St., Baltimore, MD 21231; (410) 563-7600; kalismezze.com; Mediterranean; $. As the name implies, Kali's

Neighborhood Farms Help Communities to Help Themselves

Poor urban areas are faced with a host of problems, not the least of which are empty lots that become a haven for gangs and drug addicts, and a lack of stores that provide fresh produce. Neighborhood farms address both of these issues simultaneously by turning dirty and dangerous parcels of land into fertile gardens that produce much-needed fresh fruits and vegetables for low-income residents.

The success of neighborhood farms in Baltimore can be traced to a blend of grassroots activism and government support. The **Duncan Street Miracle Garden,** for example, came to be when a local men's group known as the Pharaoh's Club decided to take over an empty lot and plant a garden. Lewis Sharpe has been a major force in turning one plot into a series of adjoining garden lots covering the entire 1800 block of Duncan Street. Even organizations like Moveable Feast and the Baltimore Child Care Resource Center have plots.

The **Ash Street Garden** (ashstreet.org) was established with the help of **Baltimore Free Farm** (baltimorefreefarm.org), a collective that is focused on sustainable lifestyles, and the city's **Adopt-a-Lot** program, which assists neighborhoods in developing empty lots into gardens by providing soil testing and reduced water rates. Their website at baltimorehousing.org/vtov_adopt lists literally thousands of potential lots in the city that could be developed. Nonprofit organizations like **Baltimore Green Space** (baltimoregreenspace .org) help communities preserve gardens by offering soil testing, liability insurance, and technical support to sustain the site.

Jason Reed was a music teacher who understood the importance of an educational component to any community farm. When he started the **Filbert Street Community Garden** (filbertstreetgarden.blogspot.com), he enlisted the help of students from the nearby Curtis Bay Elementary/Middle School. His volunteers have since formed a network with community leaders, schools, churches, and local groups to maintain and distribute the products they grow.

The 6 acres in Clifton Park known as **Real Food Farm** (realfoodfarm.org) have also combined education with community involvement. Since 2009 the farm has produced over 9,000 pounds of food. Its high tunnel hoop houses have proven to be a low-cost way to grow food, and their outreach to teens through field trips, clubs, and internships have provided a mutual benefit for the community and more than 1,000 students. The produce is distributed at local markets and through a program where residents can receive a box of fresh food each week. Local restaurants are also supplied by Real Food Farm.

Community awareness is key to the sustainability of these projects. The **Boone Street Farm**, located between 21st and 22nd Streets just east of Greenmount Avenue, grows a wide variety of produce including beets, kale, collard greens, tomatoes, cucumbers, and zucchini. Volunteers create their own dishes from these ingredients and sell them at major city events like Artscape and Hampden Fest. It is only through the time and money provided by concerned citizens that these programs can thrive.

Mezze offers up the Mediterranean version of tapas, the small plates known as *mezze*. While we love tapas, we also love having the opportunity to gorge ourselves on Greek-style dishes like the braised greens called *horta, giouvetsi* (Greek orzo) in an herbed tomato sauce, and tangy imported feta. Oven-baked oysters with feta, spinach, and a balsamic drizzle are like a Mediterranean-style oysters Rockefeller, and roasted chicken livers with oregano are an unusual and delicious way to prepare this neglected bit of poultry. For folks who have trouble making up their minds when presented with so many options, Mezze has tasting menus for both carnivores and vegetarians that do the job nicely. Oh, and the downstairs bar is constantly busy, so if you want a calmer dining experience, do sit in the upstairs dining room.

Kooper's Tavern, 1702 Thames St., Baltimore, MD 21231; (410) 563-5423; koopers.com; Burgers; $$. Named after owners Patrick and Katie Russell's beloved yellow Lab (who, fittingly, loved to eat), Kooper's has all manner of steaks, seafood, and sandwiches. Even grilled pizza. But it might be best known for its burgers (*Baltimore* magazine's Best in 2011); they even have a food truck that serves 'em up all week long to hungry downtown workers. There are beef burgers and sliders made with Angus or Kobe, lean and luscious bison burgers, even lamb burgers topped with feta and cilantro mint chutney. Tuesday's Burger Day, when you can build your own starting at $5. But let's not forget that Kooper's is a tavern, which means there are also plenty of libations to choose from. Thursday is Belgian beer night, with more than 25 available; as an appropriate accompaniment, order up some *moules frites* (mussels and fries). There's also brunch on Sunday with some interesting specialty cocktails, should you need a hair of the dog after Saturday's bender. A second location, Kooper's North, is at 12240 Tullamore Rd., Timonium, MD 21093; (410) 853-7324. See Kooper's Tavern's recipe for **Kooper's Gonzo Sliders** on p. 306.

Liquid Earth, 1626 Aliceanna St., Baltimore, MD 21231; (410) 276-6606; liquidearth.com; Vegetarian/Vegan; $$. Liquid Earth is one of a few completely vegetarian restaurants in the area, but it's not all sprouts and tofu (well, yeah, there is a lot of tofu)—meat eaters are sure to find something to enjoy. Start off your healthy meal with something from the juice menu, maybe something simple and refreshing like the apple lemonade or the Royal Flush (pineapple, pear, ginger, aloe), and try one of the amazing nonmeat sandwiches like the Philly Cheese Phake, which substitutes thinly sliced marinated organic tofu for the steak, or the tofu Reuben. Liquid Earth also offers a selection of completely raw food items, like the raw zucchini spaghetti (shredded organic zucchini, heirloom raw tomato sauce, and fresh organic baby Italian oregano). We feel healthier just reading the description. Service can be a little slow, since everything is made to order, so don't expect to be in and out in a hurry.

The Olive Room, 803 S. Caroline St., Baltimore, MD 21231; (443) 681-6316; theblackolive.com; Greek; $$$$. The space on the roof of the Inn at the Black Olive may serve as the green hotel's general dining room, but it's also a dining destination on its own. Like the celebrated **Black Olive** (p. 76) on Bond Street, also owned by the Spiliadis family, this small restaurant with a big view of the water serves Greek food. There's also a Turkish influence on the menu, which is full of shareable small plates. Try the traditional Greek melted cheese dish *saganaki,* here given a twist of sweet lobster meat; the Black Olive's famous Greek spread platter, served with pita, is also a must. If you can, snag a table on the terrace to enjoy the view without the intrusion of walls.

The Point in Fells, 1738 Thames St., Baltimore, MD 21231; (410) 327-7264; thepointinfells.com; Modern American; $$$. If you're looking for fine dining in Fells Point, there are a handful of good options, one of which is at the Point. Wait, you're wearing shorts and a T-shirt? That's OK. Despite the white tablecloths and views of the harbor in the upstairs dining room, the Point is upscale in a very casual way. The dinner menu includes both small and large plates, all of which sound so good, it's hard to decide whether a meal should be a traditional 3 courses, or just a bunch of appetizer portions. Downstairs in the Pub, the menu is shorter (burgers, salads, wings, plus a couple of surprises), which makes decisions so much easier. Brunch is pretty much served all day on the weekends (from 10 a.m. to 4 p.m.) and includes yummies like fried-green-tomato eggs Benedict and apple-pie French toast.

Riptide by the Bay, 1718 Thames St., Baltimore, MD 21231; (410) 732-3474; riptidebythebay.net; Crab House; $$. Technically situated near the northwest branch of the Patapsco River and not by the Chesapeake Bay at all, Riptide nonetheless offers Maryland crabs from April through November (and sources them from elsewhere the other four months of the year). You don't have to be proficient with a mallet to enjoy lunch or dinner at Riptide, however. While crab is everywhere on the menu, from the Maryland crab dip and crab bisque to crab mac and cheese and an Angus beef burger topped with a crab cake, you can certainly get a crab-free hamburger (on Wed you can build your own starting at a mere $5) or dishes featuring other types of seafood. In addition to the dulcet tones of crab mallet on claw, there's also live music several nights a week.

Sláinte, 1700 Thames St., Baltimore, MD 21231; (410) 563-6600; slaintepub.com; Gastropub; $$. Like beer? Love soccer? Then get thyself to Sláinte, where soccer is religion. And the food is pretty great too. You can hang out in the bar and get rowdy with the folks watching soccer, hockey, or rugby (the website has a handy TV schedule so you know exactly what will be on), or you can sit in one of the more quiet areas upstairs in this rustic gastropub. Sláinte specializes in Irish cuisine, like shepherd's pie and fish-and-chips (Fri is build-your-own fish-and-chips day, BYO boxty on Wed), but owners Patrick and Katie Russell have a couple of tricks up their sleeves. How's an Irish bibimbap, poutine with a truffled chicken emulsion, or nachos with corned beef grab ya? We're partial to the calamari with a killer smoked pepper aioli, and the award-winning gumbo, which has a real kick to it and gives good reason to sample a pint or two. See Sláinte's recipe for **Sláinte's Shepherd's Pie** on p. 327.

Sticky Rice, 1634 Aliceanna St., Baltimore, MD 21231; (443) 682-8243; bmoresticky.com; Asian Fusion; $$. While it might seem a bit odd that an Asian restaurant with the word "rice" in the name gets a nod from *Baltimore* magazine for their Tater Tots, stranger things have happened. The tots come in a bucket, accompanied by a "world-famous secret" sauce, and the proper way to eat them in this hipster-ish branch of the local MD-DC-VA chain is with chopsticks, which is probably what you'll be using to eat everything else. (OK, your hands are fine too.) While there are sandwiches, noodle dishes, and stuff like wings and pot stickers, the inventive sushi is where it's at. The signature dish, rudely called "sticky balls," are a version of inarizushi, or rice stuffed into a pouch made from fried tofu. Here, they also contain crab, the rice is flavored with Sriracha, and the whole thing is fried and topped with two sauces and scallions. Another novel take on sushi, Drawn-n-Buttered is a roll stuffed with crab and tempura shrimp and served with a cup of butter for dunking.

There are also several vegetarian and vegan options, including the slightly more polite-sounding "garden balls."

Stuggy's, 809 S. Broadway; Baltimore, MD 21231; (410) 327-0228; stuggys.com; Sandwich Shop; $. At some point during a typical Fells Point pub crawl, hunger strikes. If you don't want to deal with a full-blown meal at a sit-down restaurant, then a hot dog covered with macaroni and cheese from Stuggy's might be just the antidote. Hot dogs are the thing at this four-stool joint, which offers 11 or so specialty wieners, like the Chi Town (similar to a Chicago dog, but with corn relish and green peppers in place of the neon green relish and sport peppers) and the Bmore (grilled bologna and yellow mustard), or you can concoct your own combination from any of nearly 40 toppings. A typical Stuggy's sandwich has a ¼-pound all-beef dog that's split, grilled, and served on a squishy/delicious Martin's potato roll, but there are also veggie and turkey dogs, **Ostrowski's** (p. 98) Italian and Gunpowder bison sausages, along with fries, wings, chili, and fried pickles. And for dessert, deep-fried Oreos.

Tapas Adela, 814 Broadway, Baltimore, MD 21231; (410) 534-6262; tapasadela.com; Small Plates; $. The latest restaurant in the Kali's Restaurant Group, Tapas Adela offers small plates like Kali's Mezze, but this time with a Spanish flair. As the name suggests, Tapas Adela does indeed specialize in tapas and has quite a large selection of small plates from the land and sea, including flatbreads. There's also the option of a whole roast suckling pig, which needs 24 hours notice, and is rather the polar opposite of a small plate. However, it is done in the Spanish style, and it's terrific, so we'll allow it. The restaurant's wine list is mostly Spanish, with a couple of bottles from South America and Portugal, but a creative cocktail also goes well with a dish of grilled shrimp brochetas. Try the Pisco Ginger, which contains the South American brandy called pisco, ginger liqueur, cucumber, and lime.

Thames Street Oyster House, 1728 Thames St., Baltimore, MD 21231; (443) 449-7726; thamesstreetoysterhouse.com; Seafood; $$$. As per its name, this relatively new restaurant on scenic Thames Street specializes in oysters. There are normally 10 varieties available, many of them from local waters, and you can get them raw, fried, stewed, or given the ol' Rockefeller treatment. There's also plenty other stuff to be had, much of it with a New England rather than Mid-Atlantic angle: lobster rolls; a Rhode Island whole belly clam roll (yum!); and one of the few nonseafood items, a Portuguese chouriço sandwich. (There's also a burger and a rib eye.) Of course, there's a crab cake too, which the restaurant brazenly touts as the area's only cake made with real Maryland blue crab. Served in a cast-iron skillet, it's moist and delicious and comes with watermelon salad on the side. In warm weather grab one of the few sidewalk tables for some entertaining people-watching, otherwise, a seat in the upstairs dining room offers a great view of the water.

Tortilleria Sinaloa, 1716 Eastern Ave., Baltimore, MD 21231; (410) 276-3741; tortilleria-sinaloa.com; Mexican; $. Ignore the ugly Formstone facade and the fact that there are no tables in this Fells

Point eatery. Tortilleria Sinaloa's menu is limited to things that can be stuffed into tortillas, plus tamales and a couple of soups, but the real draw is the tacos. Belly up to the 10-seat counter and order at least a couple. Two fresh corn tortillas are stacked and filled with your choice of meat (try the beef tongue or pork carnitas), onion, and lettuce, with a side of salsa and a lime wedge to squeeze over it. Those hot and fresh tortillas, made in-house daily, are available for sale by the kilo, and meats are available by the pound, so if there's no room at the counter, you can take your taco fixins home and DIY.

Waterfront Kitchen, 1417 Thames St., Baltimore, MD 21231; (443) 681-5310; waterfrontkitchen.com; Modern American; $$. Fans of the 1990s NBC series *Homicide: Life on the Street* may recognize the building as the Waterfront Hotel, a conspicuously uncrowded (by Fells Point standards) bar owned by homicide detectives Lewis, Munch, and Bayliss. The former recreation pier across the street is still painted up like the show's police station, but the Waterfront Hotel is under new management. Now called the Waterfront Kitchen, the restaurant has undergone extensive renovation, and the elegant, Patrick Sutton–designed space is hardly recognizable as a TV bar. Local celebrity chef Jerry Pellegrino is Waterfront's consulting chef and he and Chef de Cuisine Levi Briggs have put together a seasonal menu that relies on local products, including produce from Living Classroom's BUGS program for inner-city kids.

The menu is full of comfort-food favorites with a local twist, like a porterhouse pork chop from Carroll County's Truck Patch Farm, a Chincoteague oyster stew, and a crab imperial topping that's an option for any of the grilled meat or seafood dishes. Waterfront also serves lunch 6 days a week and brunch on Sunday.

Woody's Rum Bar, 1700 Thames St., Baltimore, MD 21231; (410) 563-6800; woodysrumbar.com; Caribbean; $$. Climb to the third-floor deck and pretend you've left Fells Point for a bar somewhere on an island. This island is stocked with lots of rum that can be enjoyed neat or in a festive specialty drink like the Painkiller, which

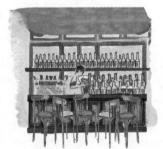

combines the Caribbean's favorite libation with cream of coconut, pineapple and orange juices, and a sprinkle of nutmeg. They still call it the Painkiller even if you order it with a triple portion of rum, but you may just find your head pounding in the morning. To stave off the hangover, nibble on some of their coconut-curry-steamed shrimp with Old Bay chili sauce, the fish tacos, or the tasty black-bean falafel tacos with spicy cucumber sauce.   If the pup on the front of the menu seems familiar, Woody's is part of the big happy family of **Kooper's** (p. 82) and **Sláinte** (p. 85), down the street, and the **Chowhound Burger Wagon** (p. 282), so rest assured that Woody's burger will be a tasty cure for that "morning after" feeling. See Woody's Rum Bar's recipe for **Woody's Fish Tacos** on p. 310.

Ze Mean Bean, 1739 Fleet St., Baltimore, MD 21231; (410) 675-5999; zemeanbean.com; Slavic; $$. Ze Mean Bean started out as a coffee shop with a case of homemade pies and cakes and a couple of Slavic specialties on the menu. Over the years, it's expanded to include a seasonal menu but one still heavily rooted in Slavic pride. When we've got a hankering for pierogies or beet borscht like Grandma's, we head over to the cozy and rustic ZMB to indulge in some childhood memories. The *golabki* (stuffed cabbage) rolls are excellent, as is the *hriby* (mushroom) dip. We have friends from New Jersey who come all the way down to Baltimore just to eat that dip (and everything else at ZMB)! The cafe serves lunch and dinner on weekdays and brunch and dinner on weekends. Sunday brunch has live jazz music, which is always a good time. And where else can you get a Polish Benedict, with kielbasa in place of the Canadian bacon?

Landmarks

Bertha's, 734 S. Broadway, Baltimore, MD 21231; (410) 327-5795; berthas.com; Seafood; $$$. For as far back as we can remember, area cars have sported bright-green bumper stickers bearing the legendary "Eat Bertha's Mussels" slogan. When Bertha's was opened in 1972 by classical musicians Tony and Laura Norris, it kick-started a minor renaissance in the then-declining Fells Point neighborhood. Now the dark and dive-y Bertha's is a Baltimore institution, serving up their world-famous mussels for locals and tourists alike. There are other seafood options as well, like creamy oysters William served with toast points, and soft-shell crabs in season. We like our mussels with a pint or two of Bertha's Best Bitter, brewed by Oliver Breweries on Pratt Street, especially when enjoyed at the bar on one of the 4 nights per week that Bertha's offers live jazz or blues.

Jimmy's, 801 S. Broadway, Baltimore, MD 21231; (410) 327-3273; Diner; $. Jimmy's, a quintessential greasy spoon across from the Broadway Square, is truly a Baltimore landmark. Baltimore's late beloved Mayor William Donald Schaefer used to dine here regularly, and occasionally the restaurant would make a cameo appearance on the NBC TV series *Homicide: Life on the Street.* Opened way back in 1948 by Jimmy Filipidis, the restaurant is now in the hands of his son, Nick, and namesake grandson. They say that breakfast is the most popular meal, and it's no wonder, considering the restaurant opens at 5 a.m. While you can get eggs, home fries, scrapple, and creamed chipped beef at that hour, you can also get a burger and a beer. Heck, or all of the above.

John Steven Ltd., 1800 Thames St., Baltimore, MD 21231; (410) 327-5561; johnstevenstavern.com; Seafood; $$$. The bar at the corner of Thames and Ann Streets has been serving up grub since

1911, which makes it a bit of a local institution. The clientele has changed a bit over the years, from merchant sailors to mostly Fells Point residents and some tourists, and the food has changed too. There was a period there when all one could get at John Steven Ltd. were steamed shellfish, and, amazingly, some very good sushi. Sushi's not on the menu anymore, but the steamed mussels are still some of the best in town. Enjoy them at the bar or while sitting in the dining room or courtyard. The menu is chock-full of seafood goodies like shrimp salad on a pretzel roll, fish tacos, and crab nachos. They also serve some pretty good crab cakes, broiled mounds of moist meat with little filler that even earned a recommendation from *Baltimore* magazine.

Peter's Inn, 504 S. Ann St., Baltimore, MD 21231; (410) 675-7313; petersinn.com; American; $$$. 504 S. Ann has had a liquor license since just after Prohibition. In the 1980s it was a biker bar. In the 1990s Bud and Karin Tiffany turned this neighborhood institution into a restaurant serving fine New American cuisine in an unapologetically quirky setting. The menu changes weekly, depending on what looks good at the farmers' markets, but always has a fillet or strip steak option, and the signature salad with garlic bread. What we love about Peter's is that there are no wings, no burgers, no typical pub grub to appease the masses, just fine cuisine. Peter's doesn't take reservations, and there are only a handful of tables and bar stools, so be prepared to wait or get there early (the kitchen opens at 6:30 p.m.).

Pierpoint, 1822 Aliceanna St., Baltimore, MD 21231; (410) 675-2080; pierpointrestaurant.com; American; $$$. Lauded local chef Nancy Longo's narrow row-house restaurant has been a Fells Point fixture since 1989. While the joint looks a little funky, especially the cluttered bar area at front and the yellow walls and purple wainscoting, appearances belie the aspirations of the menu. Seafood is handled with care here, especially crab. Longo serves up a fine crab cake, flavored by subtle smoking, that we feel is a model example of what a Baltimore crab cake should be—moist and meaty, not overly lumpy, with a crisp crust. Plump oysters, dredged in a light cornmeal coating and fried, are served with a spicy tomato remoulade. For dessert, try the chocolate plate, which includes such treats as a banana-chocolate spring roll and a chocolate gelato ice cream sandwich, served with Chef Longo's edible chocolate forks.

Specialty Stores, Markets & Producers

Agora Market, 803 S. Caroline St., Baltimore, MD 21231; (443) 681-6316; blackoliveagora.com. This specialty market in the LEED Platinum–certified Inn at the Black Olive is packed with earth-friendly, sustainable—and of course, delicious—goodies. Their inventory includes everything from soup to nuts: organic seasonings; locally produced fruits and vegetables; olive oils; wine and spirits; Greek yogurt and cheeses; fresh seafood; and local Cherry

Glen Farm goat cheese. Breakfast items like muffins and egg sand-wiches, *mezze,* sandwiches, and dessert items are also available. And if you have a hankering for a loaf of the Black Olive's amazing bread, this would be the place to purchase a loaf or 10.

Bonaparte Bakery, 903 S. Ann St., Baltimore, MD 21231; (410) 342-4000. When we want an almond croissant as big as our heads, we head to Bonaparte, where said crois-sants are buttery, flaky deliciousness. The same goes for pretty much any pastry in the case including any and all variations on croissants, palmiers, and cookies. While more often than not we lean toward noshing on their breakfast-type delights with a cup of their strong coffee or an espresso drink, we're often tempted by the jewellike fruit tarts and other sweet desserts. And of course, a crusty loaf of bread to take home. Bonaparte also serves up lunch-time goodies like quiche and pissaladière that come with a zippy, mustard-dressed side salad. There's plenty of room inside to dine, but in nice weather, we prefer to take a table on the sidewalk and enjoy the seaside view.

Broadway Market, 1640 Aliceanna St., Baltimore, MD 21231; bpmarkets.com/bwy1.html. The Broadway Market, the oldest of Baltimore's public markets, was established in 1786. At one time its four buildings stretched down Broadway to the water; these days the two remaining buildings hold only a handful of businesses, but those are worth visiting if you're in the area. Sal's Seafood is one of them; stop by for a bowl of crab soup or oysters, or pick up some fresh rockfish or salmon fillet. Another is Sophia's Polish Deli (sophiaspolishdeli.com), serving up golabki, pierogies, and liverwurst sandwiches to eat there or take home, plus an assortment of other goodies imported from Poland.

Daily Grind, 1720 Thames St., Baltimore, MD 21231; (410) 558-0399. The Daily Grind has been in Fells Point for more than 20 years now, which kinda makes us feel old. In days of yore, when the coffee shop was housed in a smaller space down the street, it was one of our favorite hangouts to grab a cup of locally roasted joe and a muffin and maybe play an intense pickup game of Scrabble. (Yes, we are hard-living folks.) Now the Grind is in a bigger, but no less funky, space, and in addition to consistently good coffee and espresso drinks, they offer salads, wraps, and sandwiches, like the veggie burger featuring **Jack and Zach**'s (p. 134) veggie patty, and turkey with pesto. There's also a location on the second floor of Johns Hopkins University School of Public Health at 615 N. Wolfe St., Baltimore, MD 21205; (410) 502-0833.

Fells Point Farmers' Market, Broadway Square, Broadway & Thames St., Baltimore, MD 21230; fellspointmainstreet.org. Every Saturday from May to September, the new Fells Point Farmers' Market brings a plethora of produce and other goods to the square at the foot of Broadway. The original farmers' market from this area dates back to the 18th century; some stall numbers can still be seen etched into the curbs around the square. While vendors back in the day probably showed up in Conestoga wagons, today's modern sellers are likely to port their wares to market in slightly more modern vehicles. Those vendors include Dirty Carrots (vegan bakery), **Atwater's** (p. 169), Blades Orchard, Gunpowder bison, and others.

Krakus Deli, 1737 Fleet St., Baltimore, MD 21231; (410) 732-7533; krakusdelibaltimore.com. Krakus Deli is a happy place. Not because the staff is particularly jovial, but because it is a palace of two of the most joy-inducing things on earth: pork and garlic. We're always fixated on the sausages hanging above the counter and occasionally forget to peruse the Polish products elsewhere in the store. After ordering a pound or so of *kabanosy,* a smoky pork sausage, we turn our attention to the beet horseradish and black currant jam and never leave without a box of Ptasie Mleczko (chocolate-covered marshmallows) and a handful of delectable chocolate-covered prunes.

Mr. Yogato, 732 S. Broadway, Baltimore, MD 21231; (410) 276-1006; mryogato-fellspoint.com. Baltimore's answer to Pinkberry and the other post-TCBY froyo shops is Mr. Yogato, which also has a location in DC. Their frozen yogurts are made fresh with real yogurt, not a prepackaged mix, in both tart and creamy (sweet) varieties. Both come in oodles of flavors, like blackberry, pistachio, and pumpkin, and even more flavor can be added via fresh fruit, candy, or cereal toppings. We're partial to the plain tart yogurt with fresh strawberries and almonds, but those looking for a more ice cream–like flavor might prefer the creamy style.

Ostrowski's Famous Polish Sausage, 524 S. Washington St., Baltimore, MD 21231; (410) 327-8935. This entry and the next one might confuse some folks, but take note: While the name is the same, the sausages are not. The original Ostrowski's has been around since the 1930s and has provided kielbasa to our family for three generations now. In the past the fatty, garlicky, porky treats were the centerpiece of every holiday meal. Other sausages, like the kishka (blood sausage), peppery Gypsy sausage, and even an andouille-style Cajun, are all delicious and worth waiting in line for.

Ostrowski's of Bank Street, 1801 Bank St., Baltimore, MD 21231; (410) 732-1118; ostrowskiofbankstreetsausage.com. The Bank Street Ostrowski's also makes delicious Polish sausage, in mild and spicy versions, plus smoked kielbasa, country sausage, and Italian sausage. Their products are available in many local supermarkets, which means kielbasa doesn't have to be just for special occasions anymore.

Pitango Gelato, 802 S. Broadway, Baltimore, MD 21231; (410) 236-0741; pitangogelato.com. This shop offers just two things, and they may well be categorized as Necessities of Life: ice cream and coffee. Technically not ice cream, gelato has far less than the legal limit of butterfat to earn that name. That means that gelato is healthy, right? (Yeah, let's run with that idea!) Two kinds of gelato are available at Pitango: the creamy variety that usually comes to mind, and sorbetto, made without milk. There are only about 16 flavors of both varieties available at any given time; our favorites are the amazingly intense Caffe Espresso gelato, the Pistachio made with special Sicilian Bronte pistachios, and the Spicy Chocolate sorbetto, a dark chocolate with a hint of heat. Lattes and such are available, but try the *affogato,* which combines a shot of espresso with a scoop of gelato.

V-No, 905 S. Ann St., Baltimore, MD; (410) 342-8466; v-nowinebar .com. At the very end of Ann Street sits an inviting wine bar/ wine shop owned by Mark and Kristina Bachman. They've smartly arranged their wares—most of which are priced under $30—by flavor rather than region or country of origin, so if you're looking for something "juicy" or "crisp," you don't have to guess or even be familiar with a particular wine to end up with something that hits the mark. Pricier bottles are also available in the "cellar room." And there's no need to go home to enjoy your selection(s)—grab a table inside or one out on the sidewalk so you can enjoy the sea air with your vino, and drink it right there. V-No also offers a limited menu of locally produced snacks, including charcuterie from **Clementine** (p. 191), bread from **Bonaparte** (p. 95) next door, and cake pops from Duff Goldman's **Charm City Cakes** (p. 165).

Canton

When we were children growing up in the 1970s, there's no way we could have foreseen that Canton would become one of the hipper neighborhoods in Baltimore. Like other areas along the harbor, Canton saw much of its industrial base decline during the last half of the 20th century, but unlike the Inner Harbor or Federal Hill, few had much interest in revitalizing Canton. Then in the 1990s, with real estate values rising in those other areas along the Patapsco River, the abandoned industrial buildings and decaying row houses in Canton looked mighty attractive. Now, Canton's newly refurbished look is a welcome backdrop to its lively bar-and-restaurant scene.

The area started as a plantation owned by John O'Donnell. Since he had once transported goods to the US from Guangzhou, China (more commonly known to westerners as Canton), the area gained that namesake once the land was sold to developers. Like Fells Point, Canton thrived during the late 19th and early 20th centuries due to the commercial business along the outer harbor. Blue-collar immigrants lived and worked in the area for generations. Just east of Canton stands Brewers Hill, so named for the National Bohemian Brewery, which gave such cultural identity to Baltimore.

Today, there's a wide range of culinary attractions available in the bars, pubs, and restaurants that surround O'Donnell Square and in the shopping center around the refurbished American Can Company building. In addition to the ubiquitous seafood, one can find Mexican, Greek, and Italian fare. High-end and eclectic dishes can also be had at places like **Langermann's** (p. 108) and **Jack's Bistro** (p. 107). Canton is a comfortable balance of urban cool and friendly neighborhood.

Foodie Faves

Annabel Lee Tavern, 601 S. Clinton St., Baltimore, MD 21224; (410) 522-2929; annabelleetavern.com; Eclectic; $$. The Annabel Lee is named after a poem by Edgar Allan Poe, onetime resident of Baltimore. (One might argue that he's a current resident, since he's buried just a few miles to the west.) This row-house restaurant, which is actually closer to Patterson Park than it is to O'Donnell Square and the majority of the other eateries in Canton, celebrates Poe with raven decorations on the outside and a portrait of the writer over the mantel indoors. The menu also manages to sneak in a few Poe references but otherwise offers an interesting selection of "upscale comfort food." Nachos are a specialty; try the applewood bacon and barbecue chicken version. The crab cakes, packed with sweet crab and little filler, are delicious, especially with a side of duck fat fries. Owner Kurt Bragunier was once general manager at **Brewer's Art**

(p. 291), so the drinks menu is definitely worth perusing, but a Resurrection draft or Natty Boh goes with everything.

Blue Hill Tavern, 938 S. Conkling St., Baltimore, MD 21224; (443) 388-9363; bluehilltavern.com; Modern American; $$$. While this Brewer's Hill restaurant is on a hill (albeit not a blue one), it's not really a tavern. But all that matters is that the kitchen in this sleekly attractive two-story space serves up food as gorgeous as its surroundings. There are multiple bars, however, which can get a bit noisy, so if you prefer to concentrate on your food, request to be seated in the upstairs dining room. Blue Hill's menu is designed to tickle the senses, starting with the knockout aromas wafting about as servers take plates to tables. The platings are little works of art, and the flavors are mouthwatering. The bread basket starts things off right and it just gets better from there. We like to start with a bowl of the tomato soup with truffled grilled cheese wedges for dipping. Many of the entree proteins are prepared *en sous vide,* which means they are cooked perfectly; if the short ribs are on offer, do try them. Blue Hill also has a great, upscale happy hour. Complimentary valet parking only enhances the experience.

Bo Brooks, 2701 Boston St., Baltimore, MD 21224; (410) 558-0202; bobrooks.com; Crab House; $$$. When we were kids, Bo Brooks was always one of the first places that would come to mind on those sultry summer nights when bashing on a pile of steamed crabs seemed like the right thing to do. Crab houses have come and gone since then, but Bo's is still around, nearly 50 years later, albeit in a new location on the water in Canton. Crabs are still steamed to order with their spicy house seasoning. They're delivered daily and graded that day, so make sure to call the day you plan to dine there for prices, sizes, and availability. There are plenty of other things on the menu besides steamed crabs. The crab soup is reliably good, and we've heard raves about the crab guacamole. There are also steaks, burgers, and chicken dishes. Make sure to try the O Rings—colossal sweet onion rings—which we think are a perfect accompaniment to just about everything on the menu.

Captain James Crabhouse & Restaurant, 2127 Boston St., Baltimore, MD 21231; (410) 327-8600; captainjameslanding.com; Seafood; $$$. At the spot where Aliceanna Street ends and meets up with Boston Street, there is a large boat . . . but not an actual sailing ship. In the late 1970s the wedge-shaped building on that corner was cleverly remodeled to resemble one of the merchant vessels that once routinely passed through the nearby harbor. On the premises are three separate restaurants. The Bayview Carry-Out is open 24 hours and offers breakfast, subs, and seafood platters. The Captain James Crabhouse is across Aliceanna Street on the water; there you can get all-you-can-eat (in 2 hours) steamed crabs from 4 to 9 p.m. Mon through Thurs (excluding holidays), plus steamed clams, hush puppies, and Boardwalk fries. We like to eat in the boat

PICKING CRABS

Here in Maryland, the act of cleaning steamed crabs, along with extracting (and eating) the meat, is known as "picking." There are two schools of thought. One involves removing the legs before cleaning and the other does not. We like to remove the legs, since any meat that comes off with them is that much less we have to dig for later. Don't just yank them out—grab a leg up high near the body and bend it downward. You should hear a small snap as it breaks away from the shell. Use a little finesse to gently wiggle the leg away from the body; hopefully there will be a hunk of meat attached to it. In the case of the backfin, there will be quite a bit of meat. If not, all is not lost—the meat is still inside. All crabs are different, so you won't get lucky every time.

Next, turn the crab so it's belly-up. Using a short, nonserrated knife, lift up the slim pointed tip of the flap-like apron (which is much larger on the female) and pull it upward until it's perpendicular to the body of the crab. At this point you should be able to slide the tip of the knife within the newly revealed gap between the bottom and top shells. Twist the knife and the halves should separate easily; remove the top shell.

What you have left will be pretty ugly, but stay with us! Use your knife or fingers to scrape off the gills or "dead man's fingers" from

proper, at Captain James Landing. The crab cakes are our favorite, but the seafood platter, which includes fish, clams, oysters, shrimp, and scallops in addition to a crab cake, is also a good choice.

both sides of the body, and remove the squiggly mess of guts in the center. What you'll have left is two halves of the body, joined by a thin piece of shell. With one half in each hand, bring them toward each other to crack the shell and separate them.

Using the knife or your fingers, remove the meat from the various chambers that make up the crab's body. The shell is quite easy to break with a little pressure, but the going might be slow until you get the hang of it.

When you've exhausted the supply of meat within the body, move on to the claws (the legs aren't really worth bothering with). Bend each "elbow" in the wrong direction to separate the top and bottom pieces of the claw. Grab the edges of the pincer (watch out, they're sharp) and pull them apart. You should be able to wiggle the "thumb" portion of the pincer away from the shell, hopefully pulling out a piece of cartilage and a chunk of meat. If you only get part of it, use your hammer to crack the shell and remove it the hard way. Use the hammer on the white portion of the bottom part of the claw to crack it in the same way. Some people like to place the blade edge of their knife against the shell and hammer that instead, which can make a cleaner break.

However you do it, enjoy!

The Fork & Wrench, 2322 Boston St., Baltimore, MD 21224; the forkandwrench.com; (443) 759-9360; Gastropub; $$. Look around this multilevel corner restaurant and you might think that parts of the interior are largely unchanged from what they might have been decades ago. But you'd be wrong. Owners Jason Sanchez and Andy Gruver spent quite a bit of time making the interior of their restaurant as interesting as the food. From the distressed wall coverings upstairs in "the study" to the seemingly random tchotchkes arranged here and there, everything has been intentionally placed. After you've done the tour and have been safely ensconced at a table or one of the three curvy booths near the downstairs bar, then it's time to turn your attention to Chef Sajin Renae's short but sweet menu. There are selections from garden, water, flock and field, and herd and pen that cover everything from salads and mussels to rabbit pie and pork chops. We love Chef Renae's always perfectly cooked scallops and think the flavorful burger made from house-ground short rib, chuck, and brisket served with bacon jam is tops.

The Gin Mill, 2300 Boston St., Baltimore, MD 21224; (410) 327-6455; ginmillcanton.com; Pub Food; $$$. Colloquially, a "gin mill" refers to a run-down bar, but the recently refurbished Gin Mill in Canton is anything but run-down. The vibe is comfortable and intimate, with a handsome horseshoe-shaped bar paneled in tin ceiling tile anchoring the main space. The bar specializes in classic cocktails like Manhattans and gin fizzes, all of which go well with the menu of elevated pub grub, like the Shropshire Blue mac and cheese, or the oven-roasted chicken wings, which can be had with a Thai chili sauce. There are more substantial dinner items like a New York strip, but you might just prefer to come in at happy hour and take advantage of the $5 appetizer specials.

Jack's Bistro, 3123 Elliott St., Baltimore, MD 21224; (410) 878-6542; jacksbistro.net; Eclectic; $$. Jack's Bistro, which claims to be Baltimore's first *sous vide* restaurant, is probably best described as eclectic. This covers both the decor, which is retro-'60s with a dash of '00s hipster, and the menu. It includes the Canadian specialty poutine, various proteins prepared with the modernist cuisine technique most commonly known as *sous vide,* and chocolate macaroni and cheese. Yes, you read that right: Chef Ted Stelzenmuller uses chocolate rather than bread crumbs to top his mac. He also offers a 100 percent beef-free bacon burger (literally, a burger made from bacon), and on the tamer side of things, a rather nice crab cake. Wash down your food with something from the fancy beer list like a Black Douglas ruby malt ale or one of several Belgian selections, or try a flight of any that happen to be on tap that evening. And be sure to check out late-night (11 p.m. to 1 a.m.) happy hour, rated one of Baltimore's Best by *Baltimore* magazine.

Johnny Rad's, 2108 Eastern Ave., Baltimore, MD 21231; (443) 759-6464; johnnyrads.com; Pizza; $$. Who doesn't like beer and pizza? Johnny Rad's has both in spades. There's only a handful of beers on tap, but the selection available in bottles and cans is impressive indeed. As for the pizza, it's Neapolitan-"style" with a thin, chewy bottom crust and soft, airy *cornicione* (outer edge). Because it's baked in a gas oven rather than the traditional wood-fired one, one might call it "Baltipolitan." Johnny Rad's owners, former skate punks Richard Pugh and Steve Ball, pay homage to famous skateboarders like Ed Templeton, Alex "Trainwreck" Gall, Eddie "El Gato" Elguera, and Christian Hosoi on their pizza menu. The latter's namesake, a combination of jalapeño, pancetta, and pineapple on tomato sauce and mozz, is one of the world's finer examples of "Hawaiian" pizza. There are also salads, plus a handful of bar snacks like some mighty-tasty hush puppies, and a spicy black-bean hummus called El Vortex that will keep vegetarians and vegans quite happy.

Langermann's, 2400 Boston St., Baltimore, MD 21224; (410) 534-3287; langermanns.com; Modern American; $$. The American Can Company building on Boston Street in Canton was once home to a tin-can-manufacturing company. Today, the Can Company complex houses several businesses, including Langermann's, a midprice restaurant and bar specializing in Southern-inspired food and good old-fashioned hospitality. One look at the menu always gets our stomachs growling because everything looks *soooo* good, from snacky things (pimento cheese! ham and cheddar beignets!) and small plates (fried green tomatoes! gumbo!) to entrees (shrimp and grits! pork chops!). One of our favorite dishes at Langermann's is the small plate they call Cape Fear Scallops, which are served with tomato and bacon in a clam broth over grits. So good! Another one we're fond of is the tuna-and-crabmeat tartar served with a creamy avocado dressing. And there's the

Low Country Louie, with crayfish and lobster added to the classic crab Louie. And . . . and . . . and . . . honestly, there's nothing we don't like at Langermann's. See Neal Langermann's recipes for **Tuna Crab Tartare** and **Cape Fear River Scallops** on p. 304 and p. 325, respectively.

Mama's on the Half Shell, 2901 O'Donnell St., Baltimore, MD 21224; (410) 276-3160; mamasmd.com/MamasSite; Seafood; $$$. Despite the plethora of seafood restaurants in the Baltimore metro area, none of them felt quite right to the owners of Nacho Mama's. They wanted a seafood restaurant to evoke the feel of old Baltimore, of classic joints that no longer exist. Acting on the maxim "if you want something done right, do it yourself," they opened their own seafood restaurant right next door. The result, Mama's on the Half Shell, has been a big hit. Oyster lovers are especially happy at Mama's, for they can get their favorite bivalves raw, fried, steamed, wrapped in bacon, grilled, with steak, in stew, and in a classic Rockefeller preparation. There aren't as many crab offerings here as at other places, but there are Maryland crab soup and crab cakes. There's meat too, for the fish-averse, but sorry, not a whole lot for vegetarians.

Nacho Mama's, 2907 O'Donnell St., Baltimore, MD 21224 (410) 675-0898; nachomamascanton.com; Mexican; $$. Nacho Mama's wants you to remember the old days. The good old days, when Elvis was king, the Colts were still in Baltimore, Johnny Unitas was their quarterback, and National Bohemian beer—Natty Boh to the locals—was the beer of choice. Today, Elvis is dead and Natty Boh is brewed in North Carolina, but they're both alive and well in this funky joint in Canton. Its decor can best be described as chaotic; kitschy and fun also come to mind. The food comes in huge portions and most of it tends to lean toward the border, with selections like enormous quesadillas with myriad fillings, tacos, enchiladas, and chimichangas. There are other items too, like Mama's meatloaf and baby back ribs. Wash it all down with a "hubcap" margarita, served in a hubcap-size plate with four straws to share (or not) or a couple a dem Natty Bohs, hon.

Of Love & Regret, 1028 S. Conkling St., Baltimore, MD 21224; (410) 327-0760; ofloveandregret.com; Gastropub; $$. There's lots to love and little to regret at this spare space across from the Natty Boh building. The decor is rather ascetic—a long exposed brick wall, wooden bar, and a few tables—because the real focus is on the beverages, most of which are the creation of owner Brian Strumke, the mastermind behind **Stillwater Artisanal Ales** (p. 295). Of Love & Regret offers more than 20 interesting artisan brews on tap, plus beer cocktails for the more adventurous drinker. We like to sample various half-pours from the draught list, starting with Stillwater Cellar Door, the "quintessential food beer," and go on to an IPA or maybe the dry Debutante, a joint venture between Stillwater and **the Brewer's Art** (p. 291). We could spend all day sampling the beer, and that's best done when there's some tasty grub on hand to absorb some of the sauce. The menu is eclectic, with interesting tidbits like strips of crisply fried pig's ear served with a poached egg, grilled duck tongues, and a nice selection of fat and juicy burgers.

Pasticcio Italian Kitchen, 2400 Boston St., Baltimore, MD 21224; (410) 522-7700; pasticciorestaurant.com; Italian; $$. This family-friendly Italian restaurant in the Can Company building serves up Italian favorites in large portions at reasonable prices. There are those who rave about the pizza, which can be bought by the slice for a quick snack or by the whole pie. Try the spicy Diavola, with Italian sausage, broccoli, and sliced banana peppers. Subs are also a good choice, particularly the meatball parmigiana. And then there are the large portions of pasta—if you start your meal off with an appetizer, you'll be taking some of your penne in vodka sauce home with you. We like the gut-busting gnocchi Sorrentina, potato gnocchi and ricotta topped with marinara and lots of melted mozzarella. Pasticcio now has a second location at 8811 Waltham Woods Rd., Parkville, MD 21234; (410) 665-0580.

Rosina Gourmet, 2819 O'Donnell St., Baltimore, MD 21224; (410) 675-9300; rosinagourmet.com; Sandwich Shop; $. If at lunchtime you find yourself with a hankering for a quick and delicious sandwich made with premium ingredients, then you might want to duck into one of the two Rosina Gourmet locations in town. Try the delicious basil pesto chicken salad, served with watercress on a baguette, or the white-cheddar sandwich with Granny Smith apple and honey mustard on multigrain. All of Rosina's breads are homemade, and they are a big part of what makes their sandwiches so good. Soups and salads are also available, as are breakfast sandwiches and a selection of pastries to nibble on during your morning commute. Rosina Gourmet's second location is at 300 E. Lombard St., Baltimore, MD 21202; (410) 244-1885.

Sauté, 2844 Hudson St., Baltimore, MD 21224; (410) 327-2883; sauteofbaltimore.com; Modern American; $$$. Judging by the lively crowd in the front room, this upper Canton corner space may seem more bar than restaurant, but the elegant dining room in back sports cozy banquettes and an ambitious Modern American menu. The "Light Fare" portion of the menu includes gussied-up bar standards like chicken wings that are smoked in-house and served with a celery salad, their version of Canadian favorite poutine, with *foie gras* gravy, white cheddar, truffle salt, and duck confit on hand-cut fries, and pulled duck nachos. Entrees shine as well, particularly the bacon-wrapped Ultimate Meatloaf with a lingonberry sauce. The bar supplies a good selection of beers, wines, and cocktails, and the popular Sunday brunch comes with bottomless Bloody Marys, mimosas, or sangria for $16.95.

Speakeasy Saloon, 2840 O'Donnell St., Baltimore, MD 21224; (410) 276-2977; speakeasysaloon.com; Eclectic; $$. On the outside, Speakeasy looks a bit like an eatery one might find in New Orleans, with its wrought-iron railing and tables on the second-floor balcony. Inside, there's a whiff of the Roaring '20s, the era when speakeasies were the only way one could find alcoholic beverages other than making them in their bathtubs at home. Now we can belly up to the bar to order our libations legally, but the dining room murals depicting what, for some, was the "bad old days," are still fun. The menu at Speakeasy leans heavily toward Mediterranean, with Greek-inspired apps like *saganaki* (flambéed cheese), and grape leaves, and Italianate entrees like veal Marsala, chicken francese, and chicken parm. Speakeasy also serves tasty homemade meatballs as an entree or in a sub sandwich. Happy hour brings a variety of cheap eats priced at $3, $4, and $5 per plate, plus discounted beverages.

Tavern on the Square, 2903 O'Donnell St., Baltimore, MD 21224; (410) 675-1880; Gastropub; $$$. This elegant gastropub belongs to Mel Carter and Brett Lockard, partners at the popular **Blue Hill Tavern** (p. 102) nearby. Former Blue Hill sous chef Jeremy Thatcher is in the kitchen, and his menu is a real multiethnic melting pot. For instance, from Mexico, there's a spicy wild-boar burrito and a *queso* dip. Asian-influenced dishes include crispy duck confit spring rolls with a teriyaki ginger dipping sauce, Thai lettuce wraps, and a sesame chicken salad. Spaghetti and meatballs and pizza are on the menu, but one can also get a good ol' American NY strip steak sandwich. And most of the brews are US-produced, including a handful of local beers. Happy hour brings half-price drinks, plus a different food special every night. Monday, for example, will get you a half-price burger, and on Wednesday a steak is a mere $12, which only leaves more money for beer or a specialty cocktail.

Landmarks

Sip & Bite, 2200 Boston St., Baltimore, MD 21231; (410) 675-7077; sipandbite.com; Diner; $. This little old-school 24-hour Greek diner has been a neighborhood institution since 1948. In our youth this was the place to go to after a night of barhopping in Fells Point; a huge, late-night breakfast was always the best hangover prevention. We like the crab cake omelette with an order of perfect, crisp, and golden home fries. Speaking of crab cakes, Sip & Bite claims to have the best in town for the price, and many of their regulars agree. Unlike most places, where you have the choice of broiled or fried cakes, they make them only one way here: grilled on the flat top, where they pick up flavors from other things that were cooked before them, and vice versa. Also good are the Greek dishes, like the gyro, the spanakopita, and the pastitsio. And in every case, the price is right—diners can gorge themselves for less than $10. A bonus for late-night diners: People-watching here can be quite entertaining.

Dangerously Delicious Pies, 2839 O'Donnell St., Baltimore, MD 21224; (410) 276-4364; dangerouspies.com. It's somewhat amazing that a person can achieve fame and fortune through something as simple and familiar as a pie, but that's exactly what Rodney Henry has done. He's competed on the Food Network's *Chopped,* had a pie *Throwdown with Bobby Flay,* and was featured on both *Road Tasted with the Neelys* and *The Best Thing I Ever Ate.* His pies are some of the best things we've ever eaten too. We're torn between the SMOG (with tender hunks of steak, mushrooms, onions, and gruyère) and the spicy pork barbecue pies as our favorite in the savory category. The local sour cherry pie is our fave in the sweet category, although the "white trash crème brûlée" custard pie is pretty amazing too.

East Baltimore City

"East Baltimore" is the blanket term used when referring to pretty much the entire area of the city that lies east of Downtown. There are dozens of tiny neighborhoods in this area, but only a few have any sort of dining scene: Highlandtown, Greektown, and Butchers Hill are three.

For many years, Thomas McGuiness was the only resident on the land known as Snake Hill. Living in a converted boat cabin, McGuiness set about planning streets and putting in trees. Soon, German brewers and butchers, along with Jewish merchants and businesspeople, moved into the area to create a thriving community. Not happy with the name Snake Hill, the neighborhood became Highlandtown due to its view of the city to the south and the farmland to the north. Once Highlandtown was incorporated into the city limits, it became a major shopping district, with Eastern Avenue as its main commercial thoroughfare. All that changed, however, when the proliferation of malls killed the shopping district. Only recently has Highlandtown begun to see some turnaround with the Markets @ Highlandtown luring both the diverse ethnic community of the area and outsiders to sample its culturally mixed wares.

Nearby Greektown was so named for the large influx of Greek immigrants to the neighborhood. Sometimes known as "the Hill," Greektown features numerous Greek restaurants, although the recent influx of Latino immigrants are beginning to make their mark as well. The big annual event for Greektown is the Greek Festival at St. Nicholas Greek Orthodox Church, where a vast array of Greek cuisine can be sampled, all made by the local parishioners.

Just north of Fells Point stands Butchers Hill. Like Highlandtown, Butchers Hill was populated by German butchers and poultry pre-parers long ago. Once more prosperous than its neighbor to the south, Butchers Hill is now a community in transition. It's mostly home to artists and students, who enjoy the quirky character of city living.

Foodie Faves

Chicken Rico, 3728 Eastern Ave., Highlandtown, Baltimore, MD 21224; (410) 522-2950; Latin; $. As whole chickens spin slowly on a rotisserie over glowing charcoal, their tantalizing smell lures people in off the street. People who didn't even realize they were hungry until they started their Pavlovian salivating. Most folks who eat at Chicken Rico order a whole, half, or quarter chicken and a couple of side dishes, take their food to a table in the brightly painted dining area, and feast on the succulent, herb-flavored meat and crisp skin. Peruvian chicken, while the most popular item at this Highlandtown restaurant, isn't the only thing on the menu. Diners can also get South American specialties like *lomo saltado* (stir-fried marinated beef with tomatoes, rice, and potatoes), and *bistec a lo pobre* (steak with fried eggs), plus more familiar dishes like chicken or steak burritos and sub sandwiches. But get the chicken—you won't be sorry.

Salt Tavern, 2127 E. Pratt St., Butchers Hill, Baltimore, MD 21231; (410) 276-5480; salttavern.com; Modern American; $$$$. While pretty much everyone is in agreement that this little row-house restaurant and bar serves up some pretty terrific food, there is one aspect of Salt that some people adamantly do not like. It's not the exposed brick or the worn wooden floors. It's not even that sometimes there's a long wait for a table. It's the rows of alien-green and purple lights that hang over the bar. While they certainly don't do much for the complexion, we think they're rather fun. And really, when we sink our teeth into the richness of a Wagyu beef and *foie gras* slider, we're not that concerned with what is hanging overhead. Pairing the slider with an order of the duck fat fries and their trio of flavored mayos makes us a bit swoony, so our eyes are closed anyway. We're also in love with the little tuna pot stickers that come with the coriander- and pepper-crusted tuna, not to mention the trio of chocolate-slicked waffle cones filled with house-made ice creams.

Zorba's, 4710 Eastern Ave., Greektown, Baltimore, MD 21224; (410) 276-4484; Greek; $$. Zorba's is a little different from other Greektown joints in that it serves spit-roasted meats in addition to all of the usual Greek goodies. If you happen to score a table near the kitchen, you can watch the spits rotating through a big glass window. (Drooling's allowed, but try not to get the floor wet.) Start your meal with a platter of appetizers that includes *melitzanosalata* (eggplant salad), *taramosalata* (fish roe salad), feta, and beautiful char-grilled octopus salad. The octopus is so amazing, you might just want to order more of it and call it a day, but don't pass over the plump and juicy lamb chops, smoke-kissed grilled fish du jour, or even the tiny but finger-licking-yummy roasted quail. And the marinated and spit-roasted pork called *kontosouvli,* a veritable mountain of meat on a plate, is not to be missed.

Landmarks

Acropolis, 4718 Eastern Ave., Greektown, Baltimore, MD 21224; (410) 675-3384; acropolisbaltimore.com; Greek; $$. Under the long blue awning at Eastern and Oldham Streets is Acropolis. Not the Acropolis, of course, but a restaurant that's a relative newcomer to Greektown, having only been open since 1987. Chef-Owner Demitrios Avgerinos's restaurant is a family affair. His son George is the manager, and his wife, Despina, makes all of the pastries by hand. Her spanakopita is rich with feta and spinach, and the crust is light, flaky, and greaseless. Demitrios' Village Salad, the authentic, nonlettuce version of Greek salad, is made extra special when topped with his creamy Greek house dressing (which is available for carryout). He also excels at simple broiled fish preparations (check the specials to see what is available), but if you want something richer, he can stuff any fish with crab imperial. And don't miss Despina's desserts, particularly the light and lemony *galaktoboureko*.

Chaps Charcoal Restaurant, 5801 Pulaski Hwy., Baltimore, MD 21205; (410) 483-2379; chapspitbeef.com; Barbecue; $. Nationally, Chaps is perhaps one of the better-known restaurants in Baltimore City. Not only has it been featured in an episode of Food Network's *Diners, Drive-Ins, and Dives,* the Travel Channel's Adam Richman chowed down here on *Man vs. Food,* as did Anthony Bourdain on *No Reservations.* Not technically barbecue, at least not in the way those in Texas, the Carolinas, or Kansas City think about it, the specialties at Chaps are pit beef, pork, and turkey. Baltimore's version of 'que. What is pit beef, you ask? Why, it's a top round of beef, slow-grilled until charred and crusty on the outside, but still juicy and pink inside. It's cut into wafer-thin slices and heaped onto a Kaiser roll before being topped with as much of the horseradish-and-mayonnaise concoction called Tiger Sauce as you need to make your nose run. Chaps has other stuff too, like ribs and chicken, but it's called Chaps Pit Beef for a reason, folks.

DiPasquale's Italian Market, 3700 Gough St., Highlandtown, Baltimore, MD 21224; (410) 276-6787; dipasquales.com; Italian; $. Almost 100 years ago the DiPasquale family opened a corner grocery store; four generations later it's still going strong. The market is full of imported Italian products, pasta makers, and espresso machines. There are also house-made sausages and pasta, fresh-baked breads, and prepared salads. Even house-made mozzarella. And don't forget lunch, like a warm porchetta sandwich with melted provolone, served on crusty bread, or the meat- and cheese-filled rice balls called *arancini* that were featured on an episode of *Diners, Drive-Ins, and Dives*. Sometimes we want something basic, like an Italian cold-cut sub. DiPasquale's calls theirs "the real Italian," and we think their combinations of meats and toppings is close to perfection. If pizza's your thing, they have that too, baked in a brick oven. There's a much smaller DiPasquale's Cafe and Deli at 3 Allegheny Ave., Towson, MD 21204; (410) 821-5352.

Ikaros, 4901 Eastern Ave., Greektown, Baltimore, MD 21224; (410) 633-3750; ikarosrestaurant.com; Greek; $$. Ikaros is one of the few Greek restaurants left in the area called Greektown. Before its recent move down the street, this venerable eatery was in the same location since 1969. Dinner at Ikaros is like dining at someone's Greek grandmother's house. The new joint is a bit swankier, with a grand wooden bar and white-tableclothed dining room, but the same chef is in the kitchen and the friendly and accommodating staff still treats guests like family. That's just one reason that people have been coming here for decades. Another reason is the

Goetze's Caramel Creams—
a Unique Baltimore Treat

Once you've tasted a Goetze's Caramel Cream, you won't soon forget it. When you first bite down on the candy, you'll find that the soft and chewy caramel is not too sweet, and the creamy and somewhat crumbly vanilla fondant in the center is sweeter. A perfect marriage. The caramel cream has been the flagship sweet of the **Goetze's Candy Company** (goetzecandy.com) for more than 70 years. When August Goetze bought the Baltimore Chewing Gum Company in 1895, however, this unique treat was a long way off.

The Goetze family started delivering a variety of candies around Baltimore by horse cart. It wasn't until 1918 that R. Melvin Goetze developed the unique caramel cream. By 1941 the candy was so popular that the company decided to make the caramel cream exclusively. Since then, other caramel flavors have been added, like chocolate, strawberry, and apple. There's even a gourmet line featuring licorice and double chocolate. In 1984 Goetze's introduced Cow Tales, which are basically the caramel cream candy in a tube form. Like the caramel creams, Cow Tales come in a variety of flavors.

Now run by the fifth generation of the Goetze family, their candy is shipped globally. However, the candy is still manufactured in Baltimore, and the company uses US-sourced ingredients whenever possible.

consistently good food. It's nothing fancy, just solid renditions of familiar favorites. The spanakopita, or spinach pie, is crisp crusted, with a dense filling of mint- and feta-seasoned spinach. *Saganaki,* an herbed cheese set aflame with brandy at tableside, is rich and delicious when slathered on some crusty bread. There's lots of lamb on the menu, plus several seafood dishes. One can choose from various whole fish, served simply broiled, but we love the shrimp Guvetsaki, a casserole of briny shrimp with tomatoes and the rice-shaped Greek pasta known as *guvetzi.*

Matthew's Pizza, 3131 Eastern Ave., Highlandtown, Baltimore, MD 21224; (410) 276-8755; matthewspizza.com; Pizza; $. Matthew's Pizza, opened way back in 1943, bills itself as "Baltimore's First Pizzeria." Over the years, this little hole in the wall has received its share of accolades, including "best pizza" raves from local media like *Baltimore* magazine, *City Paper,* and the *Sun,* even a nod in a *USA Today* article on the 51 best pizza parlors in the US. While crispy, thin-crust pizzas are all the rage these days, Matthew's remains old-school, making pies with a thick crust that has a satisfying chew. The crab pizza, topped with mozzarella, Parmesan, caramelized onions, Old Bay, and backfin crabmeat, is justifiably famous. They also offer salads, pasta, and subs, all of which can be washed down with a beer or glass of wine from a limited list.

Samos, 600 Oldham St., Greektown, Baltimore, MD 21224; (410) 675-5292; samosrestaurant.com; Greek; $$. Samos is smaller than some other Greektown establishments, so that means the dining room is occasionally quite crowded. But that's really just an indicator of how good the food is. The menu is pretty large, so you might want to go for the Tour of Samos (for 2 or more people) that includes Greek salad, tzatziki, calamari, spinach pie, chicken souvlaki, dolmades, lamb chops, garlic shrimp, gyro, roasted potatoes, and their fabulous pita. In other words, one of each! Actually, there are even more choices on the menu, all of them good. (There are even a couple of Italian pastas and fresh-dough pizzas on the menu.) You can't go wrong with the gyro, possibly the best in town, and dirt cheap at $5.50; close the meal with an order of baklava or rice pudding. Samos is BYOB, with a $2 corkage fee per drinker.

Specialty Stores, Markets & Producers

Northeast Market, 2101 E. Monument St., Baltimore, MD 21205; (410) 685-6169; bpmarkets.com/ne1.html. Fans of HBO series *The Wire* may be familiar with the Northeast Market—it's where McNulty had his kids follow Stringer Bell. The market's proximity to world-renowned Johns Hopkins Hospital has turned it into a 36,000-square-foot food court, rather than an actual place to buy raw foodstuffs, but such is the scene at markets all over town. OK

Oriental is a favorite vendor—they serve up heaps of Korean fare like chicken bulgogi and stir-fried vegetables on the cheap. There are also large slabs of lasagna and pizza to be had from Michael's, and rotisserie chicken at Bair Brothers.

Downtown–Midtown (Lombard Street to North Avenue)

Beyond the harbor area lies some hilly real estate divided into several small neighborhoods. To the west is Bolton Hill, a small community of about 2,000 residents who live in Queen Anne–style town houses and mansions along tree-lined streets. Once home to such notables as F. Scott Fitzgerald, Johns Hopkins, and Woodrow Wilson, the area is still desirable because of its close proximity to theaters like the Lyric and the Meyerhoff, and to universities like Johns Hopkins and the University of Baltimore.

Cathedral Hill is a 10-block area that is more or less in the center of the city. Named for America's first Catholic cathedral, now known as the Basilica of the Assumption, the area is a collection of mostly commercial buildings with architectural styles from Late Victorian to Georgian to Art Deco. Farther north lies Mount Vernon, named for the original Washington Monument, which towers over the four parks and picturesque architecture that make up the neighborhood. During the 19th century Mount Vernon was the posh neighborhood of Baltimore. One of its wealthiest residents, William Walters, opened his home to the public to view his vast art collection. When his son bought three more houses, the gallery expanded into what is now the Walters Art Museum. Across from the museum is the Peabody Institute, renowned for its exceptional music curriculum and library.

The dining found in these neighborhoods ranges from upscale restaurants to comfortable pubs and bistros where office workers can unwind after a long day's work. More eclectic and casual fare can be found in the artistic enclave known as Station North. This recently designated neighborhood is bordered by North Avenue and Greenmount Avenue at the north and east, and by the Amtrak Northeast Corridor train tracks to the south and west. With an emphasis on artistic ventures, old homes and warehouses have been rejuvenated into mixed work/living spaces for local artists and venues such as the Station North Arts Cafe Gallery and the Station North Arts Underground. Established nightspots like the Charles Theater multiplex and the Club Charles anchor this evolving community.

Alewife, 21 N. Eutaw St., West Side, Baltimore, MD 21201; (410) 545-5112; alewifebaltimore.com; Gastropub; $$. The word "alewife" actually refers to a species of herring, but there are none on the menu of this gastropub, located in a handsome old bank building. What Alewife has served, however, is snakehead, an invasive species that has recently made its home in local waters. After all, this is Maryland, and if it comes from the water and is edible, it will be eaten. Executive Chef Chad Wells has featured the homely beast in a special-event dinner, hoping that once diners get a taste, they'll cause enough of a demand to eventually wipe the critters out. Until that time, however, Alewife customers are happy to avail themselves of the 40 or so daily draught beer options and dozen specialty cocktails while dining on Chef Wells's other creations. The drool-worthy Smokeburger is just one of them. This 11-ounce monster, made from a house blend of local beef, is topped with smoked Gouda and gruyère cheeses, applewood-smoked bacon, caramelized cipollini onions, and a chipotle aioli, with duck fat fries on the side. Heaven on a bun.

B, A Bolton Hill Bistro, 1501 Bolton St., Bolton Hill, Baltimore, MD 21217; (410) 383-8600; b-bistro.com; Modern American; $$$.

We really wish this gem of a restaurant, tucked away in a corner row house in Bolton Hill, had been around when we were attending school a few blocks away on Mt. Royal Avenue. If that were the case, we'd have probably been spending more time eating than painting, but really, is that so wrong? Now, of course, we can come to B any time we want to enjoy an intimate dinner or Sunday brunch. It's hard not to order everything on the menu at one time, because it's exactly the food we like to eat: small plates like the country pâté with house-made pickles; a bowl of fragrant steamed mussels in green curry with a side of crisp frites; gnocchi with roasted forest mushrooms. Much of the produce used at B comes from the restaurant's own farm, Fig Leaf Farm, in Howard County. Pretty much everything else, except the meat, from pasta to pastries, is made in-house.

B&O American Brasserie, 2 N. Charles St., Downtown, Baltimore, MD 21201; (443) 692-6172; bandorestaurant.com; Modern American; $$$. B&O is one of those rare places that has both sedate fine dining and a lively bar area. Located in the building that once housed the original Baltimore & Ohio Railroad headquarters (hence the name), the restaurant is part of the Kimpton Hotel Monaco. Serving breakfast, brunch, lunch, and dinner, the B&O covers all bases, but it particularly shines at night. Chef Thomas Dunklin's menu of small and large plates changes seasonally, but there's always something on it that reflects his New Orleans roots. A recent offering that was a riff on NO-style barbecue shrimp included roasted shrimp and some of the best tiny biscuits we've ever tasted. His tuna-and-beet tartar with avocado is a delicious riot of color. Dunklin's menu also includes a section of sometimes-unusual charcuterie (the venison mortadella served with a pecorino waffle and a Pinot Noir reduction comes to mind) and popular flatbreads which also make an appearance on the bar menu. Speaking of the bar, don't forget to check out B&O's award-winning happy hour featuring the skills of master mixologist Brendan Dorr. See Chef Dunklin's recipe for **Tuna & Beet Tartare** on p. 308.

Ban Thai, 340 N. Charles St., Cathedral Hill, Baltimore, MD 21201; (410) 727-7971; banthai.us; Thai; $$. Ban Thai has been serving up the savory and complex dishes that make up Thai cuisine since the early 1990s, and we've been going there about that long. By now the tasteful decor is somewhat faded, but one can't say that about the flavors, which are still bright and bold. The menu is fairly extensive, offering classics like a very good pad thai, and a whole slew of vegetarian dishes. We're partial to the mild *tod mun pla,* curry-flavored fish cakes studded with bits of green beans; the spicy chicken *larb,* with its kicky lime dressing; and most especially the *kee mao ta lay,* or "drunken noodles," a dish of wide rice noodles with shrimp, scallops, and squid flavored with fiery chiles and Thai basil leaves. Put out the fire with a glass of Thai iced tea or coffee, both with sweetened condensed milk, or order a mai tai or other cocktail from the full bar.

The Brewer's Art, 1106 N. Charles St., Midtown, Baltimore, MD 21201; (410) 547-6925; thebrewersart .com; Modern American; $$$. Set in a historic mansion in Baltimore's Mount Vernon neighborhood, the Brewer's Art is: a lively bar, a restaurant featuring inno- vative American cuisine, and a brewery that makes some gorgeous Belgian-style ales, including our favorite, Resurrection, which is also available at select locations around town. The best place to enjoy them, 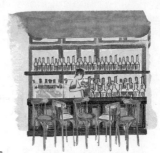 however, is on-premises, in one of *Esquire* magazine's best bars in America. You can grab a nosh from their limited bar menu (cheese- burgers, killer chili dogs) in both the cavernous downstairs space and the bright and airy upstairs bar. But if you want something fancier with your beer or wine or whiskey, then sit in the dining room and feast on roasted Berkshire pork belly, cassoulet, or ricotta gnocchi. And don't skip dessert, especially if the not-too-sweet chèvre cheesecake is on the menu.

Cazbar, 316 N. Charles St., Cathedral Hill, Baltimore, MD 21202; (410) 528-1222; cazbar.pro; Middle Eastern; $$. Cazbar serves the cuisine of Turkey, but many dishes on their menu will be familiar to lovers of Middle Eastern food in general. Those folks might be tempted to order some kebabs (kebaps here, and a specialty) and hummus and be done with it, but the vast menu begs to be explored more fully. Start off with a couple of selections from the wide variety of hot and cold *mezze,* including a spicy walnut dip called *mohamra;* flaky feta-filled cigar-shaped pastries known as *sigara borek;* and our favorite, the *manti,* beef-filled dumplings with a yogurt sauce. Try a *pide* too, one of Cazbar's boat-shaped Turkish pizzas, like the *soujuk,* with Turkish beef sausage and kasar cheese. If you're in the mood for Middle Eastern–style entertainment, Cazbar features belly-dancing shows on Friday evenings at 9 p.m. and Saturday at 10 p.m., and reservations are highly recommended.

City Cafe, 1001 Cathedral St., Baltimore, MD 21201; (410) 539-4252; citycafebaltimore.com; Cafe; $$$. The Cathedral Street side of City Cafe is a coffee shop, all blonde wood and natural light from the floor-to-ceiling windows that make up the first-floor facade of the 1920s building that houses the restaurant. Walk through the cafe to the back and find a more upscale restaurant and bar. The restaurant menu offers a nice mix of familiar dishes, and vegetarians won't feel left out; there's even a "something vegan" plate for those who eschew animal products entirely. For the rest of us, there's a panoply of goodies like cheese plates, steak frites, fried oysters, crab cakes, pasta, and burgers. The blackened turkey burger with cheddar, fried green tomato, and chipotle mayo on a cheddar jalapeño bun got a nod as one of Baltimore's Best Burgers in 2011 from *Baltimore* magazine. Sundays at City Cafe are busy, so if brunch is your thing, be prepared for a bit of a wait.

Dukem, 1100 Maryland Ave., Baltimore, MD 21201; (410) 385-0318; dukemrestaurant.com; Ethiopian; $$. Dukem, an outpost of the DC favorite, serves up traditional, beef-heavy, Ethiopian food like the sautéed *tibs,* the stew-like *wot,* and the tartare dish *kitfo.* For those not familiar with Ethiopian cuisine, eating it can be a fun experience. Generally, dishes are served communally, arranged on a spongy sourdough flatbread known as *injera,* made from a grain called teff. *Injera* also serves as the diner's utensil (no forks!); he or she tears off a piece from a flatbread with the right hand and uses it to scoop up bits of food. Ethiopian cuisine can be pretty spicy, so beginners might want to stick with the nonstarred items on the menu, like the *sambusas* (meat or veg in a pastry shell), one of the *tibs* dishes, or a dish made with chicken called *doro wot.*

Iggie's, 818 N. Calvert St., Baltimore, MD 21202; (410) 528-0818; iggiespizza.com; Pizza; $$. This casual cafe, named after the owner's pup, is a block north of St. Ignatius Church, so we sometimes find ourselves slipping and calling the restaurant "St. Iggie's." We don't find that to be so odd—eating really good pizza can be a religious experience. So it goes at Iggie's, masters of thin-crust Neapolitan pizza with interesting toppings and house-made mozzarella. We like the Anatra, with roasted duck, red onions, bleu cheese, asparagus, and mozz. There are also a couple salads and antipasto to round out the menu. Iggie's doesn't have table service, so they expect no tips. If you want to leave a gratuity, however, know that the money is donated to a different monthly local charity supporting the hungry, homeless, or animals. The one downfall we can see to Iggie's is that parking in the neighborhood can occasionally be a challenge, particularly if Center Stage is putting on a show that night.

Indigma, 801 N. Charles St., Mt. Vernon, Baltimore, MD 21201; (443) 449-6483; indigmarestaurant.com; Indian; $$. "Indigma" is a name meant to evoke both India and enigma; those familiar with the cuisines of India may well find the food here simply more intriguing than enigmatic. But first, the decor: The walls of this grand Mount Vernon town house are painted in rich hues of saffron and fuchsia, which suffuse the restaurant with great warmth. The overall look is rich and rather sexy. And frankly, so is the rather extensive menu. In addition to the usual curries, breads, and rice dishes, owner Tony Chemmanoor's fusion take on Indian food includes a selection of small plates and even some Indo-Chinese offerings. Chemmanoor, who owned Bombay Grill, a restaurant that was once downstairs in the same building, also wisely offers a selection of grilled items that please those of us who mourned when he closed that place. We're suckers for the grilled platter, which includes all manner of kebabs, and usually order it as an appetizer for the table. We also enjoy the Keralese dish, lamb *poriyal,* with its curry-leaf and ginger flavors, and the unusual sweet and savory mango *paneer.*

Jack and Zach Food, 333 N. Charles St., Cathedral Hill, Baltimore, MD 21201; (443) 615-8720; jackandzachfood.com; American; $. Friends since childhood, Jack Neill and Zachary Schoettler share a passion for sustainable food and try to use as much locally grown meat and produce as possible in their products. Their tiny shop in the Woman's Industrial Exchange building, simply named Jack and Zach Food, is open for breakfast and lunch Sun through Fri. Breakfast offerings include egg-and-cheese sandwiches, organic oatmeal, and  homemade granola with yogurt; at lunchtime there's hummus, house-made sausage, and their special veggie patties. Jack and Zach's sausages and veggie patties—which come in several delicious varieties—are also available by the pound, and they sell their pickled vegetables by the jar. The veggie patties can also be found at shops and restaurants around town, including the **Daily Grind** (p. 96) in Fells Point.

Joe Squared, 133 W. North Ave., Station North, Baltimore, MD 21201; (410) 545-0444; joesquared.com; Pizza; $$. When Joe Squared opened its doors on North Avenue near Howard Street, not exactly the most secure corner in town, some of us were skeptical. But Joe Squared has not only thrived as the Station North neighborhood took off, it also won national accolades for its perfectly square ultrathin-crust pizzas made with a 200-year-old sourdough starter. The signature pizzas, like the bacon and clam, are perfect marriages of sauce and toppings, but you can also create your own with ingredients as diverse as apples, tofu, andouille, and sage Derby cheese. If a thin-crust pizza doesn't have enough carbs to satisfy, Joe's also has 17 flavorful risottos on the roster, all of which are gluten-free. Folks don't just go to Joe Squared for the food. They also go for the hip artsy vibe that includes a new monthly art exhibit and live music after 7 p.m. most nights of the week. There's another location at Power Plant Live, 30 Market Place, Baltimore, MD 21202; (410) 962-5566.

Joss Cafe, 413 N. Charles St., Cathedral Hill, Baltimore, MD 21201; (410) 244-6988; josssushi.com; Japanese; $$. The serene Joss Cafe distinguishes itself from the pack of sushi restaurants in Baltimore by offering unusual items that aren't necessarily found everywhere else. For instance, among the many items available as nigiri sushi and sashimi are the not-oft-seen (at least in Baltimore) *ankimo* (monkfish liver) and *kurage* (jellyfish). Another somewhat unusual item for the area, this time on the kitchen menu, is *takoyaki* (bits of octopus cooked in a batter, what we like to call octopus donuts). The *ankimo* is also available as a steamed trio served with 3 sauces and 3 colors of roe. More standard items are not so standard; rolls labeled "spicy" deliver a nice kick, and the escolar (also called white tuna) is the epitome of buttery smoothness. The original location is at 195 Main St., in Annapolis (410-263-4688), and was featured on an episode of the Food Network's *Best Thing I Ever Ate*.

Maisy's, 313 N. Charles St., Cathedral Hill, Baltimore, MD 21201; (443) 220-0150; maisysbaltimore.com; American; $$. Maisy's, named after owner Matt Helme's daughter (the restaurant's Ox Lounge is named after son Maddox), is one of those warm and inviting neighborhood restaurants that we're drawn to even when we're not particularly hungry. When that happens, we like to sit at the bar with a beer and nibble on an order of the beef short-rib spring rolls. When we *are* hungry, pizza is the way to go. The brick-oven-fired crusts are thin and nicely chewy, and toppings are flavorful. We like the simple Margherita pie but have also enjoyed the Bianco (garlic butter, provolone, mozzarella, goat cheese, and Parm). Maisy's has some good daily specials, and the Ox Lounge is the place to hang during Ravens games, especially when beer, wings, and pizzas come at bargain prices.

Mekong Delta, 105 W. Saratoga St., Midtown, Baltimore, MD 21201; (410) 244-8677; Vietnamese; $. There's an unfortunate dearth of Vietnamese cuisine in Baltimore; thankfully, Mekong Delta is there to fill the niche. This little mom-and-pop restaurant is a bit off the beaten path, but the food of Chef Tuyen Vo and her husband, host/server Luan Nguyen, is worth the walk from Charles Street (aka, the beaten path). Most people go there for the pho, the iconic soup dish of Vietnam; Mekong Delta offers a couple of varieties, including one with tiny meatballs and another with rare beef and tendon that is rich, delicious, and positively transportive. The light and fresh summer rolls, made with translucent rice paper and stuffed with a variety of fillings including shrimp or lemongrass beef, are also a favorite, as well as a perfect summertime delight.

MemSahib, 400 W. Lexington St., Baltimore, MD 21201; (410) 576-7777; memsahibrestaurant.com; Indian; $$. Once inside this serene space at the southeast corner of Lexington Market, you would never imagine the clamor just outside the doors. During the week, MemSahib is a popular lunch spot for University of Maryland employees and students, as well as other workers in the area. We think they have one of the tastiest lunch buffets in the city, with everything from tandoori chicken to *saag paneer,* plus salads, pickles, breads, and samosas. Enjoy your lunch while seated at a booth filled with colorful, plump pillows, and hopefully you'll be able to see the large screen showing Bollywood videos at the back of the restaurant. (We like to sing along, despite the fact that we don't speak Hindi.) Mon through Sat from 6 to 8 p.m., MemSahib offers a 3-course prix-fixe dinner, by reservation only.

Minato, 1013 N. Charles St., Mt. Vernon, Baltimore, MD 21201; (410) 332-0332; minatosushibar.com; Japanese; $$. We love eating at Minato, partly because of the funky decor. The front dining room has a ceiling fixture that's like a crazy quilt of light and the seats are lime green, but the ornate architectural touches of the building are still firmly in place. The back dining room is a bit more sedate and cozy. Happy hour brings great prices on select items, plus deep discounts on special maki rolls, and the saketinis are delicious. While we love the always-fresh sushi and sashimi options, we're also fond of the restaurant's bento boxes, which are available at both lunch and dinner. At $16.95 for 4 items of your choice (dinner), plus rice, it's a steal.

Mughal Garden, 920 N. Charles St., Baltimore, MD 21201; (410) 547-0001; mughalgarden.com; Indian; $$. This spacious restaurant has evolved over the years from one serving pretty standard Indian-style dishes to one that tries to be a bit more creative with the cuisines of the subcontinent. The name of the restaurant implies that it serves Mughlai cuisine, which is rooted in the north of India, but the weekend buffet also features southern Indian specialties like *dosas, uthappam,* and *sambar.* The daily lunch buffet is the big draw here. For about $9, diners can choose from 25 or so items, both vegetarian and nonvegetarian. The vegetable korma is a favorite, and the tandoori chicken is some of the best in town.

The Owl Bar, 1 E. Chase St., Mt. Vernon, Baltimore, MD 21202; (410) 347-0888; theowlbar.com; American; $$. This handsome brick-walled dining room at the historic Beaux Arts–style Belvedere Hotel has a lot of history. Most notably, the Owl Bar functioned as a speakeasy during Prohibition. It survived that era but almost didn't survive the early 1990s, when the owner removed the famous owls, replaced them with coyotes, and dubbed the place "Taos Cafe." That didn't last long. Today, the owls are back, and there's the addition of a brick pizza oven. Excepting the familiar Margherita, the pizza choices are all rather unique. For instance, the Georgian has peaches and bacon, the Spicy Latino has chorizo and pico de gallo, and still another pizza is topped with crab dip. The Owl Bar's burger is a whopping 10 ounces, with bacon and cheese, and is a bargain at $10.99, including a pickle spear and chips or fries. Everything tastes best with one of the several beers available on tap, including the beer closest to many Baltimore hearts, Natty Boh.

Sascha's 527 Cafe, 527 N. Charles St., Mt. Vernon, Baltimore, MD 21201; (410) 539-8880; saschas.com; Cafe; $$. The high-ceilinged town houses of Mount Vernon make for spectacular homes; they also make for some pretty snazzy restaurants. Inside Sascha's you'll find a large gold- and red-decorated space with a crystal chandelier and 16-foot columns. Rather than being grandiose, the feeling is warm and comfortable. Sascha's seasonally minded menu is generally small, with a selection of "taste plates," like shrimp and grits, that can be shared as appetizers or ordered in multiples in place of an appetizer and entree. Mini-burgers made with bison from local Gunpowder Farms or duck confit pot stickers are also a delicious nibble to go along with one of Sascha's interesting cocktails, like the Pear Manhattan. Monday through Thursday Sascha's offers some unbelievably inexpensive specials, like Wednesday's fillet and martini for less than $20.

Sofi's Crepes, 1723 N. Charles St., Station North, Baltimore, MD 21201; (410) 727-7732; sofiscrepes.com; French; $. For Sofi's Crepes owner Ann Costlow, cooking seemed like the perfect antidote to years spent within the hubbub of the financial world. When she opened her first creperie in a tiny space between the Charles Theater and the Everyman Theatre, Baltimore discovered that crepes are the perfect portable snack for munching before, during, and after a show. Sofi's, named after Costlow's beloved dog, fills tender crepes with a wide variety of both savory and sweet yummies. Cinnamon and sugar or Nutella fillings are simplicity itself, a perfect light dessert. For something heartier, there's the bacon, avocado, tomato, and sour cream, or the Kevin Bacon (turkey, bacon, cheese, tomatoes, and Thousand Island), named after the actor who seems to be filming something or other in Baltimore on a regular basis. Other Sofi's locations can be found at 5911 York Rd., Baltimore, MD 21212, (410) 727-5737; 9123 Reisterstown Rd., Owings Mills, MD 21117, (410) 356-4191; and in Annapolis.

Sotto Sopra, 405 N. Charles St., Cathedral Hill, Baltimore, MD 21201; (410) 625-0534; sottosopra.us; Italian; $$$. Despite a whole neighborhood dedicated to Italian food located just a mile south, we're going to come out and say that Sotto Sopra, situated at the top of Cathedral Hill, is one of our favorite Italian restaurants in the city. We love the long, narrow dining room decorated with colorful murals, the knowledgeable and friendly staff, and especially the food. Executive Chef and owner Riccardo Bosio serves up contemporary Italian dishes such as organic chicken stuffed with fennel and sausage, and grilled veal chops with gremolata mashed potatoes. Though there's plenty of silky house-made pasta on the menu, red sauce is not the norm. Instead, pasta may be dressed with a decadent porcini cream sauce or a simple veal jus. To go along with the food, try something from the small but well-thought-out wine list; selections are helpfully arranged by style, with suggestions for food pairings. See Sotto Sopra's recipe for **Lemon Basil Sorbetto** on p. 329.

Stang of Siam, 1301 N. Calvert St., Mt. Vernon, Baltimore, MD 21202; (443) 453-9142; stangofsiam.com; Thai; $$. The three-level Stang of Siam is probably the most attractive Thai restaurant in town, its chic chocolate-hued walls decorated with artistic carvings. Even the menus, presented in wooden binders, are works of art. Fare is both familiar and new, with dishes like the spicy and pungent *larb gai*, a minced chicken dish seasoned with lime, and a fine version of pad thai. Stang's "signature dishes" are items not usually seen on the menus of most Baltimore Thai restaurants. Of them, we like the crispy boneless duck with chili and basil, called *gra prao ped*. The grilled lamb in tamarind sauce is also a novel dish. The usual iced tea or coffee makes a great accompaniment to the spicy food, but if you'd like something with a little more of a kick, make sure to check out the menu of specialty cocktails.

Tapas Teatro, 1711 N. Charles St., Station North, Baltimore, MD 21201; (410) 332-0110; tapasteatro.net; Small Plates; $$. Located right smack next door to the Charles Theater, Tapas Teatro is the ideal spot to grab a snack or full meal pre- or post-show. There's even a convenient entrance to the restaurant from the theater lobby. The very first place in Baltimore to offer the popular Spanish-inspired small plates known as tapas, Quayum Karzai's restaurant is probably still the most popular. In warm weather the sidewalk tables are packed with chatting diners enjoying dishes of *albondigas, tortilla espagnola,* and dry-cured Serrano ham with glasses of Tempranillo or sparkly Cava. Often there is a wait, particularly if you hit the place on weekends or before the evening showings. During these times try for a seat at the bar. You might miss out on people-watching, but you'll be closer to the source for your refills of the tasty red and white sangrias.

Two Boots, 1203 W. Mount Royal Ave., Bolton Hill, Baltimore, MD 21217; (410) 625-2668; twoboots.com; Pizza; $. Baltimore's *City Paper* gave an award to Two Boots for having the Best Pizza in 2010, which is something to brag about because it has some stiff competition in this town. Named for the footwear-shaped geography of Italy and Louisiana, this small chain with New York origins makes thin, cornmeal-crusted pizza that combines the best of both regions. The decor is artsy-eclectic, which suits its location a block from the Maryland Institute College of Art just fine. Pizzas are named after eccentric characters like the Dude, Mr. Pink, Larry Tate, and Baltimore's own Divine, but the Cleopatra Jones, with Italian sausage, roasted peppers, and onions, is the top seller here. We're partial to the Old Bay Beast: Topped with crab, crawfish, and andouille, it mixes the best of Charm City and the Big Easy.

Woman's Industrial Kitchen, 333 N. Charles St., Cathedral Hill, Baltimore, MD 212101; (410) 244-6450; womansindustrialkitchen .com; American; $. The Woman's Industrial Exchange was part of a nationwide post–Civil War movement to help women in need to discreetly earn a living. The Baltimore Exchange has been in its stately brick building since 1887, selling handcrafted goods and offering lunch in the tearoom. Over the past several decades, during which time the tearoom was featured in a scene in the movie *Sleepless in Seattle,* the restaurant portion of the Exchange changed hands a few times. It's now run by Irene Smith, owner of the popular **Souper Freak** (p. 287) food truck. Her Woman's Industrial Kitchen, open only for lunch Mon through Fri, reemphasizes the need to provide women with a way to make a living. She's also made sure to keep the friendly old-fashioned feel that the restaurant had in the mid- to late 20th century. The menu has changed somewhat but still includes the famous chicken salad and aspic. There are also new but similarly homey items like light-as-air broccoli cheese casserole and meatloaf wrapped in bacon. After lunch make sure to check out the jewelry and hand-knit items, among other things, available in the shop up front.

XS, 1307 N. Charles St., Baltimore, MD 21201; (410) 468-0002; xsbaltimore.com; Eclectic; $$. XS is one of those quirky places that can't really decide what it wants to be, so it becomes all of them. Part of this multiple-personality syndrome (can't really call it a disorder, because it's not exactly a problem here) may be due to the proximity of the Maryland Institute and University of Baltimore; it's well documented that students may have unique nutritional requirements. (OK, we made that up.) In any case, this Asian coffee bar/cocktail lounge/breakfast spot not only has multiple dining options but also multiple places in which to dine. The first floor houses the coffee and sushi bars. A mezzanine and third floor are reserved for dining. The latter also has a bar and evening DJ. A fourth-floor loft area has still more dining space. So find a table and order up some triple-thick French toast with sweet cinnamon apples and a Pearl Moon sake while your friend enjoys her rainbow roll, fried tofu, and a sugar-cookie latte. Heck, why not? On weekends there's complimentary valet parking, which is a good excuse to check the place out.

Zhongshan Restaurant, 323 Park Ave., Baltimore, MD 21201; (410) 223-1881; zhongshanrestaurantbaltimore.com; Chinese; $$$. Once upon a time, Baltimore had a small but thriving Chinatown. Now, all that's left are a couple of entranceways still decorated with Chinese-style curved roof tiles and Zhongshan Restaurant. Zhongshan doesn't look like much on the inside, and it's rarely crowded, but the food can be very good. Among the most popular dishes here are dim sum, which is available all day. The crowds aren't thick enough here to require the customary stainless carts full of lidded containers, even on the weekends, despite being the only game in town. However, ordering off the menu means your siu mai and chicken feet, steamed buns, and fried shrimp balls arrive at your table hot and fresh. And everything on the extensive menu (dim sum included) is available for carryout. Delivery is also available after 5:30 p.m.

Landmarks

Akbar, 823 N. Charles St., Ste. B, Mt. Vernon, Baltimore, MD 21201; (410) 539-0944; akbar-restaurant.com; Indian; $$. We've been going to this cozy basement-level restaurant pretty much since the day it opened 25 years ago. If we find ourselves in the Mount Vernon neighborhood at lunchtime, bellying up to Akbar's lunch buffet is pretty much a no-brainer. We love dinner there too. Their *bengun bharta,* a dish of seasoned mashed eggplant, is as delicious cold as it is piping hot; "it's not as good as Akbar's" is a phrase oft said when trying the dish elsewhere. We're also fans of the chicken tikka masala, the tandoori chicken, and the vegetarian thali (a selection of vegetarian dishes, bread, and dessert, served in small bowls on a traditional Indian tray). Akbar has another location in Howard County at 9400 Snowden River Pkwy., Columbia, MD 21045; (410) 381-3600.

Club Charles, 1724 N. Charles St., Midtown, Baltimore, MD 21201; (410) 727-8815. Eclectic; $. A blogger once described the Club Charles as being like the Mos Eisley cantina in *Star Wars,*

except populated by hip and unpreten-
tious humans rather than aliens. (This
has been Baltimore director John Waters's
hangout, and he's about as hip and unpre-
tentious as they come.) And a recent review
in the *Baltimore Sun* suggested that the Club Charles
has a "1920s art deco meets *The Shining* vibe." Both
descriptions conjure up some pretty fun images, and you'll
have to be the judge as to which is more accurate. In any case while
you're bellied up to the bar, checking the crowd for roguish smug-
glers and their Wookiee pals, and listening to some Tom Waits from
the jukebox, order yourself up a Zodiac pizza, loaded with cheese,
andouille, caramelized onions, smoked mozzarella, and basil. There
are also several vegetarian selections, like the vegan crab cake
made from zucchini. Unlike many bars, the Club Charles doesn't
open until 6 p.m., so catch a movie at the Charles Theater across
the street in the meantime.

The Helmand, 806 N. Charles St., Mt. Vernon, Baltimore,
MD 21201; (410) 752-0311; helmand.com; Central Asian; $$.
Specializing in Afghan cuisine, the Helmand has been around since
1989, and it's one of those restaurants that seems to be on every-
one's list of favorites. Like **B** (p. 128) and **Tapas Teatro** (p. 142)
up the road, it's owned by a member of the Karzai family, a brother
to Afghanistan's current president, and it's clear that this family
knows food. If you've never tried Afghan cuisine, it bears a simi-
larity to other cuisines of the Middle East, but it might also remind

you a little of Indian food, with more subtle spicing. All we know is that when we eat at the Helmand, we're going to emerge from its cozy environs full and happy. A must-try is the *kaddo borawni,* a pumpkin preparation that is both sweet and garlicky and has the texture of silk. Equally delicious are the ravioli-like *aushak* filled with leeks and served with minty yogurt and ground beef sauces . . . and just about everything else on the menu too.

The Prime Rib, 1101 N. Calvert St., Midtown, Baltimore, MD 21202; (410) 539-1804; theprimerib.com; Steakhouse; $$$$. From leopard carpeting and black walls to crisp white tablecloths, the Prime Rib oozes old-school elegance. As in men in suits and women in furs, no doubt the usual attire when this restaurant opened in 1965. Today, the dress code is relaxed (business casual) but we still feel the need to be formal. Service is impeccable but not at all stuffy. We love to be taken care of by Chuck, who's like a favorite uncle we want to visit frequently. When we order something to split, he makes sure the food is divided in the kitchen, even if that includes making two small crab cakes out of one. Those cakes are full of moist lump crab, lightly seasoned, with little filler. In another app, oysters Rockefeller, 4 huge specimens are topped with enough spinach and cheese to still allow the flavor of the delicate creatures to shine. The signature prime rib comes in a giant, tender, 26-ounce bone-in slab with a flurry of freshly shaved horseradish. And don't miss the crisp Greenberg potato skins with their DIY topping of sour cream and horseradish sauce. See the Prime Rib's recipe for **Imperial Crab** on p. 321.

Tio Pepe, 10 E. Franklin St., Cathedral Hill, Baltimore, MD 21202; (410) 539-4675; coloquio.com/coloquioonline/tiopepe.htm; Spanish; $$$. Tio Pepe is one of the few truly classic Baltimore restaurants that are still in operation. Opened in 1968, the restaurant is still going strong and making *Baltimore* magazine's best-restaurant list year after year. The secret? Consistency. The current chef, Emiliano Sanz, has been at the restaurant for more than 35 years, taking over the kitchen in 1989 when his cousin Pedro, the original chef and owner, passed away. Much of the staff has worked there for decades, the decor is old-school, but the most consistent thing has been the menu, where dishes like *gambas al ajillo* (shrimp and garlic sauce) and the fillet of sole "Alcazar," served with sautéed bananas and hollandaise sauce, still reign supreme. Chef Emiliano has added some modern touches like fresh stone-crab claws and tilapia and mahimahi dishes, but go for broke and order the tender and aromatic roast suckling pig, and don't pass on the luscious pine-nut roll for dessert.

Specialty Stores, Markets & Producers

Baltimore Farmers' Market & Bazaar, Holliday and Saratoga Streets, Baltimore, MD 21202; (410) 752-8632. Every Sunday from April through December, people congregate under the Jones Falls Expressway for Maryland's largest producer-only farmers' market. While spring through summer is peak time for fruits and vegetables, the vendors who sell dairy and meat products are popular all year. There are also a plethora of food vendors, including vegan bakery Dirty Carrots, **Dangerously Delicious Pies** (p. 115), Ruben's Crepes, **Zeke's Coffee** (p. 197), and dozens more. The bazaar part of the market, which started in 2009, offers crafts and collectibles like clothing, pottery, stained glass, and jewelry items. Parking for the event is courtesy of Mercy Medical Center; the lot is located at Guilford Avenue and Pleasant Street, accessible via Guilford Avenue.

Lexington Market, 400 W. Lexington St., Baltimore, MD 21201; (410) 685-6169; lexingtonmarket.com. One of Baltimore's oldest markets, the Lexington Market started back in 1782 when farmers and merchants would bring their wares to sell in Conestoga wagons. The first shed was erected in 1803 and soon grew to include multiple buildings and more than 1,000 stalls. Today, there are 140 merchants in 2 market buildings, including 10 produce merchants, 11 delis, 6 stalls selling fresh fish, 5 with fresh poultry, and 6 selling fresh meat, plus 8 bakeries and 3 candy stalls. Among the best known are Faidley's Seafood, which arguably serves the best crab cakes downtown, Mary Mervis Deli (marymervis deli.com), Polock Johnny's (polockjohnnys.com) hot dogs, and Berger's Bakery (bergercookies.com), where one can get cakes as well as Berger's famous fudge-topped cookies. There are also gifts, accessories, and beauty products available, plus two banks, shoe repair, and tax services. While the market is enticing, we would be remiss if we didn't tell you that, despite the University of Maryland Baltimore campus nearby, this isn't the safest neighborhood in town. Try not to travel alone, particularly after dark.

Milk & Honey Market, 816 Cathedral St., Baltimore, MD 21201; (410) 685-6455; milkandhoneybaltimore.com. Many local restaurateurs have really embraced the whole "locavore" movement, as have residents who swarm the weekend farmers' markets on a regular basis. Milk & Honey also offers dozens of locally grown products for those of us who prefer much of our food to come from sources within our community and state. Among the many local brands they carry are **Taharka Bros.** (p. 187) and **Prigel Family Creamery** (p. 244) ice creams, Roseda beef, Gunpowder bison, Fischer's Apiary, Michele's Granola, and Mouth Party Caramels. Milk & Honey also has a full coffee bar and a menu of sandwiches for a quick—and local—breakfast or lunch.

Trinacria, 406 N. Paca St., Baltimore, MD 21201; (410) 685-7285; trinacriabaltimore.com. Italian products galore line the shelves in this beloved Baltimore deli that opened back in 1908. They're famous for their deli sandwiches, so grab a number from the ticket machine at the front door and wait for your number to be called. In the meantime browse the selection of fresh and imported pastas, sauces, and vinos. When it's your turn, order a prosciutto sandwich and you'll be rewarded with a fresh roll smeared with pesto and packed with prosciutto and mozz. Or, if you're on a budget, shell out less than $4 for a 6-inch Italian cold cut (salami, capicola, prosciuttini, provolone) and dine happy.

Hampden & Remington

No neighborhood embraces Baltimore kitsch like Hampden. This is likely due to the influx of artists into the primarily white, blue-collar area during the last 30 years. What was everyday for the indigenous residents was seen as ironic and iconic to the new-comers. As a result, Hampden hosts events like HonFest, where each year people dress up in beehive hairdos, cat's-eye glasses, and leopard-skin capris and greet everyone with a hearty, "Hi hon, welcome to Bawlmer!"

Hampden started out as a mill town for the workers who toiled in the grain and cotton mills along the Jones Falls. Most of the residents came from places like Kentucky and West Virginia, so the area was seen as solidly white and blue-collar. When companies moved their mills south after World War II, Hampden went into decline, but the abandoned buildings were soon converted into artist studios and office space, bringing a new eclectic vibe to the area. Thirty-sixth Street, known to the locals as "the Avenue," is packed with boutiques, art galleries, coffee shops, and restaurants. At Christmastime one must-do activity is to visit what is known as the "Miracle on 34th Street." One block of 34th Street is festooned with thousands of Christmas lights, and each house is uniquely decorated. Some feature kitschy, blow-molded Santas and reindeer, while others fill their yards and porch roofs with Christmas trees made of hubcaps or snowmen made of bicycle wheels. We don't feel the Christmas spirit until we visit Hampden.

Just south of Hampden is another old mill town known as Remington. Unlike the primarily brick row houses found around the harbor, Remington's row houses feature elaborate details like Formstone, marble, and stained-glass. The "daylight" row houses are appealing because they have windows in every room and some sport skylights. While Upper Remington is primarily residential, Middle and Lower Remington are more commercial and industrial.

Foodie Faves

Alchemy, 1011 W. 36th St., Hampden, Baltimore, MD 21211; (410) 366-1163; alchemyon36.com; Modern American; $$$. Alchemy, owned by Michael and Debi Matassa, who act as chef and sommelier, respectively, is one lovely restaurant. The decor of this small space on Hampden's "Avenue" is modern and sophisticated, done in shades of white and silver, with a sexy tufted leather booth along a side wall and animal-print chairs opposite. The kitchen turns out modern American cuisine with global touches and an eye toward sustainability. Don't miss the mojito mussels flavored with Kaffir lime, blood orange, and roasted-garlic chipotle butter (we don't think they taste like a mojito at all, but that's ultimately a good thing), the butterscotch bean hummus, or the chile-rubbed pork tenderloin. And make sure to get dessert, particularly if they're offering their outstanding blackberry Cabernet sorbetto. Alchemy also offers lunch on weekdays and Sat and brunch on Sun.

Baltimore Burger Bar, 830 W. 36th St., Hampden, Baltimore, MD 21211; (410) 878-1266; baltimore burgerbar.com; Burgers; $. Not one to rest on her laurels, pastry chef Anisha Jagtap decided to transform her bakery, Puffs and Pastries, into the Baltimore Burger Bar because she was bored. While she loves being a pastry chef, she also loves burgers. The Burger Bar is basically a carryout—the only seating comes in the form of a few chairs on the front porch—and there's certainly no bar. But there are burgers, including the standard (grass-fed) beef variety, plus vegetarian burgers and those made from more esoteric ingredients (which could be anything from rabbit to cod or even scrapple). Toppings are inventive (tomato dill relish, curried crème fraîche, champagne caviar aioli) and selections change monthly. Chef Jagtap also has periodic 5-course Tuesday Tasting dinners for a maximum of 15 diners per seating. Make sure to check the website for dinner announcements.

Corner BYOB, 850 W. 36th St., Hampden, Baltimore, MD 21211; (443) 869-5075; cornerbyob.com; American; $$$. As the name implies, this tiny 36-seat restaurant does not serve alcohol, but you are certainly welcome to bring your own. Belgian-born Chef Bernard Dehaene prepares inventive continental fare influenced by his homeland and with a special emphasis on exotic meats. As in kangaroo, muskrat, snake, and . . . rabbit ears. The restaurant even has a special "Gastronaut Society" that offers special prix-fixe dinners to its exotic-meat-loving members. Never fear, Corner also serves tamer fare like duck, pork, and mussels by the kilopot. The servers are all very knowledgeable about the various ingredients and preparations and you may find them able to persuade you to try something you might never have tried before. And like it. Now for the fine print: There can be fees involved, for instance, if you want a to-go container, or if you want to pay by a means other than cold hard cash. And of course, corkage fees apply as well.

Daniela's Pasta & Pastries, 900 W. 36th St., Hampden, Baltimore, MD 21211; (443) 759-9320; danielaspastaandpastries.com; Italian; $$. Sfogliatelle? Yum! You hear that a lot when Daniela's is mentioned. Those heavenly, crunchy, multilayered, seashell-shaped Italian pastries filled with ricotta cheese are one of the many sweet choices offered by Daniela Useli at her charming little carryout on Hampden's Avenue. There are a few tables—two inside, and on nice days, two outside—but they are usually occupied, so it's probably best to plan to buy some of Daniela's food and take it elsewhere to eat. The day's specials are posted on a chalkboard and might include *saccottini,* or "little sacks," made from pastry and stuffed with a savory mixture of spinach, bacon, and cheese, or there might be a sweet version with lemon cream. Many of Daniela's recipes come from her Sardinian family and are made from scratch in the upstairs kitchen, including the pasta. Try one of the several varieties of lasagna that are usually available or the fist-size ravioli.

The Dogwood, 911 W. 36th St., Hampden, Baltimore, MD 21211; (410) 889-0952; dogwoodbaltimore.com; Modern American; $$$. Galen and Bridget Sampson's restaurant, located in a space that boasts one of Hampden's few private parking lots (around the back), is a neighborhood gem. The Sampsons are mindful restaurateurs who advocate sustainable, artisanal, organic, and local products, which they turn into interesting and innovative cuisine. Some examples from a recent menu include gingered sweet-potato spring rolls, "dolmades" made from Big City Farms collard greens, and pan-seared Maryland black bass. Many items are vegetarian or vegan friendly. While entrees are delicious, we like to make a meal out of several starters, perhaps whatever escargot dish happens to be on the menu, plus fried oysters, and maybe a hearty salad or two, like the farro and roasted beets. Dogwood has also started serving brunch on weekends, and the menu is large and definitely worth checking out.

Emporio Grano, 3547 Chestnut Ave., Hampden, Baltimore, MD 21211; (443) 438-7521; granopastabar.com; Italian; $$$. Turn onto Chestnut Avenue from 36th Street and you'll immediately see the big sign yelling "Grano" affixed to the top floor of two adjacent Hampden houses. Inside, Emporio Grano is much more subtle, with multiple cozy dining areas painted in secondary colors. The menu here is straight-up Italian, with a regularly changing list of antipasti, pasta, proteins, and side dishes. We love the deceptively simple but full-of-flavor farfalle tossed with caramelized onions, Springfield Farms pancetta, and peas, and their twist on a Caesar salad made with an eggless yet still authentic-tasting dressing. If you're in the mood for an even cozier experience, check out **Grano Pasta Bar** around the corner (p. 159).

The Food Market, 1017 W. 36th St., Hampden, Baltimore, MD 21211; (410) 366-0606; thefoodmarketbaltimore.com; American; $$. Chef Chad Gauss won *Baltimore* magazine's Best New Chef award when he worked for **City Cafe** (p. 132) downtown. Now he's working his magic in Hampden, transforming what was a sad space into a modern, hip, trendy, and very popular restaurant with an innovative menu. Not content with merely small and large plates, the Food Market also has a category of "little" plates that are primarily carb-o-licious (loaded fries, popcorn with truffle oil) and another called "in between" that includes burgers and such. While the "big" plates like the pork schnitzels and wild salmon are fab, the funky small-plates menu is where it's at. Here are four words for you: duck confit potato skins. 'Nuff said. The restaurant serves brunch on the weekend, including Friday, and during the week yummy food can be ordered until 1 a.m. Parking is a bit of a bear in Hampden, so the Food Market's free valet parking makes us very happy.

Golden West Cafe, 1105 W. 36th St., Hampden, Baltimore, MD 21211; (410) 889-8891; goldenwestcafe.com; Eclectic; $. The Golden West has morphed over the years from a tiny storefront restaurant with a fairly limited menu to a much larger, rather eclectic space down the street. The menu got bigger too, with selections leaning toward the American Southwest: burritos, quesadillas, green chile cheeseburgers. But there are also BLTs and catfish po' boys available, plus a selection of vegetarian items. Even carnivores like the buffalo tofu, deep-fried hunks of airy tofu tossed in a spicy sauce and served with ranch dressing and celery. The restaurant is also very popular at breakfast time, with vegetarian chorizo available as a substitute for meat in several of the offerings. Late-night diners can check out the Long Bar side of the room, which serves food up until 2 a.m. on Fri and Sat.

Grano Pasta Bar, 1031 W. 36th St., Baltimore, MD 21211; (443) 869-3429; granopastabar.com; Italian; $$. Affectionately called "Little Grano," Emporio Grano's wee sister doesn't have enough room in its tiny kitchen to serve anything much more complicated than pasta and sauce. But a small restaurant with little storage space means everything is super fresh. Choose your favorite pasta (linguine, fettuccine, fusilli, etc.) and a sauce that floats your boat (Bolognese, puttanesca, pesto, and several others), maybe a green salad on the side, and you have a quick, filling, and wallet-friendly meal. The cozy and intimate atmosphere makes Little Grano a sweet spot for a date night, especially if you remember to bring a nice bottle of wine to share (the restaurant is BYOB).

Luigi's Italian Deli, 846 W. 36th St., Baltimore, MD 21211; (410) 814-0652; luigisdeli.net; Deli; $. While a lot newer and a whole lot less famous than some of the other Italian delis in Baltimore, Luigi's ranks among the best in one important category: sandwich deliciousness. Their menu is pretty limited—16 or so sandwiches, a handful of salads, and cannoli for dessert—but more options would only make choices more difficult. As it is, we vacillate between the Lorenzo (a panini filled with eggplant and other veggies, cheese, pesto, and balsamic dressing) and Guiliano's meatball chub (meatballs stuffed into half a loaf of Italian bread, with cheese and sauce). But then there's the Vesuvio, a sandwich full of hot stuff like pepper turkey, pepper cheese, and spicy mustard. Luigi's also sells olive oil, cookies, meats, and other Italian goodies to take home.

Meet 27, 127 W. 27th St., Remington, Baltimore, MD 21218; (410) 585-8121; meet27.com; Eclectic; $$. This casual restaurant, decorated with murals of famous Baltimoreans painted by Maryland Institute students, serves American food with a strong South Asian influence. For instance, there are vegetable fritters on the appetizer menu that elsewhere would be called *pakora,* and super-fiery vindaloo pork is an entree option. People with dietary restrictions—vegetarians, the soy intolerant—will find that Meet 27 is more than happy to accommodate their needs. For instance, two of the several burgers on the menu are meat-free; the Indian-style spiced potato patty called *vada pao* is delicious. And the bread it's served on—house-made focaccia—is gluten-free. Actually, everything served at Meet 27 is 100 percent gluten-free, including the desserts from **Sweet Sin Bakery** (p. 162) next door, so there's never need to worry about cross-contamination.

Rocket to Venus, 3360 Chestnut Ave., Hampden, Baltimore, MD 21211; (410) 235-7887; rockettovenus.com; Eclectic; $. Back in 1928 three enterprising Baltimoreans attempted to launch a rocket to Venus fueled with a mere 50 gallons of gasoline. Needless to say, they didn't make it very far out of the neighborhood, but the trip has been commemorated by this eclectic restaurant. The decor is retro-modern, with a little bit of underwater dungeon thrown in for good measure, but the menu is indefinable. There's all manner of pan-global foodstuffs available, like Singapore noodles, Vietnamese *banh mi,* and Korean bulgogi. But it's not just a random tour of Asia; one can also get crispy hot wings, mac and cheese, and a chicken biscuit sandwich. And house-made pierogies! Among their most popular dishes are the roasted brussels sprouts with balsamic vinegar and olive oil, which are positively addictive.

Spro, 851 W. 36th St., Baltimore, MD 21211; (410) 243-1262; spro coffee.com; Coffeehouse; $. This small space on Hampden's Avenue is home to the big, bold flavor of coffee. None are locally produced, but Spro's coffees do come from some of the best roasters in North America, including Vancouver's Hines/Origins, NY's Stumptown, California's Ecco Caffe and Barefoot, and Chicago's Intelligentsia. While nonlocal coffee is the focus at Spro, the short food menu does include local products from places like Kite Hill, One Straw, and Breidenbaugh Farms, plus baked goods from **Pâtisserie Poupon** (p. 71).

Sweet Sin Bakery, 123 W. 27th St., Remington, Baltimore, MD 21218; (410) 464-7211; sweetsinbakery.com; Cafe; $. Sweet Sin is a completely gluten-free bakery that specializes in cupcakes. In addition to lacking gluten, many varieties are also soy- and lactose-free. While baked goods are the primary focus of Sweet Sin, this funky little cafe also offers savory meals influenced by several world cuisines. For instance, tacos, pizzas, Malaysian fish curries, chana masala, chicken Wiener schnitzel, Penang chicken, and chicken parm. There's also break-

fast, with selections like vegan crepes and nonvegan huevos rancheros and omelettes. The cupcakes, however, are what keep people coming back, even those without dietary restrictions. We recommend any of the chocolate varieties, like the chocolate/chocolate, chocolate/orange, or pumpkin/chocolate.

13.5% Wine Bar, 1117 W. 36th St., Hampden, Baltimore, MD 21211; (410) 889-1064; 135winebar.com; Wine Bar; $$. 13.5% (the average alcohol content of wine) is a hip and modern hangout for Baltimore's oenophiles. Owner Wayne Laing aims to feed the wine maven's passions with selections that are affordable, offering low corkage fees to promote quaffing the goods in-house. There are also enticing daily specials, such as waived corkage fees on Tues and $2 off on wines by the glass from 4 to 6 p.m. on Thurs. There are plenty of beverages to choose from, with around 40 wines available by the glass and more than 200 by the bottle, plus a nice selection of beers and cocktails. In most cases man doesn't live by wine alone, so there is also a variety of bar snacks like pork belly sliders, duck confit tacos, and 9-inch pizzas with toppings like buttered turnips or smoked tomatoes and coppa that make tasty accompaniments to your libations.

Landmarks

Cafe Hon, 1002 W. 36th St., Hampden, Baltimore, MD 21211; (410) 243-1230; cafehon.com; Cafe; $$. It's hard to miss Cafe Hon, what with that giant pink flamingo attached to the front of the building.

Fans of *Gordon Ramsay's Kitchen Nightmares* are probably already familiar with the restaurant, which was featured in an episode in early 2012. Cafe Hon didn't suffer from the same issues as Ramsay's typical client; what they did have was a serious PR problem. But now, with the "hon"troversy over, Denise Whiting and her crew are once again dishing up lunch, dinner, and brunch with Baltimore favorites like crab cakes, hot crab dip, and salads with their signature dill vinaigrette. Don't miss Friday at the bar, with karaoke and raw oyster specials.

Holy Frijoles, 908 W. 36th St., Hampden, Baltimore, MD 21211; (410) 235-2326; holyfrijoles.net; Mexican; $. We were regulars back in the day when dining at Holy Frijoles was a lot like trying to have a nice dinner on a school bus. The restaurant was noisy and crowded and impossibly tiny, but the chile rellenos and super-oniony salsa were completely addictive. Thankfully, the restaurant has expanded into the space next door, which doesn't exactly lower the sound level, but there is a bit more elbow room. According to *Baltimore* magazine, Holy Frijoles has one of Baltimore's best happy hours, especially on Wednesday, when tacos are $1 and margaritas are $3 from 4 to 7 p.m. The rest of the week, prices are still low, and we still like to order the chile rellenos and sometimes a crispy-fried chimichanga with black beans and chorizo.

Charm City Cakes, 2936 Remington Ave., Baltimore, MD 21211; (410) 235-9229; charmcitycakes.com. While bakery tours aren't available, we can't talk about Remington without mentioning Charm City Cakes, one of the best-known places in all of Baltimore, thanks to the Food Network show *Ace of Cakes*. Duff Goldman and his gang have been turning out fabulous and fancy cakes from this Remington shop since 2005, and they're happy to make something for you if you call and ask nicely. We suggest if you're interested in having them put something together for you that you check the FAQ on the website because there are lots of rules. The bakery is generally booked for about a month from the current date, so keep that in mind. But how cool would it be to have Duff and his team put together a special-occasion cake for you? Very cool.

Northern Baltimore City

The northern edge of Baltimore City is filled with a cluster of neighborhoods once known as the "streetcar suburbs" because the streetcars carried wealthy residents from their quaint, tree-lined neighborhoods to the congested downtown area where they shopped and worked. In fact, the first streetcar line in the US ran from the neighborhood of Waverly to downtown Baltimore. Waverly may be best known as the home of the old Memorial Stadium where the Baltimore Orioles and the Baltimore Colts played some historic games. It's now home to the extremely popular 32nd Street Farmers' Market, where farmers from across the state come to sell their wares.

The first planned suburban community in the US was Roland Park, an upper-class neighborhood with fine private schools and a quaint shopping center believed to be the first in the world. Nearby Tuscany-Canterbury is a 90-acre section of the city that provides Tudor-style homes and high-rise apartment living for people who teach and learn at Loyola and Johns Hopkins Universities. Charles Village is also an enclave for university staff and students, best known for its multicolored row houses and the 2-block shopping center on St. Paul Street. Farther north is Govans, home to Loyola University, College of Notre Dame, the historic Senator Theatre, and the Belvedere Square Market. And in the northwest corner of the city is the quaint and rather serene neighborhood of Mount Washington Village.

Foodie Faves

Alonso's, 415 W. Cold Spring Ln., Roland Park, Baltimore, MD 21210; (410) 235-3433; alonsos.com; Eclectic $. Alonso's is really two restaurants in one. The popular neighborhood bar, long known for its humongous 1-pound burger (which also comes in an 8-ounce size), has had for the past several years a Siamese twin called Loco Hombre. The restaurants share a kitchen but not a menu, so if you're feeling like a rack of lamb, or Cajun chicken and shrimp Alfredo, then eat on the Alonso's side of the building. But if you'd rather have fish tacos or a south-of-the-border potpie with corn-bread crust, then it's Loco Hombre you want. Fortunately, burgers, pizza, wings, and selected menu items are available on both sides of the equation. OK, so we lied. It's really three restaurants. Recently, Alonsoville opened upstairs, offering cheesesteaks, tots, and hot dogs in addition to the 26 varieties of burgers available downstairs. Let's not forget that the place started out as a bar, so they have a nice selection of beers, including the locally produced **Brewer's Art** (p. 291) Ozzy on tap, and domestic microbrews like the unusually floral Buffalo Bill Orange Blossom. Packaged goods are available too.

Ambassador Dining Room, 3811 Canterbury Rd., Tuscany-Canterbury, Baltimore, MD 21218; (410) 366-1484; ambassador dining.com; Indian; $$$. This quiet neighborhood just north of the Johns Hopkins University Homewood campus is home to director John Waters. (We're not telling you which house is his.) Another notable fixture in Tuscany-Canterbury is the Ambassador Dining Room, located in a 1930s-era apartment building. This elegant and romantic restaurant serves favorite Indian dishes like chicken tikka masala and lamb *saag,* but the menu also lists more unusual specialties like Bengali swordfish with mango salsa and lobster tail with fennel sauce. Then there's the whole pan-fried fish topped with a mixture of roasted garlic, tamarind, and scallion, called Goa fish. Local celebrity cake guru Duff Goldman drooled over this dish on the Food Network's *Best Thing I Ever Ate.* In nice weather there is outdoor seating on the lovely garden patio, which might make you forget you're still in the city.

Atwater's, 529 E. Belvedere Ave., Govans, Baltimore, MD 21212; (410) 323-2396; atwaters.biz; Cafe; $. Atwater's is here, there, and everywhere in the Belvedere Market. There's the original Atwater's, where you can get soups, salads, and sandwiches at the counter or a loaf of delicious bread to go. The adjacent Farmstead Cheese is also an Atwater's business, as is Market Bakery, over on the far right side. We have a friend who is a soup fiend and can often be found here or at the Towson location ordering up some chicken-noodle or mushroom-barley soup to go, maybe with a chicken and Granny Smith apple salad sandwich. We're usually there for the breads; the slightly sweet struan (Celtic harvest bread) is our all-time fave. Sometimes we wander over to Market Bakery, but that's a dangerous thing to do because we can't go home without buying something— or several somethings—sweet. There are also other Atwater's locations around town, including 798 Kenilworth Dr., Towson, MD 21204, (410) 938-8775; 815 Frederick Rd., Catonsville, MD 21228, (410) 747-4120; and 1407 Clarkview Rd., Ste. 600, Baltimore, MD 21209, (410) 296-0373.

Chocolatea Cafe, 3811 Canterbury Rd., Tuscany-Canterbury, Baltimore, MD 21210; (410) 366-0095; chocolateacafe.com; Cafe; $$. Chocolatea is a cute little cafe located in the same apartment building as the **Ambassador Dining Room** (p. 168). As the name suggests, the specialties of the house are chocolate and tea. The latter is available in all the usual suspects—Earl Grey, chamomile, Lapsang souchang—but there are also all manner of exotic teas, like an aromatic wild-rose-infused white tea or a roasted green known as Houjicha with accents of roasted barley and chocolate. Speaking of which, there are fancy chocolate drinks called "coco-lattes" that are made from chocolate melted into milk, with added flavorings like fresh ginger or strawberry puree. Yum. Chocolatea also offers breakfast items like waffles and egg sandwiches, and Asian-style lunch items like shrimp dumplings, udon soup, and teriyaki bowls.

Crepe du Jour, 1609 Sulgrave Ave., Mt. Washington, Baltimore, MD 21209; (410) 542-9000; crepedujour.com; French; $$. Provincial French cuisine is on offer at Crepe du Jour, a cheery (and occasionally crowded) little bistro in Mount Washington. Plump, grit-free mussels are available prepared five ways. The Toulousain version with tomatoes, sausage, and cream is pretty decadent, with a sauce begging to be mopped up with a chunk of baguette. And while there's also duck confit and trout almandine, we go to Crepe du Jour for the crepes. Savory crepes come in myriad varieties, like the La Provencale with shrimp and scallops in a rich cream sauce, and the Crepe Jeanne d'Arc, filled with a ratatouille-like mixture of vegetables. Then there are the dessert crepes—ooh la la! There's everything from a very simple Crepe au Sucre, with butter and sugar, to the decadent Crepe Caramel, filled with peaches and almonds and topped with caramel sauce, Melba sauce, ice cream, and whipped cream. If you're creped out from dinner, you might prefer profiteroles, instead. Crepe du Jour has a small list of wines, but you can get a very French Orangina with your meal too.

Crush, 510 E. Belvedere Ave., Belvedere Square, Baltimore, MD 21212; (443) 278-9001; crush-restaurant.com; Modern American; $$. This restaurant is one of those places that every neighborhood needs. Housed in a former Hess shoe store across from the Belvedere Market, Crush is an ideal spot to grab a great burger—or an even better salmon BLT—but is also a fine choice for a special-occasion dinner. We've always been thrilled with any risotto Executive Chef Dan Chaustit puts on the menu, especially the bacon and egg. The shrimp and grits is another favorite app. Simple, elegant preparations of roasted chicken, salmon, and steak always please, and someone at our table usually goes for the gusto by ordering a side of the truffle fries or the evilly decadent lobster mac and cheese. Or both. (But nobody will stop you from ordering the arugula salad with poached pears if you're feeling more virtuous.)

Donna's, Cross Keys, 5100 Falls Rd., Baltimore, MD 21210; (410) 532-7611; donnas.com/crosskeys; Mediterranean; $. Donna Crivello and Alan Hirsch opened the first Donna's restaurant and coffee bar downtown in Mount Vernon in the 1990s and expanded from there. Our favorite location is at the Village of Cross Keys, a posh little housing and shopping complex in the northern part of Baltimore City. The dinner menu at Donna's changes weekly but always includes their famous roasted vegetable salad, full of caramelized onions, beets, potatoes, and peppers and served on mixed greens with a balsamic vinaigrette. At lunchtime it's also available as a sandwich. We're big fans of another lunchtime treat, the chicken salad with pistachios and couscous. Vegetarians can find lots to be happy about at Donna's: In addition to the various roasted veg concoctions, there are usually a couple of pastas, flatbreads, and specials that are meat-free, like beet ravioli with sautéed kale, or spaghetti with arugula pesto. But our all-time favorite thing to order at Donna's is a bowl of custardy bread pudding. There's another Baltimore-area Donna's in Charles Village at 3101 St. Paul St., Baltimore, MD 21218; (410) 889-3410. See the recipe for **Donna's Bread Pudding** on p. 328.

Egyptian Pizza, 542 E. Belvedere Ave., Govans, Baltimore, MD 21212; (410) 323-7060; egyptianpizza.com; Middle Eastern; $. "Egyptian" and "pizza" don't seem like two words that should ever be seen side by side, but there they are. This rather flamboyantly decorated restaurant in the Belvedere Square complex, with antiqued faux stone walls and columns, giant papyrus flower lamps, and artwork that might be more comfortable in a pyramid, is no joke. In addition to more than 30 varieties of flatbread-like pizzas with such toppings as curried lamb, fresh crab, and Boursin cheese, Egyptian Pizza also serves up Middle Eastern dishes like hummus, foul, baba ghanoush, fattoush, and tabouli. Then there's the soups, salads, calzones, burgers, pasta, pizza, and dessert. The kitchen seems tiny, so it's like the 8th wonder of the modern world that they can produce so many items. We're partial to the pizza, either the India with tandoori chicken and a side of mango chutney, the Al Pacino with shrimp, dill, and lots of garlic, or the appropriately named 8th Wonder with chicken, potatoes, and pesto.

Ethel & Ramone's, 1615 Sulgrave Ave., Mt. Washington, Baltimore, MD 21209; (410) 664-2971; ethelandramones.com; Cajun; $$. You won't find Ethel or Ramone behind the counter or even in the kitchen at the little Mount Washington eatery that bears their names. That's because they don't exist. The restaurant, named after nobody, is owned by Jeff Berkow and Ed Bloom, whose menu of "Chesapeake Creole" foods like gumbo and po' boy sandwiches have been pleasing Baltimoreans since 1993. The gumbo is a thing of beauty, a thick stew made with a traditional dark roux and blend of vegetables, with your choice of proteins, including chicken, andouille, and seafood. The jumbo portion of jambalaya tickles the palate with its piquant sauce, and the pan-fried oysters are spiced with both Old Bay and Cajun seasonings, for a little South-meets-Mid-Atlantic magic. On Sunday Ethel & Ramone's eats can also be found at the downtown **Farmers' Market** (p. 150).

Gertrude's, 10 Art Museum Dr., Homewood, Baltimore, MD 21218; (410) 889-3399; johnshields.com/restaurant/rest/gertrudes.html; American; $$. Local celebrity chef John Shields opened Gertrude's—named after his grandmother—at the Baltimore Museum of Art in 1998, coinciding with the release of his PBS series and companion cookbook, *Chesapeake Bay Cooking with John Shields*. Naturally, the restaurant specializes in Maryland seafood, including crab, oysters, and rockfish. We like starting a meal there with a bowl of Miss Jean's red crab soup or maybe an order of the "zuchettes," which are small zucchini fritters flavored with Old Bay, a traditional Maryland crab cake seasoning. Gertrude's also offers an entree-size version, touting them as "I Can't Believe It's Not Crab." Even if you're not fooled, they're still pretty tasty. If you really want the full Chesapeake Bay treatment, order the Chesapeake Rockfish Imperial or the cornmeal-crusted Chincoteague oysters. Of course, if you're not all that into seafood, burgers, poultry, and vegetarian options are also available. And if you're lucky, you'll get to sit outside and enjoy the BMA's vaunted sculpture garden, featuring works by Rodin and Calder, among others.

Grand Cru, 527 E. Belvedere Ave., Govans, Baltimore, MD 21212; (410) 464-1944; grandcrubaltimore.com; Wine Bar; $$. Belvedere Square is a place where the locals like to hang out, and Grand Cru allows you to hang out in style. Generally serving more than 50 wines by the glass, with several beers on draught and in bot-

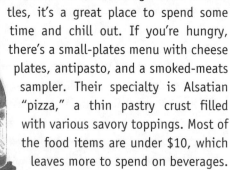

tles, it's a great place to spend some time and chill out. If you're hungry, there's a small-plates menu with cheese plates, antipasto, and a smoked-meats sampler. Their specialty is Alsatian "pizza," a thin pastry crust filled with various savory toppings. Most of the food items are under $10, which leaves more to spend on beverages.

Of course, you can always pick up some delectable morsels from the specialty stores in the Belvedere Market and enjoy them with your wine. Grand Cru is also a full-service wine shop with more than 300 wines at competitive prices. Most liquor stores in Baltimore are closed on Sunday, but Grand Cru is open 7 days a week, so if you need a last-minute bottle to go with Sunday dinner, this is your place.

Haute Dog Carte, 6070 Falls Rd., Mt. Washington, Baltimore, MD 21209; (410) 608-3500; hautedog carte.com; Sandwich Shop; $. This little restaurant (well, we guess we can call it a restaurant despite it being located in a garage next to **Bonjour French Bakery Cafe** [p. 184]) specializes in one thing: the hot dog, which it sells daily from 11 a.m. to 2:30 p.m. Customers line up at lunchtime to enjoy the fancy wieners, which might just be the best around. The signature ¼-pound Angus dog is topped with tomato onion jam and bacon marmalade plus Dijon mustard, making for a sweet, tangy, meaty delight. Three other regular menu items include a veggie pup, a spicy Italian-style dog, and a Filipino dog called the Maharlika, topped with a delicious miso ginger concoction. There are also a couple of special daily dogs, which might include kielbasa, chicken sausage, or a hot dog made with bison. Seating is limited, but aren't hot dogs really the perfect food to eat while on the go?

Jong Kak, 18 W. 20th St., Charles Village, Baltimore, MD 21218; (410) 837-5231; jongkak.99k.org; Korean; $$. While most Maryland-area Korean barbecue places use gas-fired grills, Jong Kak is the real deal, specializing in "soot-bool," or mesquite-wood-fired grills. So the food tastes just a little more authentic. The downside: You'll smell a little more authentic when you leave, but hey, sometimes a little wood smoke and garlic in the hair is the price you pay for a good meal. Besides, if you're enjoying your *gal bi* at 3 a.m., you're probably just going to go home and pass out anyway. That's right, Jong Kak is an ideal place to ward off that impending hangover because they are open until 4 a.m. Every day. Korean barbecue can sometimes be a little spendy, but at Jong Kak $25 is usually enough to feed one very amply, including meat and a variety of the tasty little pickled vegetables and whatnot called *panchan*. The Korean-style Chinese dishes like the noodle dish *ja jang myung* and bibimbap served in a hot stone bowl will set you back less than half of that.

La Famiglia, 105 W. 39th St., Tuscany-Canterbury, Baltimore, MD 21210; (443) 449-5555; lafamigliabaltimore.com; Italian; $$$. When Little Italy's Boccaccio closed down suddenly in 2008, regulars missed their dining-room-away-from-home. That restaurant's former GM, Dino Zeytinoglu, decided there was a need to reunite the family—former staff included—and opened his own restaurant several miles north of downtown. Despite the striking mod interior, La Famiglia's roots are firmly set in familiar northern Italian cuisine, serving richly sauced pastas like a creamy penne

alla vodka and fettuccine Alfredo, and meat dishes like veal scaloppine piccata or Marsala. In the Lounge one can order smaller portions of pastas like the rich gnocchi in a Gorgonzola and cream sauce, or fried shrimp with a zippy dipping sauce. Because diners here are treated like family, don't be surprised to see Zeytinoglu visiting tables like a proud papa. Another nice touch: If you feel as if you've indulged a bit too much in selections from the ample wine list, management will make arrangements to get you safely home again.

Loco Hombre, 415 W. Cold Spring Ln., Roland Park, Baltimore, MD 21210; (410) 235-3433; alonsos.com; Eclectic $. See Alonso's (p. 167).

Nak Won, 12 W. 20th St., Charles Village, Baltimore, MD 21218; (410) 244-5501; Korean; $$. Unlike other Korean restaurants in the area, Nak Won's raison d'être isn't their barbecue, although they do offer it. Instead, they concentrate on authentic versions of other Korean favorites, like *ddukbokki* (chewy rice cakes in a spicy sauce), *yuk gae jang* (spicy beef and scallion stew), and our favorite, *soondooboo chigae* (spicy soft tofu soup). No wait, scratch that—our real favorite is the scallion-and-seafood pancake called *haemul pajeon*. At Nak Won it's pizza-size, crisp without being greasy, and chock-full of seafood and scallions. We also appreciate that the restaurant's *panchan* (side dishes and salads) are so generous and varied. And that it's open until 4 a.m.

Nam Kang, 2126 Maryland Ave., Charles Village, Baltimore, MD 21218; (410) 685-6237; Korean; $$. Nam Kang's been around for a while, and for some, it's the favorite of the Korean restaurants that make up a sort of Koreatown in the lower part of Charles Village. The decor is a tad strange, sorta '70s-ish, with Korean posters on the wall. So they couldn't afford a posh decorator—you're there for the food anyway, right? Nam Kang's menu is huge, offering sushi, udon, and Korean-style Chinese dishes as well as several pages worth of Korean hotpots, casseroles, stews, and barbecues. The dolsot bibimbop (rice, meat, and seasonings served in a piping hot stone bowl) is particularly good, as are the various hot pots. Like its competition around the corner, Nam Kang stays open until 4 a.m. to feed those late night bulgogi jones.

One World Cafe, 100 W. University Pkwy., Homewood, Baltimore, MD 21210; (410) 235-5777; one-world-cafe.com; Vegetarian; $. One World Cafe is a pretty popular place, particularly for students from nearby Johns Hopkins University. We really can't understand how they can get any studying done when it's sometimes very noisy, but we presume that the alcohol at the full bar helps. Just about all of the eats here are vegetarian, with several dishes vegans would be happy with as well. For the meat eaters, well, apart from the occasional fish dish, there's plenty of alcohol at the bar. Honestly, there's nothing wrong with meat substitutes; the tempeh Reuben is very tasty, and you'll never miss the meat in the eggplant gyro. There are oodles of things available for breakfast and weekend brunch too, and there's a pastry case chock-full of sweets, vegan, gluten free, and otherwise.

Pete's Grille, 3130 Greenmount Ave., Waverly, Baltimore, MD 21218; (410) 467-7698; Diner; $. Legend has it that local boy and winner of 14 Olympic Gold medals Michael Phelps routinely packed away enough food at this cash-only Waverly eatery to feed a forest full of lumberjacks. We don't recommend that you eat three egg sandwiches, grits, pancakes, French toast, and an omelette at the same sitting unless you're doing some serious swim training, but you might want to try all of the above on separate occasions. Seating at the narrow restaurant consists of a row of stools at a counter, and it gets pretty crowded in the morning and on weekends, but the wait for a short stack of thick and fluffy blueberry pancakes is well worth it. Pete's wasn't voted Baltimore's Best Breakfast 2011 by *Baltimore* magazine for nothin', you know.

Petit Louis Bistro, 4800 Roland Ave., Roland Park, Baltimore, MD 21210; (410) 366-9393; petitlouis.com; French; $$. Petit Louis is one of several restaurants owned by Baltimore's own culinary Dynamic Duo, Cindy Wolf and Tony Foreman. Each of their restaurants has a different theme cuisine, this one being *naturellement,* *francais.* It's like they plunked an actual French bistro down in residential Roland Park. While the restaurant is ordinarily free of French accents, there is no shortage of convivial spirit, great food, and, of course, wine. (Tony Foreman owns a wine shop in Harbor East, Bin 604.) We go as much to soak in the atmosphere as to enjoy a plate of steak frites, a frisée salad *aux lardons,* or a croque monsieur. And we love the special prix-fixe dinners offered from time to time, say, to celebrate the latest Beaujolais nouveau. The staff is friendly and knowledgeable and always ready to make a recommendation, which comes in handy when choosing something from their very large, very French wine menu.

S'ghetti Eddie's, 410 W. Cold Spring Ln., Roland Park, Baltimore, MD 21210; (410) 235-5999; sghettieddies.com; Italian; $$. S'ghetti Eddie's, sister (brother?) restaurant to **Miss Shirley's** (p. 38) down the street, is a fine place for hungry families, college students from nearby Loyola and Notre Dame Universities, and just about everyone else to enjoy a bowl of, err, s'ghetti or an order of wings. But we go for the pizza, which we like to design ourselves, piling on the Italian sausage, roasted red peppers, and artichoke hearts. Every once in awhile, we go for the Philly-style hoagie, offered with a choice of provolone or Whiz; some consider it to be the best cheesesteak outside of Philadelphia. All we know is that everything tastes better at S'ghetti Eddie's in the summer if there's an egg-custard snowball with vanilla soft serve at the bottom for dessert.

Sushi Hana, 6080 Falls Rd., Mt. Washington, Baltimore, MD 21209; (410) 377-4228; sushihanabaltimore.com; Sushi; $$. This serene restaurant is located at the back of a small shopping center on a busy stretch of Falls Road and is a perfect place to stop for lunch after a visit to the hair salon across the way or before a trip to the bustling Whole Foods down the street. Grab one of the well-priced lunch combos, maybe the tuna roll with chicken teriyaki, soup, salad, and rice, or order an inventive roll or two from their large selection. We like the soft-shell-crab roll and the "I Like That Roll," a deep-fried concoction containing shrimp and avocado and topped with lump crab and hot sauce. Another reason to visit one of *Baltimore* magazine's best sushi restaurants for 2011—it's very kid friendly. There's another location at 6 E. Pennsylvania Ave., Towson, MD 21204; (410) 823-0372.

Toss, 5716 York Rd., Govans, Baltimore, MD 21212; (410) 433-8677; tossthepizza.com; Pizza; $. Blink and you'll miss Toss, located in a small storefront on York Road not far from the Senator Theatre. We love Toss because they deliver, but you can certainly enjoy your pizza, calzone, or sandwich at one of the handful of tables on the premises. They bill themselves as "gourmet," which to some simply means "toppings other than pepperoni." Toss, however, takes care with their fresh dough, turning out thin-crust pizzas with a nice combination of crispness and chewiness. Those qualities are also present in their pillowy ciabatta-like bread, which in our opinion is reason enough to order one of their warm and delicious sandwiches, particularly the roasted eggplant or portobello mushroom versions. Another reason to order a sandwich: It's the only way to get some of their yummy herb-and-garlic-flavored Mediterranean fries.

Woodberry Kitchen, 2010 Clipper Park Rd., Clipper Mill, Baltimore, MD 21211; (410) 464-8000; woodberrykitchen.com; Modern American; $$$. After opening and closing several well-received restaurants in the Baltimore area, Spike Gjerde finally hit pay dirt with Woodberry Kitchen, his rustic restaurant in Clipper Mill. Housed in a renovated 1870s foundry building, Woodberry Kitchen offers homey dishes made with seasonal ingredients from local growers, pasture-raised animals, and sustainable seafood. Whether you're in the market for dinner or just drinks at the bar, be sure to try a flatbread, which on any given night could be topped with air-dried beef, fresh farm eggs, or locally grown beets. And save room for dessert. The CMP (malt ice cream, chocolate sauce, marshmallow fluff, and wet peanuts) was declared "the best thing I ever ate" by local celebrity baker Duff Goldman on the Food Network show of the same name.

Thai Restaurant, 3316 Greenmount Ave., Charles Village; Baltimore, MD 21218; (410) 889-6003; Thai; $$. This little joint was the first Thai restaurant in Baltimore. While not in a very, er, posh neighborhood, it's still worth a visit. Park in the private lot around back and ignore the dated decor inside. Order the coconut-rich *tom ka gai* soup to start and the *gai sawan,* chicken wing drumettes stuffed with shrimp and crab, deep-fried, and served with a sweet and sour dip. The pad thai is usually pretty good, but if you're more adventurous, go for the spicy drunken noodles with basil and your choice of protein. Spicy dishes here tend to be moderately hot; if you want something closer to genuine Thai hot, make sure to tell them you want your food *pet mak mak* (very, very spicy—personally, that scares us a little bit).

Specialty Stores, Markets & Producers

Belvedere Square Market, 518 E. Belvedere Ave., Govans, Baltimore, MD 21212; (410) 464-9773; belvederesquare.com. The Belvedere Square complex holds about two dozen businesses including restaurants, boutiques, and a gym. About a dozen of these businesses are within the Belvedere Market, including **Atwater's**

(p. 169) and **Grand Cru** (p. 174), which are spoken of elsewhere in this chapter. Other businesses in the market include Ceriello's, a purveyor of quality meats, Italian groceries, and a selection of prepared items like salads and pasta dishes. We regularly buy their aged sirloin steaks for special occasions. Neopol Savory Smokery specializes in all things smoked, both seafood and meats. The hot smoked salmon, which comes in several flavors, is outstanding. Ikan Seafood offers super-fresh sushi and sushi-grade fish to take home. The Peanut Shoppe has been selling freshly roasted nuts since the 1930s, plus candies, dried fruits, and chocolates.

Bonjour French Bakery Cafe, 6070 Falls Rd., Mt. Washington, Baltimore, MD 21209; (410) 372-0238; bonjourbakerycafe.com. This very purple shop was awarded Baltimore's Best Macarons in 2011 from *Baltimore* magazine, but they are so much more than that! For one thing, Thursday is crepe night; sweet and savory flavors change regularly but have included coq au vin, smoked salmon, and Asian pork barbecue. The rest of the week, stop by for a flaky croissant or a slice of ham-and-cheese quiche and a cup of coffee from local Maryland fair-trade roaster, Orinoco. Bonjour also sells decadent desserts to take home, like Sacher torte and apple tarts, and freshly baked bread from their sister bakery, the French Oven. And of course, they are more than happy to talk with you about ordering one of their exquisite wedding cakes, created by Paris-born pastry chef Gerard Billebault.

Charm City Cupcakes, 340 Smith Ave., Mt. Washington, Baltimore, MD 21209; (410) 435-8790; charmcitycupcakes.com. Specialty cupcake bakeries are all the rage, and Charm City Cupcakes makes some of the best in town. There are more than 65 varieties available, including "Charm City classics" like the Baltimore Black Bottom and the Pimlico, "breakfast cupcakes" in Espresso and Lemon Ginger, "black tie" flavors like Limoncello Chiffon and Ouzo Peach, plus lots of other favorites like pistachio, almond raspberry, and German chocolate. Charm City Cupcakes also offers cupcake-decorating classes at their Charles Village location, 3215 N. Charles St., Baltimore, MD 21218; (410) 889-8080.

Dominion Ice Cream, 3215 N. Charles St., Charles Village, Baltimore, MD 21218; (410) 243-2644; dominion icecream.com. When you were a kid, wouldn't you have rather eaten ice cream than vegetables? Fess up: You still feel that way. How about eating them both at the same time? Dominion Ice Cream believes that ice cream can be both healthy and tasty, and they prove it by fortifying their frozen treats with actual veggies, including spinach, carrot, and red cabbage. Truthfully, the veggie taste is largely hidden, except in the cucumber, beet, sweet corn, and sweet-potato flavors, but those are still pretty subtle. Dominion also serves non-veggie ice creams, but what's the fun in that?

Druid Hill Farmers' Market, Howard P. Rawlings Conservatory, Druid Hill Park, 2600 Madison Ave., Baltimore, MD 21217;

druidhillpark.org; (443) 469-8274. Most farmers' markets are open early in the morning, but the one at Druid Hill Park is held in the afternoon, making it super-convenient for working stiffs like us. Open Wed from 3:30 to 7:30 p.m. from June through Sept, the market offers oodles of fresh produce, prepared foods, and crafts. There's also live music, family yoga, and workshops—check the Market Event calendar on the website for more details.

Greg's Bagels, 519 E. Belvedere Ave., Govans, Baltimore, MD; 21212; (410) 323-9463. Don't be fooled by the no-nonsense look of Greg's Bagels: Their bagels are fresh, soft, and chewy and come in a variety of sweet and savory flavors. One of the more popular choices is the Vidalia onion bagel, and their everything bagel has the distinct flavors of cumin and fennel. Bagels can be had with numerous toppings, from smoked salmon paired with various chutneys and preserves to eggs, bacon, havarti cheese, duck confit, and, oh yeah, the ubiquitous cream cheese. There are literally oodles of topping + bagel flavor combinations, so you can personalize your nosh in exactly the way you want. There are some who say these are the best bagels this side of New York City and, while they may not sway a hardened New Yorker, in our opinion, Greg's bagels are pretty darn good.

Roland Park Bagel Company, 500 W. Cold Spring Ln., Baltimore, MD 21210; (410) 889-3333; rolandparkbagelcompany.com. Part of the Crazy Man Restaurant Group along with **Miss Shirley's** (p. 38) and **S'ghetti Eddie's** (p. 180) down the street, Roland Park Bagel Company offers breakfast and lunch as well as bagels by the one or by the dozen. Any of 17 flavors of bagel can be had with the usual selection of plain or flavored cream cheeses, smoked salmon, or hummus, but you can also get eggs, cheese, bacon, even Taylor Pork Roll (New Jersey's salty—and possibly superior—answer to Canadian bacon). Lunchtime brings more sandwich options, which can come on a bagel, ciabatta, pretzel roll, flat bread, or good old rye. We're kinda partial to that pork roll ourselves. . . .

Taharka Bros., 1405 Forge Ave., Mt. Washington, Baltimore, MD 21209; (410) 433-1673; taharkabrothers.org. Taharka Bros. is operated by the Sylvan Beach Foundation, a local nonprofit organization that helps young men between the ages of 18 and 22 who are considered to be at risk. Using ice cream shops as a training ground, these young men learn about business strategy while getting the benefits of education and hard work. Not only that, Taharka uses only milk and cream from grass-fed cows. So while the ice creams are rich and delicious, they can be eaten nearly guilt-free. Except for, well, the calories. (Why does there have to be a downside to everything?) Flavors are seasonal; we love the key lime pie, which tastes like the real thing, including the crust. Salted caramel and pumpkin pie are also pretty delish. If you can't make it to the ice cream shop in Mount Washington but want to try Taharka Bros.

ice cream for yourself, it's served at dozens of restaurants in the Baltimore/Washington area and can be bought by the pint at the **Milk & Honey Market** (p. 151).

32nd Street Farmers' Market, 400 E. 32nd St., Waverly, Baltimore, MD 21218; (410) 889-6388; 32ndstreetmarket.org. Since 1980, farmers and local vendors have been gathering at the parking lot on East 32nd and Barclay Streets to sell everything from fresh strawberries to strawberry basil hummus, from croissants to curry. Also known as the Waverly Farmers' Market, the 32nd Street market is open every Sat year-round, from 7 a.m. to noon, rain or shine.

Woodlea Bakery, 4905 Belair Rd., Baltimore, MD 21206; (410) 488-7717; woodleabakery.com. If you are looking for a custom cake for a wedding, birthday, or special event, Woodlea Bakery can design one for just about any occasion. Established in 1943 by John and Dorothy Hergenroeder, the bakery is now operated by grandson Charlie and his wife Concetta. With its old-school design, you might feel as though you've walked into an earlier time when family-run businesses were the norm. The family pride in quality doesn't just extend to their cakes; they offer any number of delicious pastries, doughnuts, and desserts. The cupcakes are a favorite, with a melt-in-your-mouth texture and rich, creamy icing. The fruit-filled turnovers are another must with their flaky pastry and not-too-sweet filling. Woodlea Bakery also has a location in Belair at 548 Baltimore Pike, Belair, MD 21014; (410) 420-2203.

Hamilton & Lauraville

Harford Road was once the main thoroughfare connecting Baltimore City and Harford County. The farmland along this corridor was eventually developed into suburban villages to handle the ever-growing population of Baltimore. Lauraville was officially named a village shortly after the Civil War. When the post office requested a name for the village, local lumberyard owner John Henry Keene suggested his daughter's name, and Lauraville was born. During the early 20th century, large single-family homes were built to appeal to the upper middle class who wished to move out of the congested city. Today, the area retains the same mix of urban and suburban charms.

Nearby Hamilton has long been a mixed-race middle-class neighborhood. However, in recent years a concerted effort by area artists and artisans to bring a more eclectic feel to the neighborhood has paid off. Unlike Station North downtown, which had a well-publicized plan to create an artistic community, Hamilton has experienced a more grassroots evolution. Now the neighborhood is populated with well-regarded restaurants like Clementine, art galleries like the Hamilton Arts Collective and the Hamilton Gallery, and theater like the Performance Workshop Theatre. It's a welcoming balance of a hip, stimulating art scene with a serene suburban backdrop.

Foodie Faves

Big Bad Wolf's House of Barbecue, 5713 Harford Rd., Baltimore, MD 21214; (410) 444-6422; Barbecue; $$. The yellow-painted building is tiny, but it serves up some big barbecue flavors. When Chef Scott Smith and his brother Richard opened up their little joint in 2004, they helped fill a niche for barbecue in this town. Other than **Andy Nelson's** (p. 214) way out in Cockeysville and **Harborque** (p. 23) downtown, there's no place else in Bawlmer that can feed a jones for good 'que. Brisket, pulled pork, and ribs are standouts, but Eastern Shore chicken flavored with Old Bay is pretty fine too. Sauce your meat with any of BBWs various regional choices, like Texas barbecue, Carolina mustard, KC-style (sweet or spicy), and North Carolina vinegar sauce; the occasional seasonal sauce is usually quite special, like the bourbon cherry or blueberry. Try the eponymous sandwich, which includes brisket, pulled pork, and a couple of slices of bacon(!) with your choice of sauce (KC spicy!).

The Chameleon Cafe, 4341 Harford Rd., Lauraville, Baltimore, MD 21214; (410) 254-2376; thechameleoncafe.com; Modern American; $$. One thing we would never have expected to see on this particular stretch of Harford Road is a restaurant with a prix-fixe menu. Back when we were in high school, all we could find in the area was fast food or pizza. But today, should we not be in a pizza kind of mood, we can dine on house-made charcuterie, rich pork rillettes, or duck confit, washed down with a fun cocktail like the Prince of Lauraville (the Balvenie "Double Wood" Scotch, Maraschino liqueur, Ramazotti Amaro, lemon peel), at Chameleon. Chef-Owner Jeff Smith and the folks at Chameleon are serious about serving locally sourced ingredients and hit the local farmers' markets every week, a practice that earned them well-deserved accolades as *Baltimore* magazine's Best Farm to Table Restaurant 2011.

Clementine, 5402 Harford Rd., Hamilton, Baltimore, MD 21214; (410) 444-1497; bmoreclementine.com; American; $$. Clementine serves somewhat eclectic food in a somewhat eclectic (part country, part kitsch) space. Where else can you get Korean hot pot, smoked duck nachos, escargot in a Dijon-thyme cream sauce, and old-fashioned yellow cake with peanut butter chocolate frosting, while your kids play (hopefully quietly) in the toy-filled area set aside just for them? Hmmm . . . nowhere? Clementine also serves cage-free eggs at breakfast, and uses all-natural, hormone-free meats, locally sourced produce, and fair trade coffee. And did we mention that they make their own charcuterie? Oh, how we love a plate of house-made pork sausage and some chicken liver pâté, hopefully spiked with Baltimore's own Pikesville Rye whiskey! Sometimes they offer a seafood charcuterie plate too. Mmm . . . smoked trout salad. But enough about the savory stuff. Let's get to the two words probably uttered most often in this restaurant, "coconut cake." Even coconut-haters seem to love the moist yellow cake with boiled frosting and the perfect amount of grated coconut, made by owner Winston Blick's very own mom. There's a second location in the Creative Alliance at the Patterson, 3134 Eastern Ave., Baltimore, MD 21224; (410) 276-1651.

Hamilton Tavern, 5517 Harford Rd., Hamilton, Baltimore, MD 21214; (410) 426-1930; hamiltontavern.com; American; $. The focal point of this homey bar and restaurant is the fabulously simple Art Deco bar back. The warm wood is a soothing visual counterpoint to the Tavern's other decorative elements: various sharp and pointy tools. Owned by **Brewer's Art** (p. 291) partner Tom Creegan, that bar serves up a nice selection of American craft brews, including, naturally, Brewer's Art Resurrection Ale. The food menu is short but sweet and changes seasonally, but the must-try at Hamilton Tavern is their Crosstown Burger. A thick and juicy patty of local Roseda Farms beef is cooked perfectly to order, topped with a generous portion of horseradish cheddar, shredded lettuce, and onion, and served on a sesame seed bun from **Hamilton Bakery** (p. 197) up the road. There's also the option of topping your burger with a fried egg, and/or slices of sweet and sticky bacon (yes and yes!).

It's making us drool just thinking about it. Start your meal out with an order of the fried dill pickle chips with goat cheese sauce for dipping, or a half pound of perfectly steamed shrimp, and you'll be happy (and full) campers.

Red Canoe, 4337 Harford Rd., Baltimore, MD; 21214; (410) 444-4440; redcanoe.bz; Cafe; $. In an era when even the big nationwide booksellers can't hold their own against Internet retail giants, it's a breath of fresh air to see a cute little independent like Red Canoe thriving. Not only do they offer literature for all ages and a selection of books and toys for the kiddies, Red Canoe also serves breakfast and lunch 7 days a week (dinner too, if you're inclined to eat by 5 p.m.). The menu includes a selection of wraps, salads, and sandwiches, but Red Canoe is probably best known for their muffins, both sweet and savory. The blueberry is a favorite, as is the coffee cake, but every variety of the house-made treat is uniformly moist and delicious. On Thursday pizza is on the menu, with inventive combos like bleu cheese, figs, and bacon, or apple butter with chicken and three cheeses.

Tooloulou, 4311 Harford Rd., Lauraville, Baltimore, MD 21214; (443) 627-8090; tooloulou.com; Cajun; $. Tiny doesn't begin to describe Tooloulou; the whole restaurant could probably fit in our town-house living room with space left over. But apparently square footage isn't a requirement for churning out big Cajun flavors.

Tooloulou's menu is spare, offering sandwiches, pizzas, wings, and sides like dirty rice and Old Bay fries, many with a distinct New Orleans bent. Most of the sandwich selections are po' boys, Louisiana-style subs served on French bread with pickles, Tabasco remoulade, lettuce, and tomato, with your choice of protein (shrimp, oyster, catfish, roast beef . . . even gator). Pizzas come in 12- and 16-inch sizes and are not your mama's pizza, unless she uses toppings like homemade sausage and aged provolone. We love the namesake pie, which heaps crab, Andouille sausage, banana peppers, mozzarella, and a sprinkle of Old Bay on a thin crust smeared with white sauce. If you choose to take your food home rather than eat at one of the four tables and counters, the smell will drive you insane until you reach your destination.

Landmarks

Koco's Pub and Grill, 4301 Harford Rd., Baltimore, MD 21214; (410) 426-3519; kocospub.com; Pub Food; $$$. What's yellow and blue on the outside and chartreuse on the inside? Koco's Pub. This colorful sliver of a restaurant, decorated with painted foliage and parrots, has one of Baltimore's best crab cakes. Seriously, it blew us away. Koco's is a neighborhood bar, full of friendly patrons who are willing to debate you on the merits of current and former Baltimore Orioles players, but it's also a popular spot for lunch and dinner, in no small part due to that crab cake. It's huge, as big as two cakes

CRAB CAKE WARS

While reading this book, the reader might notice that many, if not most, restaurants in the Baltimore area serve crab cakes. A goodly number of these places, both plain and fancy, claim to serve the best crab cake in the area. There can really only be one "best" of anything, so these restaurants can't all be right.

So who does have the best crab cake in town?

We have our favorites, but we can't pick just one to call the very best. After all, personal preference does come into play here. There may be folks who prefer the somewhat dryer cakes that result from being made with jumbo or colossal lump crabmeat and very little binder. Still others might like the addition of vegetables like bell peppers. (We don't— it detracts from the flavor of the crab itself.) After trying dozens of crab cakes while writing this book, we can make some recommendations.

We feel that truly superlative examples of Maryland's ubiquitous patty of crabmeat include those served at **Koco's Pub and Grill** (kocospub.com) in Lauraville and **Pierpoint** (pierpointrestaurant.com) in Fells Point. Other highly recommended cakes are served at **G&M Restaurant & Lounge** (gandmcrabcakes.com) in Linthicum, **Faidley's** in the Lexington Market (lexingtonmarket.com), **Pappas Restaurant** (pappascrabcakes.com) in northern Baltimore County, and the **Prime Rib** (theprimerib.com) downtown. And we wouldn't turn our nose up at the specimens found at **Mr. Bill's Terrace Inn** and **By the Docks** (bythedocks.com) either.

anywhere else, and chock full of sweet blue crab with little filler. Their meaty chicken wings are worth a mention too, as is Mom's crab soup. While Koco's is by no means fancy, you just might want to make a reservation if you plan to belly up to a crab cake or 8-ounce burger. Oh, and there's a dress code: Gentlemen, don't even think of wearing a tank top.

Specialty Stores, Markets & Producers

Green Onion Market, 5500 Harford Rd., greenonionmarket.net. Green Onion is probably a lot like the kind of market that our great-grandparents shopped in. One of those little corner stores that got their goods from local farmers, where everything was super-fresh. Green Onion offers meats by Glen Arm's Genuine Food Co. and Mt. Airy's Wagon Wheel Ranch, eggs from Harford County's Andy's Eggs and Baltimore County's Mingodale Farm, and ice cream from Glen Arm's **Prigel Family Creamery** (p. 244). There is also a selection of goodies from **Clementine** (p. 191) down the street, including their amazing charcuterie and pickles. Coffee comes from **Zeke's** (p. 197), which is a bit farther down Harford Road. OK, you're probably getting the picture by now: Green Onion is making old-fashioned new-fashioned again and is a very welcome addition to the Baltimore area.

Hamilton Bakery, 5414 Harford Rd., Baltimore, MD 21214; (410) 254-0797; hamiltonbakery.com. Hamilton Bakery is so serious about freshness, they even mill their own organic flour on-premises every morning! With it—and lashings of real butter, eggs, and vanilla—they bake everything from breads and cookies to gourmet pastries to wedding cakes. And of course, cupcakes. Their versions of the popular treat are so good, *Baltimore* magazine named them among the top 10 cupcakes in the area for 2011 (#2!), and the bakery had only been open for a handful of months at that time. So if you find yourself in the neighborhood with a hankering for something sweet, pop into Hamilton Bakery and order yourself up a cup of locally roasted Zeke's coffee and a strawberry shortcake or a banana nut muffin. You might also be tempted to buy a loaf of black olive ciabatta to nosh on, by the hunk, right out of the bag.

Zeke's Coffee, 4607 Harford Rd., Baltimore, MD 21214; (410) 254-0122. Local coffee roaster Zeke's has only been around since 2005, when they started peddling their wares at the Baltimore Farmers' Market. Zeke's uses quality Arabica beans that are roasted locally in very small batches using a fluid bed roaster. They offer signature blends with names that reflect landmarks in our fair city, such as Shot Tower espresso or the natural fair trade blend Montebello Reserve, plus more conventional varieties like Moka Java or Sumatra Mandeling. While this location is primarily a retail establishment where one can pick up a few pounds of beans to go, there's also room to sit and enjoy a cup or two, perhaps accompanied by a treat from nearby Hamilton Bakery.

Eastern Baltimore County

Much of Baltimore County's history is tied to the "flight to the suburbs" so many major cities experienced during the mid–20th century. The town of Dundalk, however, has a history more closely tied to the neighborhoods of Baltimore City. Established in 1856 when Henry McShane set up his Bell Foundry on land near the body of water known as Patapsco Neck, Dundalk became a prime site for new industry. After Bethlehem Steel built a plant in Sparrows Point, plans were put in motion to develop a residential community for its employees modeled after Roland Park. The shopping center at Shipping Place still bears some resemblance to its older cousin. Dundalk thrived in the years after World War II, its population swelling to over 80,000 during the 1960s and 1970s. Its affluent residents could support landmark restaurants like the Brentwood Inn. Major companies like Bethlehem Steel and General Motors eventually left the area, and the town has seen some decline.

The Brentwood Inn is gone as well, but restaurants like Jimmy's Seafood, Squire's, and the Poplar Inn still flourish.

Nearby Essex started out as a 10-block area set aside for housing but quickly swelled thanks to industrial jobs and the Glenn L. Martin Airport. Farmland was sold off to create more residential housing. The desire for waterfront property caused development along Middle River as well.

Similar history is shared by places like Overlea, Rosedale, and Perry Hall. Acres and acres of farms were converted into housing developments and strip malls. White Marsh is the most recent development, started in the 1970s with the concept of putting a shopping mall at the community's center. Since then, the area has grown with commercial interests firmly in mind. Although much of the dining there leans toward national chains, the occasional culinary gem can be found within its borders.

Foodie Faves

Al's Seafood, 1551 Eastern Blvd., Essex, MD 21221; (410) 687-3264; als-seafood.com; Seafood; $$. Al's started out as a carryout in Fells Point, where our families routinely bought crab cakes and coleslaw. The Essex location started out as a carryout too, expanding into a full-service restaurant in the early 1980s. All of the usual Maryland seafood favorites are available at Al's, including steamed crabs. Buy them individually, by the dozen, or pig out on the "all-you-can-eat" (in 2 hours) deal. Another pig-out opportunity comes with Cap't Doc's Broiled Seafood Medley, which includes a crab cake, flounder, crab imperial, shrimp, scallops, and a lobster tail, all served with drawn butter, plus a salad and a veg. More delicate eaters might prefer oysters on the half shell and a cup of Maryland crab soup, but when such a bounty of seafood items is available in one place, we say go for it.

Arigato Hibachi & Sushi, 7698 Belair Rd., Fullerton, MD 21236; arigatoblt.com; Japanese; $$. A friend of ours recommended this little strip-mall restaurant, saying that the sushi she ate there was so good it made her cry with happiness. With a recommendation like that, we dropped what we were doing and headed out to Fullerton. She was not wrong. Arigato's sushi is some of the best we've eaten in Baltimore. The portions are properly petite and easy to eat, the fish is amazingly fresh and tender, and the rice is usually still a bit warm, which makes everything melt in our mouths. We've also sampled the hibachi meals, which are cooked on a flat-top grill like those used in Benihana-type places, but without the spectacle of onion ring volcanoes and flying shrimp. Portions are generous—your choice of protein(s) comes with clear soup, salad with a yummy sesame dressing, noodles, various vegetables, and a huge pile of white or fried rice. A single order is ample enough to share, especially if you're ordering sushi too.

Boulevard Diner, 1660 Merritt Blvd., Dundalk, MD 21222; (410) 285-8660; boulevarddiner.com; Diner; $$. It always surprises us that all diners, while outwardly similar, have their own personalities. Take the Boulevard Diner. It's typically shiny with chrome and neon lights, but it's not open 24/7 (except on Fri and Sat). And the menu is long, but it's not mind-boggling. In fact, it's just right. One page points out the specialties that were prepared for Guy Fieri on a 2012 episode of *Diners, Drive-Ins, and Dives:* the sour beef and dumplings and the grape leaves. Those grape leaves are made from owner Marc Tsakiris's family recipe, which includes ground pork as well as the usual beef, plus lots of dill, and are served five to an order with a topping of tart avgolemono (egg and lemon) sauce. If that's too dainty for you, try the Big A$$ sandwich, topped with several pounds of pit beef, pot roast, and corned beef, plus fried onions, cheese sauce, and horseradish mayo. And you might want to bring your family to help you eat it.

Broadway Diner, 6501 Eastern Ave., Dundalk, Baltimore, MD 21224; broadwaydiner1.com; (410) 631-5666; Diner; $$. The Broadway Diner has only been around for a handful of years, yet it has all of the trappings of a much older, classic diner. Lots of shiny chrome? Check. Open 24 hours? Check. Breakfast all day? Check. Huge portions of food? Check. What's most impressive about modern diners like the Broadway, though, is that not only can they churn out a huge variety of dishes, from pancakes to filet mignon, they also make dishes just as good as those in more expensive, fancy places. We tend to be a little piggy at the Broadway, ordering fat 18-ounce NY strips that come with not only onion rings and mushroom caps but also soup or salad, potato, and a veg, for $22. All that food means that two can eat quite well, or one person will have enough leftovers for lunch the next day. We also like the fancypants Angus burgers and have to admit a fondness for the evil barbecued pulled pork and mac-and-cheese sandwich. Yes, both, on one sandwich. Guy Fieri is fond of the restaurant's Hungarian Goulash, which he proclaimed "goulishious."

By the Docks, 3321 Eastern Blvd., Middle River, MD 21220; (410) 686-1188; bythedocks.com; Seafood; $$$. Despite the name, By the Docks isn't by the docks at all (it's not far), but you have to admit it's a catchier name than "Sorta Close to the Docks" or "By Bengie's Drive-In." The restaurant's not much to look at inside, but it's usually so packed full of hungry people that nobody notices. Most folks are there to dine on the crab cakes, which are a full half pound of lump blue crab (from the Chesapeake, in season) and very little filler, and generally one of the best cakes in the area. By the Docks also has some nice weekly specials that might tempt people into ordering something other than crab cakes. Monday is Greek Night, which brings a small selection of Greek specialties to the menu. Tuesday is Italian night, and on Wednesday ribs and steak are featured. Seafood's day comes on Thursday, and the weekend specials include items not on the regular menu.

Chopstix Gourmet, 5002 Honeygo Center Dr., Perry Hall, MD 21128; (410) 256-9136; chopstixgourmet.com; Chinese; $$. The mix of Japanese and Chinese decor (shoji-screen-like partitions and replicas of the Chinese Qin dynasty terra-cotta warriors), lots of wood, and soothing lighting belies the fact that Chopstix is in a strip mall. The decor is fusion, and so is the menu. Not all restaurants can do both cuisines right, but Chopstix does; we always end up ordering a couple of pieces of nigiri sushi and a roll (try the Baltimore, with shrimp, crab, and avocado, flavored with Old Bay and topped with crunchy tempura flakes) as appetizers before ordering entrees from the Chinese side of the menu. A favorite is, believe it or not, the shrimp egg foo young, smartly served with the lightly curry-flavored sauce on the side, so the omelettes stay delightfully crisp.

Costas Inn, 4100 N. Point Blvd., Dundalk, Baltimore, MD 21222; (410) 477-1975; costasinn.com; Seafood; $$$. The sound of mallet on crab is like music to our ears, which is a good thing, since that's pretty much all one hears at Costas Inn on any given summer day. Oh, there are plenty of other things on the menu (including some near-pornographic photographs of crab cakes and stuffed lobsters), and it's all good—crab soup, crab dip, crab cakes, pit beef or turkey sandwiches—but when we go to Costas, we tend to order only two things: crabs and onion rings. (Three things, if you count beer.) The crabs, which are served caked in enough crab seasoning to have your lips and hangnails tingling halfway through the first steamed beast, are available year-round. They're flown in from the Gulf daily and sorted at the restaurant, so you won't find any puny or weird crabs in your two dozen extra larges. If you're a novice at the whole business of crabs, a server will be more than happy to demonstrate the proper picking technique so you don't miss any sweet and luscious morsels of meat.

Fiesta Mexicana, 8304 Philadelphia Rd., Rosedale, MD 21237; (410) 686-0134; Mexican; $. Federico Lopez's homey little restaurant specializes in authentic Mexico City–style street food, or *antojitos*. The key word here is "authentic," which translates as "delicious." The various fried and stuffed treats we know as flautas, enchiladas, and tacos are all available, along with some less-familiar specialties like sopes and tortas. There's also the *pambazo:* a fresh roll coated with a sauce made from mild guajillo chiles, which is then flash-fried and stuffed with sausage, potato, lettuce, crema fresca, and cheese. It's a messy delight. Less messy but no less delightful are the quesadillas, made from raw, fresh corn tortillas filled with your choice of goodies (try the chorizo and potato), folded in half, fried, and served with a drizzle of crema and *queso Oaxaca*. Samplers are also available, like the Paquet Eduques, which will get you two enchiladas, a quesadilla, a flauta, a sope, and a taco. Everything is made to order, while you watch, which is all part of the fun.

The Snowball

Many places have created their own icy dessert like the Italian ice or the Hawaiian shave ice, but Baltimore can lay claim to creating the snowball. Before the invention of refrigeration, huge blocks of ice were hauled from New York down the East Coast to Florida on wagons. When the ice wagons passed through Baltimore, children would run up to them hoping to collect some of the ice scrapings. After a while mothers started making flavorings to put on the small mounds of chipped ice. Later, the summer treat was commercialized when theaters began offering the snowballs to lure customers into their stuffy venues. Early snowballs were made by hand-shaving the ice, but by the end of the 19th century, electric ice-shaving devices were invented.

Early flavorings were fairly simple, with the earliest being a combination of egg, vanilla, and sugar known as egg custard. It's still one of the most popular flavors today, but snowball purveyors have become quite inventive. Visit a snowball stand today and you may find exotic fruit flavors like mango or blood orange and even cocktail tastes like piña colada and amaretto (nonalcoholic, of course).

A traditional topping for a snowball is gooey marshmallow, but some stands offer to put a scoop of ice cream in the cup as well. At **Stouten's Shaved Ice Snowballs** in Dundalk, Maryland, you can get a "Milky Way" snowball featuring ice cream, marshmallow, caramel, and Hershey's chocolate.

The popularity of the snowball spread beyond Baltimore during the Depression when cheap treats were a necessity. Once World War II began, most of the ice cream in the US was shipped to the servicemen, leaving snowballs as the only frozen option for many Americans. Today, snowballs have the greatest popularity in two places: Louisiana and Baltimore.

Frank's Pizza & Pasta, 6620 Belair Rd., Overlea, Baltimore, MD 21206; (410) 254-2900; frankspizzaandpasta.com; Pizza; $$. It looks much like any other strip-mall carryout on the outside, but inside Frank's you'll find amazingly friendly folks who are truly thrilled to feed you one or more of their specialties. The pizza comes in both a thin-crust Neapolitan style and the more bread-like thick-crusted Sicilian style; strombolis and calzones are also available. And then there's the pasta, including a lovely fettuccine dish with shrimp, scallops, and crab in a creamy pink sauce. The subs at Frank's are good too, particularly the meatball parmigiana. There's no table service, so be prepared to run back and forth to the counter to fetch your food, drinks, etc. But look on the bright side: Maybe you'll burn off a couple of calories' worth of cheese.

Michael's Steak & Lobster House, 6207 Eastern Ave. #9, Baltimore, MD 21224; (410) 633-6485; michaelssteakandlobster .com; Steakhouse; $$$. While overindulgence isn't necessarily the in thing to do these days, every once in a while you just want to eat a giant steak as big as your head. Michael's is the place to do just that without forking over a lot of dough. This old-fashioned Baltimore steakhouse has a 40-ounce porterhouse that will make you feel like Fred Flintstone. And it costs about 20 bucks. How about a 32-ounce crab cake, which better resembles an entire meatloaf than the Maryland specialty? There are more delicately proportioned items available, like the comparatively tiny 10-ounce fillet and 8-ounce lobster-tail combination. If you want steamed crabs, they have those too. And Greek food. The appetizer platter has some lovely spinach and cheese pies, stuffed grape leaves, and *taramosalata,* but that won't leave much room for steak now, will it?

Mr. Bill's Terrace Inn, 200 Eastern Blvd., Essex, MD 21221; (410) 687-5994; Crab House; $$$. Get to Mr. Bill's early (the restaurant opens at 4:15 p.m.) and put your name on the waiting list (at 4 p.m., there will already be 10 parties ahead of you). Once seated, get your crab and beer order in right away and only then peruse the menu for accompaniments to your crabtastic feast. We like the spicy Maryland crab and smooth cream-of-crab soups. Crab cakes are tasty too. Even if they do have a bit more breading than is currently in vogue, they're also full of giant lumps of flavorful backfin. Just when you're finishing your appetizers, your crabs will arrive, screaming hot and thickly coated with a proprietary blend of seasonings that's much less salty than other crab-house blends and that doesn't muffle the sweet, sweet taste of the crab's moist meat. Crack, pick, enjoy, and repeat until all crabs are gone.

Vinny's, 6212 Holabird Ave., Dundalk, Baltimore, MD 21224; (410) 633-7763; Italian; $$. Vinny's is quite the charming little restaurant. We get a kick out of the interior decoration, with murals of the Italian countryside on one wall and a replica of Michelangelo's famous image of the Creation of Adam from the Sistine Chapel on another. The chow is classic: cold antipasto platters, marinara everywhere, and veal Parmesan. Familiar comfort food Italian. We like the hearty potato gnocchi smothered in tomato sauce and topped with melted mozzarella and Parmesan cheeses. Vinny's also has pizza, the kind with a thin crust that's perfect for folding. It's so good, we dare say even fussy New Yorkers would be happy with it. There's a pretty good square Sicilian-style pie too. Vinny's also offers an extra-large pizza that measures a whopping 30 inches across, for those with really hearty appetites. Or a bus-load of kids to feed.

Landmarks

Jimmy's Famous Seafood, 6526 Holabird Ave., Dundalk, Baltimore, MD 21224; (410) 633-4040; jimmysfamousseafood .net; Seafood; $$$. Jimmy's has been serving steaks, seafood, and steamed crabs since 1974. For some locals, it's their go-to place for hard crabs, which are steamed with Jimmy's own blend of seasonings. (Wednesday is crab night, when individual crustaceans can be had for a mere dollar each.) Other folks go there for the crab cakes, which are large, full of sweet crabmeat and little filler, and come individually or in pairs. There are also crab fluffs, in which they take those crab cakes, dunk them in beer batter, and deep fry 'em until crispy. Still others eschew seafood altogether and order a juicy T-bone. We like them "Pittsburgh-style" (despite the connotations to local football fans), which is charred on the outside and medium-rare on the inside. And the folks who like both steak and seafood at the same time show up on Thursday nights to take advantage of the surf-and-turf special, which gets them a cup of soup, a side, and their choice of several meat and fish pairings. Not bad for $20.

Poplar Inn, 7700 Wise Ave., Dundalk, MD 21222; (410) 285-2590; poplarinn.com; American; $$. We're always amused when other Marylanders tell us that they thought this Dundalk institution was really called the "Popular" Inn because with the local accent, *popular* and *poplar* sound much the same. And popular it is. Since 1963 folks have flocked to the Poplar Inn for friendly, attentive service and good, solid food.

Menu selections are familiar Maryland home-style favorites like sour beef and dumplings, crab-stuffed shrimp, fried oysters, and spinach pie. And of course, crab cakes. There's also a lengthy list of sandwiches that includes everything from a basic BLT to gyros and a French dip. The Poplar's bar is popular too, especially on Friday and Saturday nights when live music is the big draw.

Schultz's Crab House, 1732 Old Eastern Ave., Essex, MD 21221; (410) 687-1020; schultzs.com; Crab House; $$. Crabs are in Steve McKinney's blood. He and his siblings have been sorting and steaming the delicious critters since they were kids. Seems appropriate that when he grew up, he'd own a crab house of his own. Schultz's started out as a cafe in 1950 but became a crab house in 1969 when Steve's family bought the business. Ever since then, customers, some of whom have been coming for decades, flock to Schultz's to dine on all manner of crabby goodness. The biggest draw is the fat steamed crabs, full of succulent meat, that are best enjoyed with a pitcher or two of ice cold beer, and a cup of the slightly spicy Maryland crab soup to start.

Squire's Italian Restaurant, 6723 Holabird Ave., Dundalk, Baltimore, MD 21222; (410) 288-0081; squirescafe.com; Italian; $$. This large and bustling restaurant has been making diners happy for a couple of generations already. The very unfancy menu is full of classic Italian-American offerings like meat lasagna with homemade pasta and eggplant parmigiana platters, plus diner-style offerings like hot beef sandwiches and cheeseburger subs. We tend to order pizza more often than not. There's just something about their savory sauce and crispy crust, especially when piled high with homemade sausage, pepperoni, and mushrooms, that always hits the spot. Another favorite is Squire's meatballs, especially when cleverly stuffed into a hollowed-out heel of Italian bread with some tomato sauce, making a sandwich that should be quite messy to eat actually rather neat.

The Mallow Bar, 8767 Philadelphia Rd., Rosedale, MD 21237; (443) 231-7399; themallowbar.com. Most of us grew up helping our moms make those sweet bars of crispy rice cereal and marshmallow. Nikki Lewis enjoyed the experience so much, she's not only continued the tradition with her own children, but she's also sharing her confections with the rest of us. Her Mallow Crunchies are made with handmade marshmallows, which keep them delectably gooey and moist. Nikki and her husband, Antre, started selling her crispy treats at farmers' markets. Now they've expanded into a retail outlet where she dispenses them along with goodies from other local producers like Dirty Carrots, Mouth Party caramels, and **Zeke's Coffee** (p. 197). Mallow Crunchies come in six flavors including caramel-topped, and the Mallow Softies (handmade marshmallows) come in flavors like banana pudding, pistachio, and cinnamon. Buy them to go, or enjoy them in the cute brown-and-pink-decorated cafe, which is also available for dessert parties and private meetings.

Richardson Farms, 5828 Ebenezer Rd., White Marsh, MD 21162; (410) 335-8837; richardsonfarms.net. Richardson Farms serves double-duty as a place to pick up accoutrements to make tonight's dinner at home or simply to pick up tonight's dinner. The Farm Market boasts 10,000 square feet of locally grown produce, jams and jellies, and fresh poultry (chicken and turkey). The Kitchen and Deli portion of the business showcases the culinary talents of Chef Ben Simpkins, whose menu includes rotisserie chicken, delicious potpies, and tasty sandwiches. His braised greens with bacon and turkey are outrageously good, and we're partial to the house-roasted sirloin sandwich with caramelized onions, spinach, horseradish cheddar, and Dijon mayo. And we appreciate that prices are crazy cheap too.

Yia Yia's Bakery, 9415 Philadelphia Rd., Rosedale, MD 21237; (410) 238-2253; yiayiasbakery.com. Full disclosure: For the past several years, our Thanksgiving pies have come from Yia Yia's. In fact, we can't even drive by without stopping in for one of those pies. The pumpkin pie is rich and spicy, and the cherry and apple pies are full of fruity goodness. Breads are pretty good too, especially when used as a container for any number of sandwich fillings that are available at the deli counter. Yia Yia's also does specialty cakes for birthdays, weddings, and whatever other holiday you deem special enough for cake (that's all of them). There's a second location at 3010 E. Joppa Rd., Carney, MD 21234; (410) 668-1199.

Northern Baltimore County

Just north of the city line lies the Baltimore County seat of Towson. Some may know it as the hometown of Elaine Benes from the TV series *Seinfeld,* but we know it as a dense cluster of really interesting restaurants. Founded by the Towson family in the mid-1700s, Ezekiel Towson built a hotel on the land for farmers who were transporting their goods to the Port of Baltimore. A lavish mall complex known as Towson Town Center stands on the same site today. Within the handful of streets at the heart of Towson proper, one can find an impressive array of dining choices covering virtually every ethnic cuisine and ranging from tasty takeout to white-tablecloth service. Oh, and the "tow" in Towson is pronounced as in "towel" and not "toe."

Moving north along the York Road Corridor, Lutherville-Timonium is best known for the Maryland State Fairgrounds, where the state fair is held each year around Labor Day. Cockeysville is named after the Cockey family. Thomas built a hotel, his son built a train station, and Joshua F. Cockey III founded the National Bank of Cockeysville. Once a limestone and marble quarry, the area is now mostly residential. Although some think of Hunt Valley as part of Cockeysville with a special name made up for marketing purposes, everyone knows it's a prosperous community with major corporations like Sinclair Broadcasting Group and McCormick & Co. headquartered there. Hunt Valley is also home to a sprawling open-air shopping center with a Wegmans supermarket and numerous restaurants.

Foodie Faves

Andy Nelson's Barbecue, 11007 York Rd., Cockeysville, MD 21030; (410) 527-1226; andynelsonsbbq.com; Barbecue; $. Considering how close Cockeysville is to the Mason-Dixon line, one might not expect to find authentic Southern barbecue, cooked low and slow over hickory wood. But that's what you'll find at Andy Nelson's. Former Baltimore Colt Andy Nelson is more famous for his Memphis-style 'que than his work on the football field. And with good reason: It's delicious. We're partial to the ribs, which are smoky and tender but still need a little tug of the teeth to work the meat from the bones. They're good both sauced and with dry rub alone. Other favorites are the thick-sliced beef brisket and the pulled-pork barbecue, both of which we think taste best without sauce, so you can get the pure smoky essence of the meat itself. And don't forget to try the sides—the tangy coleslaw, collard greens, cornbread, and tater wedges should not be missed.

Bluestone, 11 W. Aylesbury Rd., Timonium, MD 21093; (410) 561-1100; bluestoneonline.net; American; $$$. Bluestone is in a large stand-alone building surrounded by strip malls. Perhaps an odd location, but it actually makes getting to the restaurant a lot easier than if it were situated directly on the area's very busy major thoroughfare, York Road. Inside, the decor is hip, with cool blues, blonde woods, and metallic accents. The bar scene is lively, so if you don't like crowds, ask to be seated at a table in the dining room, or in the sunroom. The menu features a nice selection of seafood items, among them 5 or 6 different fin fish preparations. We like to start off our meal with a salad comprising 3 kinds of roasted beets called "the beet collection," and go on to the Crisfield Stew of various fish and shellfish in a tomato-based broth. We also like the seafood club, a monster of a sandwich filled with shrimp salad and a crab cake, plus the standard club sandwich fixin's of bacon, lettuce, and tomato.

Burger Bros., 14 W. Allegheny Ave., Towson, MD 21204; (410) 321-1880; burgerbrosburgers.com; Burgers; $. Burger Bros. is a small, no-frills restaurant where one can get a nice char-grilled burger that's more like one you'd cook up in your own backyard than any of the ones you'll find at the many fast-casual burger joints that seem to be popping up everywhere these days. The meat is juicy and the brioche-style buns have the perfect amount of squishiness but are still able to stand up to several layers of cheeses and condiments. While burgers are their specialty, Burger Bros. also offers wings, both with and without bones, broiled or crispy chicken sandwiches, Vienna beef hot dogs, salads, and, of course, generous portions of crisp french fries and onion rings.

Cafe Troia, 31 Allegheny Ave., Towson, MD 21204; (410) 337-0133; cafetroia.com; Italian; $$$. Towson restaurants tend to be pretty casual. Not so at Cafe Troia. Even if it is in a rather squatty office building, this trattoria is elegant. Fancy even, with a space suffused with warmth by the golden walls and wood furnishings. The menu features modern interpretations of old-world Italian classics and has done away with the conceit that diners will order pasta as a *primi* (first course) and follow it up with a *secondi* of meat. The calamari Vesuvio, with tender squid in a spicy tomato sauce, is a treat as an appetizer or served over linguine as an entree. When we're in the mood for something more substantial and meaty, the *braciole,* wrapped around a filling of spinach and pine nuts before being braised to tenderness in a tomato sauce, works very well, particularly with its accompaniment of tender gnocchi. And if there's enough room for dessert, the tangy lemon Napoleon or the rich chocolate flan always hit the right spots.

Christopher Daniel, 106 W. Padonia Rd., Timonium, MD 21093; (410) 308-1800; christopher-daniel.com; Steakhouse; $$$. Like most Baltimore County restaurants, Christopher Daniel is located in, you guessed it, a strip mall. Yes, the interior is a little boring, but it's comfortable, the staff is very pleasant, and the food is good. On a recent trip we enjoyed a wedge salad that was so large, it looked like a slice of birthday cake with bacon and tomato in place of the edible confetti. We also had a nicely charred New York strip with an unusual cap of fried oysters and bleu cheese (other toppings and sauces are available). The buttery and decadent lobster mac and cheese makes a nice side, especially if you plan to hit the gym the next day. If you'd prefer lighter fare, head to the lounge area, called Five. The food menu there has lots of sandwiches, flatbreads, small plates, and raw-bar items that make fine accompaniments to their specialty: martinis. We like the delicious Spring Fig, made with fig vodka, St. Germain, pomegranate, and champagne. It goes surprisingly well with an order of fried pickles and okra with a spicy chipotle remoulade.

Earth, Wood & Fire, 1407 Clarkview Rd., Baltimore, MD 21209; (410) 825-3473; earthwoodfire.com; Pizza; $$. For a town not known for its pizza, Baltimore sure has a lot of terrific pizza restaurants. One of the newest is Earth, Wood & Fire, located in an area of Baltimore County halfway between Towson and Pikesville and not far north of Mount Washington. The spacious restaurant has a spare, industrial feel, with little decoration other than the food on the plates. Without a lot of sound-absorbing materials around and being rather on the kid-friendly side, EW&F can get pretty noisy. However, the food is terrific so we don't mind the extra decibels so much. Pizzas are baked with intense heat in a coal-fired oven that gives the thin, chewy crust a nice bit of char and caramelization. Toppings, even the ones labeled "standard" on the menu, are anything but, with options like roasted fennel or eggplant, capers, and Gorgonzola. We love the super-garlicky "scampi" white pizza with shrimp and garlic chips. We're also fond of the juicy burgers, interesting salads (try the Lorenzo), and small plates, like the grilled asparagus with shiitake "bacon" and caramelized shallots.

El Salto, 8816 Waltham Woods Rd., Parkville, MD 21234; (410) 668-3980; elsaltomexicanrestaurant.com; Mexican; $. There are three words to describe El Salto: fast, cheap, good. Fast, in that your order comes to the table lightning quick, almost before you've ordered. Cheap, well, that should be self-explanatory, but here's an example: The special dinner for 2—which reads like a K-Tel greatest-hits album and includes a chile relleno, a chalupa, a burrito, an enchilada, a tamal, and 2 tacos—is a whopping $15.95. Oh yeah, and it includes rice and beans. And everything's good. We really like the *queso con chorizo* and tend to order it every time because the menu is so large and busy, we have a hard time coming to a decision otherwise. It's even got a whole page of beverages and booze—a couple of wines, a selection of classic mixed drinks, and of course, Mexican beer and margaritas. Any of those will do very nicely, thank you.

Fazzini's Italian Kitchen, 578 Cranbrook Rd., Cockeysville, MD 21030; (410) 667-6104; fazzinis.com; Italian; $$. A relative used to rave about the meatball pizzas served at this little strip-mall eatery out in the 'burbs, but by the time we decided to try one for ourselves, the restaurant had closed. A few years later it reopened by popular demand, making lots of Baltimore County residents very happy. From the bowls of olive oil dotted with whole cloves of roasted garlic to the homemade pasta, we understand why. Portions are huge, the food is good, and there's a conveniently located liquor store down the strip (Fazzini's is BYOB)—what more can one ask for? We like the chicken Francaise Michael, in which panko-coated chicken cutlets are topped with asparagus, prosciutto, capers, and a flavorful lemon butter sauce. Meatballs are still available as a pizza topping, but the more gluttonous among us prefer the pound of homemade pasta with choice of sauce and meat, or the stacked eggplant parmigiana.

Gino's Burgers & Chicken, 8600 LaSalle Rd., Towson, MD 21286; (410) 583-0000; ginosgiant.com; Burgers; $. Back in 1957 two former Baltimore Colts players, Gino Marchetti and Alan Ameche, opened the original Gino's in Dundalk with business partner Louis Fischer. The chain grew quickly, but after nearly 30 years of satisfying people all over the Mid-Atlantic with burgers and Kentucky Fried Chicken, Gino's was acquired by Marriott and closed. Flash-forward almost 30 years later,

Spotlight on Area Pick-Your-Own Farms

Huber's Farm, *11898 Philadelphia Rd., Kingsville, MD 21087; (410) 538-7725; hubersfarm.com.* Run by third-generation farmers Steve and Ethel Huber, the farm offers a staggering array of fruits, vegetables, and herbs from early April through November. From turnips and radishes in the spring to strawberries and cucumbers in the summer, right on to pumpkins and cauliflower in the fall, there will always be something worth picking. The crops vary according to the season, of course, so it's best to check their website to see what is currently available. It's also recommended that you call before visiting to find out picking times. Visitors must bring their own cutting tools and containers, and shuttles are provided to reach the fields that are out of walking range.

Hybridoma Organic Fruit Farm, *13734 Baldwin Mill Rd., Baldwin, MD 21013; (443) 902-0370; hybridomafarm.com.* Certified organic by the Maryland Department of Agriculture, the 50-acre farm grows blackberries, blueberries, and red and black raspberries. Michigan native R. G. Hamilton started growing Christmas trees on the land but found it more satisfying to grow sustainable fruit familiar to his Michigan roots. The farm is open to pickers starting in June and running through September. Containers are provided, but you are welcome to bring your own.

Mingodale Farm, *17201 Masemore Rd., Parkton, MD 21120; (410) 357-0403; mingodalefarm.com.* John Foster's family has worked Mingodale Farm for generations and take pride in the quality of their naturally grown produce. Some of their specialties include asparagus, tomatoes, garlic, herbs, and gourmet peppers. In addition to the prepicked produce on sale, visitors can pick their own blackberries and flowers. Produce is usually available from July through September.

Rodgers Farm (North Run Farm), *1818 Greenspring Valley Rd., Stevenson, MD 21153; (410) 241-3392; northrunfarm.com.* Since 2002, Patrick and Brooke Rodgers have opened their farm in September and October to visitors who want to pick their own pumpkins. Other family fun includes hayrides and a corn maze.

Weber's Cider Mill Farm, *2526 Proctor Ln., Parkville, MD 21234; (410) 668-4488; weberscidermillfarm.com.* Steve and JoAnn Weber's farm offers a wide variety of fruits and vegetables during the summer and fall, in addition to freshly baked pies, apple cider made on the premises, and fresh turkeys for Thanksgiving. Visitors can pick apples on Saturday and Sunday until the supply runs out (usually at the end of Sept).

Wind Swept Farm, *14517 Hanover Pike, Upperco, MD 21155; (410) 833-7330.* This farm has a variety of prepicked produce such as sweet corn, cucumbers, peppers, summer squash, and tomatoes, but you can pick your own pumpkins in the fall. Crops are usually available from July through December. You can also pick and cut your own Christmas tree from the day after Thanksgiving to Christmas Eve.

and we find that Gino's is back, this time as a fast-casual burger joint. Marchetti and Fischer are still around, as is old company COO Tony Romano, but other things have changed. Today's Gino's has burgers that are bigger and juicier, plus hand-breaded chicken, hand-cut fries, onion rings, salads, and umpteen flavors of shakes. To Baltimoreans of a certain age, it's a welcome bit of nostalgia. There's another location at 5001 Honeygo Center Dr., Perry Hall, MD 21128, (410) 870-2746, and one at Oriole Park at Camden Yards.

The Grille at Peerce's, 12460 Dulaney Valley Rd., Phoenix, MD 21131; (410) 252-7111; thegrilleatpeerces.com; American; $$$. For decades, Peerce's Plantation was the area's special-occasion restaurant of choice, the site of many a birthday, anniversary, and wedding reception. Sadly, that restaurant closed in 2001. Signature Catering bought the space in 2008 to use as a catering venue, then a couple of years later added a full-service restaurant that they called the Grille at Peerce's. And the crowds—former Plantation customers included—have been flocking back. The venue might be the same, but the menu has been updated for the 21st century. There are a couple of old-style dishes, like oysters Rockefeller, crab fluffs, and surf and turf, but there's more-contemporary fare as well. The Firecracker calamari (or shrimp) appetizer comes with a spicy Thai dipping sauce and slices of banana pepper. There's a hefty short rib, glazed with a sweet and spicy "Mongolian" sauce. Another classic offering, the crab cake, is full of sweet meat and lightly seasoned.

Havana Road, 8 W. Pennsylvania Ave., Towson, MD 21204; (410) 494-8222; havanaroad.com; Latin; $. Cuban-born Chef-Owner Marta Ines Quintana learned to cook from her grandmother, which is always the best way to learn how to do things right, if you ask us. Quintana's delicious and authentic Cuban food shows that she really paid attention during her cooking lessons. Her ink-black, almost perfectly smooth black-bean soup is subtlety itself, hearty yet delicate at the same time, and gently flavored with cumin. Quintana's cozy storefront restaurant has walls the color of her rich and satisfying *ropa vieja* (shredded beef in a savory sauce), which is served with caramelized sweet plantains, black beans, and rice. We've also enjoyed the classic pressed sandwich that combines pork, ham, swiss cheese, and pickles and is known simply as a Cubano. It's delightfully hot and gooey and made even better by the side of garlicky mojo sauce. *Baltimore* magazine rated it as the best sandwich of 2011. And don't forget to try the yucca fries, which are crisp on the outside and fluffy on the inside and beat the usual french fries any time. See Chef Marta Ines Quintana's recipe for **Ropa Vieja** on p. 316.

Kitchen of India, 1842 E. Joppa Rd., Parkville, MD 21234; (410) 663-6880; kitchenofindiaus.com; Indian; $$. Owners Salma Khanam and Chef Mohammed Rahman arrived in the US from Bangladesh determined to open a restaurant, which they did most successfully. Ignore the fact that Kitchen of India is on a swath of Joppa Road that is otherwise filled with strip malls and car dealerships, and stop inside for a taste of the subcontinent. There's a lunch buffet 7 days a week, but we like to go for dinner. Kitchen of India is one of the few restaurants in town that offers goat; it and other meats on the menu are Halal. We like the goat curry, which is in a deep-brown sauce redolent of cloves. As with most Indian restaurants, there's also a nice array of vegetarian choices. The bhindi masala, a dry fry of okra, is buttery and rich and a perfect match for the basmati rice that comes with every meal.

Kyodai Rotating Sushi Bar, 1 W. Pennsylvania Ave., Towson, MD 21204; (410) 339-7500; Japanese; $. There are a lot of sushi restaurants in the area. A lot. But Kyodai has a gimmick that sets them apart—their kaiten. On one side of the room is a rectangular bar around which travels a conveyor belt laden with plates of sushi rolls. Diners choose plates that look appetizing and when finished dining, one of the friendly and efficient waitstaff counts the color-coded plates and tallies up the bill. It's great for lunch, when people don't have that much time to dine, and it's affordable too—the most expensive plate is under $7. One can also order nigiri or sashimi, or kitchen items like soups and teriyaki dishes. There are tables too, but it's so much more fun to sit at the conveyor. We always order some special items like the spicy, sesame-flecked tuna tartare, and the broiled bundles of shredded crab-stick-filled salmon topped with a mayonnaise sauce and called salmon imperial, all the while keeping an eye on that conveyor belt for another tasty treat.

Liberatore's, 9515 Deereco Rd., Timonium, MD 21093; (410) 561-3300; liberatores.com; Italian; $$$$. Liberatore's seems unusually

fancy for an Italian restaurant in the 'burbs. The walls are decorated with murals of the Tuscan countryside, waiters are dressed formally, and there's a leather-couched lounge with a dance floor and live music. There's even a romantic patio with seating in warm weather. That all makes it sound like Liberatore's is the perfect place for a special-occasion meal. And it is. But it's also a good idea for a weeknight dinner. The menu is full of all the familiar classics: lasagna, fettuccine Bolognese, linguine with white clam sauce, chicken Marsala—you get the picture. And if it's not on the menu, the kitchen may be able to make it for you. There are four other Liberatore's in Maryland, including one other Baltimore County location: 5005 Honeygo Center Dr., Perry Hall, MD 21128; (410) 529-4567.

Michael's Cafe Raw Bar & Grill, 2119 York Rd., Timonium, MD 21093; (410) 252-2022; michaelscafe.com; Seafood; $$$. Michael's is famous for two things: their crab cakes and their bar scene. Indeed, we knew of one gentleman who considered Michael's to be the best place in town to meet ladies of a certain age. We go for the crab cakes. They are lumpy, have very little filler, and are available either broiled or fried (fried crab cakes seem to be increasingly more rare all the time) in either 5- or 10-ounce sizes. If you really enjoy their crab cakes, Michael's is happy to ship them anywhere in the continental US. There's plenty of other stuff on the menu too. We like the seared ahi tuna appetizer and the cream of crab soup. There's also a nice burger, made with 8 ounces of luscious local Roseda beef. Oh, and it's a raw bar, so there's always plenty of oysters ("ersters" in the local patois) and clams on hand too.

Mo's Seafood, 1528 E. Joppa Rd., Towson, MD 21234; (410) 823-2200; mosseafood.com; Seafood; $$. Mo's has been around for a while, and we often found ourselves gorging on seafood at the original Towson/Parkville location . . . which despite having white tablecloths had no ambience. The old Mo's has been replaced by a newer restaurant down the road, one with a much cheerier vibe, 2 nice outdoor seating areas, and a more straightforward menu. The emphasis is still on seafood, starring at least 14 types of fin fish, cooked and sauced your way, plus every shellfish imaginable, fried, broiled, or steamed. And just about everything on the menu is available "stuffed," or topped with a decadent amount of crab imperial. A handful of chicken, beef, and Italian dishes are available too, for folks who prefer turf over surf. But we like to have it both ways with the steak Christopher, a béarnaise- and imperial-topped filet mignon. There are several other Mo's in town, including Mo's Crab and Pasta Factory at 502 Albemarle St., Baltimore, MD 21202, (410) 837-1600; Mo's Seafood Factory, 7600 Eastern Ave., Baltimore, MD 21224, (410) 288-2424; and Mo's Fisherman's Wharf, 219 S. President St., Baltimore, MD 21202, (410) 837-8600.

Nautilus Diner, 2047 York Rd., Timonium, MD 21093; (410) 561-9236; thenautilusdiner.com; Diner; $. Sometimes you need pancakes for dinner, and if that's the case, the Nautilus is your place. But if you want pancakes and your companion wants lamb chops, the Nautilus is still your place. There are lots of diners around, but few of them do so many things as well as Nautilus. We're partial to their lasagna, which has a sauce that definitely tastes long-simmered and homemade. The same goes for their tender moussaka. They also do a nicely roasted half chicken, and a whole brook trout that you can get stuffed with crabmeat. And you can't beat the prices—most entrees cost under $20 and come with choice of soup or salad and 2 sides. Those salads are so large, we're usually full before we get our main course; that means we get to take home leftovers for lunch (sometimes 2 lunches). While the meals are huge and filling, save room for a house-made dessert from the somewhat obscenely full pastry case out front. Rice pudding, anyone?

Ocean Pride Seafood, 1534 York Rd., Timonium, MD 21093; (410) 321-7744; oceanprideseafood.com; Seafood; $$. It's very rare to drive past Ocean Pride and see anything but a completely packed parking lot. We're going to be honest and tell you that it's not the ambience that brings the crowds to Ocean Pride. Floors can be damp, and the service is occasionally . . . let's just call it "cranky." The thing that does draw folks in is the year-round crabfest. There are steamed crabs to be had by the dozen, plus crab cocktail, crab pretzels, crab flatbreads, and of course, the ubiquitous crab cake. Crabs are usually large and heavy specimens coated with Ocean

Pride's own blend of herbs and spices. Be prepared to wait on weekends and especially during the warmer months when Marylanders' clamor for crustaceans reaches a pinnacle.

The Oregon Grille, 1201 Shawan Rd., Cockeysville, MD 21030; (410) 771-0505; theoregongrille.com; American; $$$$. This handsomely appointed restaurant, its light walls trimmed with dark wood and decorated with equestrian prints, feels like a fancy country club, one in which you speak in quiet tones about deep subjects. Subjects like finance and which wine from the nearly 30-page tome goes best with the prime aged bone-in rib eye steak and the pan-fried rockfish with crab hash. The rest of the menu is similarly posh, with an emphasis on red meat and rich seafood dishes. There are a few lighter dishes on the lunch menu, like the crispy shrimp tacos and a crab and avocado Louis, but let's be honest here: The Oregon Grille is a place for celebrating an engagement, a new job, the sale of a stallion. Even brunch is rich and a bit over-the-top, but anywhere we can get a lobster cocktail before our eggs Florentine is A-OK by us.

Pasta Blitz/Il Basilico, 49 W. Aylesbury Rd., Timonium, MD 21093; (410) 453-6603; pastablitztimonium.com; Italian; $. This unassuming eatery, tucked away in a shopping center with an REI as its main attraction, doesn't exactly beckon diners with either its name or Disney-ish signage. Once inside, however, one forgets the "Blitz" and is enveloped in the charms of "Il Basilico" with its terra-cotta walls and fake grapevines. The menu emphasizes pasta dishes and pizza, and it's hard to choose one over the other. We usually get both a New York–style thin-crust pizza (like the "Di Pierno's" white pizza with arugula and shrimp) and a pasta to share. Our favorite pasta dish, the linguine with shrimp fra diavolo, looks innocent enough, but it's positively incendiary, and no, they won't make it mild. Devouring the basket of amazingly crusty Italian bread (ask for seconds!) helps put out the heat a bit. Like the bread, the pizzas have a nice crisp crust and there's usually a near-perfect crust-to-cheese ratio.

Pho Dat Thanh, 510 York Rd., Towson, MD 21204; (410) 296-9118; Vietnamese; $. Vietnamese restaurants are few and far between in Baltimore, which is a shame because the vibrant yet light flavors of garlic, lemongrass, and cilantro are often the perfect antidote to hot, muggy Baltimore summers. This tidy restaurant just south of the traffic circle on busy York Road has become our source for the cool little packages of translucent rice paper filled with shrimp or barbecue pork and herbs known as "summer rolls." We're also fans of the *bò lá nh*, juicy beef wrapped in grape leaves that have a bit of nice, smoky, char, and the *bun thit nuóng cha giò,* a huge portion of slender rice noodles topped with thinly sliced and smoky grilled pork, raw bean sprouts and cilantro, and a bowl of the goes-with-everything Vietnamese condiment *nuoc cham* to drizzle on top. Parking might seem a bit challenging in this area, but several of the side streets have small lots, and there's a large one right behind the Recher Theatre next door, so it behooves Towson visitors to check out an online map ahead of time to make things easier.

Pho Towson & Bar, 1100 Cromwell Bridge Rd., Towson, MD 21286; (410) 832-2788; photowsonbar.com; Vietnamese; $. One of a handful of Vietnamese restaurants in the area, the somewhat oddly named Pho Towson & Bar is on the ground floor of a Best Western. The pretty dining room, walls bedecked in an aqua-and-chartreuse striped paper, is bright and airy and is a fairly chic place to enjoy a steaming bowl of pho. That's the restaurant's specialty, of course, and the menu lists a dozen or so variations of the noodle-filled soup that include different permutations of beefy goodness. There are also other noodle dishes, including *mi* and *bun,* and several rice dishes, or *com,* on the menu. We especially enjoy the *bun tom thit heo nuong,* a bowl of slender rice vermicelli served with a topping of grilled shrimp and strips of pork belly, a generous handful of chopped peanuts, and a bowl of *nuoc cham* on the side. And we like to order one of their frosty milkshake-like beverages, flavored with everything from taro to avocado, to cool the fiery peppers, or simply to sip as dessert.

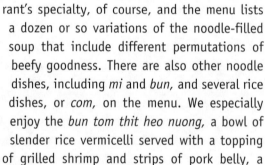

Razorback's Raw Bar & Grill, 826 Dulaney Valley Rd., Towson, MD 21204; (410) 821-9550; www.razorbacksgrill.com; Barbecue; $$.

Razorback's is set in a rather pleasant strip mall across from the hubbub of Towson Town Center. The comfortable bar in the front is usually full of regulars, so we prefer to eat in the much quieter and quite nicely appointed dining area in the back. The shiny wooden tables and cloth napkins make the place seem a lot fancier than it is, but what's wrong with enjoying oysters or clams on the half shell in nice surroundings? Seafood options are solid (try the crab cakes) but our favorite menu item is the baby back ribs. Baltimore is no barbecue mecca, so we're not even going to pretend that Razorback's fall-off-the-bone tender ribs are anything close to 'que. But they're plenty tasty, especially with sides of crisp Boardwalk-style fries and good, fresh coleslaw.

San Sushi Too/Thai One On, 10 W. Pennsylvania Ave., Towson, MD 21204; (410) 825-0907; Japanese; $$. Want sushi? You've come to the right place. Wait, you want Thai? You're still in the right place! Whether you sit on the Thai side or the sushi side, you can order anything from either menu. So if you're in the mood for a spicy tuna roll and a red curry, you can have both. We like sitting on the sushi bar side, with its colorful fish murals, regardless of what we order. The maki rolls are rather busy with ingredients, the way we like 'em, and all of the various sauces used on them are house-made. And if you don't see the roll you want on the menu, they'll be glad to make it for you. We like the Terp, with shrimp tempura, avocado, tobiko, and scallions, topped with fresh crabmeat and teriyaki sauce. Sometimes we follow it with the *penang ped,* an incendiary duck curry, and wash it down with a Thai iced coffee. Best of both worlds.

7 West Bistro Grille, 7 W. Chesapeake Ave., Towson, MD 21286; (410) 337-9378; 7westbistro.com; Mediterranean; $$. Located in a rather cavernous brick-walled space across York Road from the Towson Library, 7 West specializes in Mediterranean cuisine with a strong Greek bent, like souvlaki, *pastitsio, taramosalata,* dolmades, and tzatziki. They also serve favorites like seared ahi tuna, fettuccine Alfredo, and crab cakes, plus several items that are straight-up bar food: coconut shrimp, Southwestern egg rolls, Buffalo wings, jalapeño poppers, burgers. Basically, there's something for everyone. The bar scene at 7 West is pretty lively, even on a weeknight, which might be due in part to the great 3-to-7 p.m. happy-hour specials, including half-price appetizers. Enjoy a couple bottles of Corona and the garlicky and filling dip sampler platter (with tzatziki, *taramosalata,* eggplant dip, and hummus) for less than $20 total, and you won't even need dinner.

Spice & Dice, 1220 E. Joppa Rd., #108, Towson, MD 21286; (410) 494-8777; thaispiceanddice.com; Thai; $$. We're big fans of Thai food and usually don't wait long before checking out any new Thai restaurants in the area. So when Spice & Dice opened in a little strip mall nearby, we were on top of it. The restaurant space is more than a little quirky, with bright colors and patterns on the walls and tables; it would not be hard to imagine it as a day-care center. The staff is equally cheerful and very accommodating. But ignore the decor and concentrate on the menu, which lists a number of curries, "big bowl" soups, and duck dishes, among others. Everything we've tried at Spice & Dice has made us happy, from the aromatic Jasmine rice soup to the drunken duck with Thai basil sauce, and the spicy minced chicken salad known as *larb*. Do try the jungle curry, which is free of the usual coconut milk and has a more herbal, less sweet flavor than some of the other curry dishes. Spice & Dice also offers a number of dishes that can be made gluten-free or vegan.

Tark's Grill, 2360 W. Joppa Rd., Ste. 116, Timonium, MD 21093; (410) 583-8275; tarksgrill.com; Steakhouse; $$$. We've always been fond of this restaurant's logo because that white *T* on a red field so cleverly screams "steakhouse!" And the interior is dark and kinda clubby, with burgundy walls and nifty photomurals. But Tark's Grill is more than a steakhouse. Sure, there's gorgeous aged beef, a chopped salad, and onion rings, typical steakhouse fare, but there are also a couple of comfort-food favorites that float our boat. One is the chicken potpie, made traditionally with roast chicken, veg like peas and carrots, creamy gravy, and covered with a buttery crust. Nothing weird or nouveau or deconstructed about it. That chopped salad is pretty yummy too, and includes unusual ingredients like coleslaw, pickles, and jalapeños. For a real kitchen-sink meal, try it with blackened chicken or shrimp on top. At lunchtime the fancy steaks are replaced by several sandwiches, and brunch is completely traditional (omelettes, pancakes, eggs Benedict).

Thai One On/San Sushi Too, 10-11 W. Pennsylvania Ave., Towson, MD 21204; (410) 825-0907; Thai; $$. *See* **San Sushi Too/ Thai One On** (p. 231).

Towson Tavern, 516 York Rd., Towson, MD 21286; (410) 337-7210; towsontavern.com; American; $$$. Scott Recher, owner of music venue the Recher Theatre and the Rec Room next door, decided to switch up a few things in his establishment. He removed pool tables from part of the Rec Room and replaced them with a rather swank dining room with lots of dark tones, wood, and a dark marble bar. He hired Executive Chef Daniel Henry, formerly of the Capital Grille downtown, and voilà! The Towson Tavern was born. The menu, divided into sections of small, medium, and large plates, lists upscale treats like an heirloom tomato gazpacho with spiced shrimp, a fillet tartar served with brioche and a sunny-side-up egg, and a Duroc pork tenderloin with an apricot demi-glace. All of which pair nicely with one or more selections from the extensive beer and wine list.

Umi Sake, 9726 York Rd., Cockeysville, MD 21030; (410) 667-6585; umisake.com; Japanese; $$. Even though this popular sushi restaurant in the northern suburbs also offers a fusion-Asian selection of tasty dinner entrees like Peking duck and pad thai, we just go for the sushi. Umi Sake's maki menu features several exotic combinations; one of our favorites is called Eight Is Enough. It features 8 pieces of 4 different rolls, all of which are inventive, and might include crispy spicy tuna served on crunchy fried rice cake, or a roll wrapped in cucumber rather than nori. Other exotic rolls on the menu might include mango or rice paper wrappers. It's hard to be bored at Umi Sake. Proof? There are chicken fingers and mac and cheese for the kids, and even a Sunday brunch menu that includes bagels and omelettes in addition to sushi and stir-fried entrees.

Vito's Cafe, 10249 York Rd., Cockeysville, MD 21030; (410) 666-3100; vitos-cafe.com; Italian; $$$. We're always surprised to find flavors straight outta Little Italy hiding in a suburban strip mall in Cockeysville. The chef at Vito's, Luca Pesci, once worked in Baltimore's Little Italy, at the late, lamented Boccaccio. He also did some time at Cafe Troia in Towson. Now he's combining those restaurants' northern and southern Italian flavors on a menu that should please just about every tomato- and cheese-loving palate.

We like the pappardelle with local Gunpowder bison and marinara sauce, and the whole, oven-roasted branzino. At lunchtime there are panini and sandwiches, including a yummy veal meatball sub. Vito's also serves pizza, and there are usually a couple of folks waiting to pick up their crisp-crusted brick-oven pizzas to take home.

The restaurant is BYOB, but there's a liquor store practically next door that will give a discount to Vito's diners.

Yamato Sushi, 51 W. Aylesbury Rd., Timonium, MD 21093; (410) 560-0024; yamatosushionline.com; Japanese; $$. Tucked away in a shopping center near the Fairgrounds is this small but popular sushi restaurant that always seems to be packed with families. Who knew kids loved sushi so much? While the nigiri and sashimi at Yamato is always very fresh and delicious, it's their maki rolls that keep us coming back for more. Like the Hula roll, for instance, stuffed with shrimp tempura, crab, avocado, and cucumber and topped with spicy tuna and orange wasabi sauce. It's crispy, creamy, spicy, and seafoody, all at the same time. If there's someone in your party who's not as much into sushi as you are, then they might be happy with one or more of the pan-Asian selections, like pad thai or a Korean-style beef rib. There's also teriyaki anything and big bowls of udon soup. The service is pretty great too—you will never run out of green tea.

Landmarks

The Corner Stable, 9942 York Rd., Cockeysville, MD 21030; (410) 666-8722; cornerstable.com; Barbecue; $$$. Yeah, yeah, barbecue snobs, we've heard it a million times before. We know that grilling is not the same as barbecuing, but this ain't the Carolinas or

Texas. And we like when our rib meat falls off the bone without any effort at all. At the Corner Stable, imported Danish baby back ribs are slow-cooked for 24 hours, grilled, and served with your

choice of spicy or nonspicy sweet and tangy sauce. A full rack, served up with a side of crispy Stable fries, a dish of coleslaw, and a pile of napkins, is our idea of heaven. Sometimes we gild the lily and get the ribs and one of Corner Stable's 8-ounce crab cakes too. There's a second Corner Stable in Howard County: 8630 Guilford Rd., Columbia, MD 21046; (240) 755-0188.

Manor Tavern, 15819 Old York Rd., Monkton, MD 21111; (410) 771-8155; themanortavern.com; American; $$. Back in the 18th century, the building housing the Manor Tavern was a stable. It was then a tavern for many years before becoming a full-service restaurant in 1986. Today the current owners, a group of successful local restaurateurs and businesspeople, are breathing new life into the place with a complete remodel and a "farm to fork" concept for the food. The menu of pub and steakhouse favorites includes dishes created with locally raised ingredients like Berkshire pork from owner Jim Franzoni's nearby Verdant Valley Farms, Albright Farms chicken, and Gunpowder bison. We like the burgers, especially the one offered at Triple Crown time that's topped with a savory combination of roasted-garlic cream cheese, bacon, arugula, and truffle oil. We also like their brunch, particularly the "wings & waffles"

McCormick & Co. Add Local Spice

Located in Hunt Valley, Maryland, McCormick & Co. (mccormick .com) has been a Baltimore fixture for more than 120 years. Willoughby M. McCormick started his business with one room and a basement, making products like root beer, fruit syrups, glue, and liniment and selling them door to door. When he bought a Philadelphia spice company in 1896 and had the equipment shipped to Baltimore, his spice business began.

For decades the air in Baltimore was perfumed by the spices produced in their factory at the Inner Harbor. Through much of the last century, McCormick & Co. expanded and acquired other companies around the globe, and now the fragrances of pepper and cinnamon waft around the plant's new location in Hunt Valley. While the familiar "Mc" logo appears on a myriad of products, McCormick also produces brands like Billy Bee, Zatarain's, Lawry's, and Thai Kitchen.

One of its most famous products was not acquired by the company until 1990. Old Bay seasoning was invented by Gustav Brunn in the 1940s to be used by bars that offered crabs and shrimp as bar snacks. Named after a steamship line that once ran between Maryland and Virginia, the spice mix became synonymous with Baltimore seafood. About 50 million ounces of the stuff are sold each year.

McCormick is also known for its annual report on flavor trends known as *The Flavor Forecast*. The food industry eagerly awaits this report each year to find out what flavor combinations are most appealing to consumers. Using an extensive research network, McCormick compiles not only food trends but suggestions on how to make healthy food more appealing through the use of spices and food combinations. In 2012 a global edition of *The Flavor Forecast* was produced.

combo of Albright Farms chicken wings and savory waffles with hot sauce, washed down with bottomless Bloody Marys.

The Milton Inn, 14833 York Rd., Sparks, MD 21152; (410) 771-4366; miltoninn.com; American; $$$$. The Inn has a long and interesting history, starting back in the 1740s when it was used as a coach stop for local Quakers. Much later it became a boys' school called the Milton Academy (after English poet John Milton) and was attended by John Wilkes Booth. In the 1940s the building was turned back into the inn it had once been, and today the Milton Inn continues a tradition of being a place for special celebrations. Executive Chef-Co-owner Brian Boston was named the Restaurant Association of Maryland's Chef of the Year in 2011 for dishes like his seafood Andor, comprising various shellfish and rockfish in a dill sauce with a side of risotto. The Inn also features hefty steaks, which can be topped with seared *foie gras* or lobster (or both!), and rich sauces. It can get quite expensive, but there's a $45 prix-fixe menu that allows diners to taste fancy food at a not-so-fancy price.

The Orient Restaurant, 319 York Rd., Baltimore, MD 21204; (410) 296-9000; theorientrestaurant.com; Chinese; $$. The Orient has been around almost as long as we can remember. It's one of those increasing number of Chinese restaurants that recognizes the popularity of sushi; in fact, it's the first Chinese restaurant in the area to include a sushi bar. We love having the ability to start a meal with a steaming bowl of wonton soup, then enjoy a fancy maki roll before going on to our main course of Peking duck. All of the typical Chinese-American dishes are solid, like the Szechuan string beans and moo shu pork, and the sushi and sashimi are always very fresh. The Orient has one other area location, in Perry Hall: 9545 Belair Rd., Baltimore, MD 21236; (410) 256-8100.

Orchard Market & Cafe, 8815 Orchard Tree Ln., Towson, MD 21286; (410) 339-7700; orchardmarketandcafe.com; Middle Eastern; $$. Don't be fooled by its location in a strip mall off the beaten path. "Baltimore's premier Persian restaurant" has been pleasing patrons with their Persian cuisine both authentic and innovative since the late 1980s. In the pretty cream-and-celadon dining room decorated with tapestries and replicas of Persian art, one can dine on the classic duck fesenjune, with its flavors of walnut and pomegranate, or enjoy a selection of mixed kebabs. If you've never tried Persian cuisine, it bears a similarity to other Middle Eastern cuisines in that chickpeas and eggplant are staples, as are flatbreads, but dishes are more saucy, with an emphasis on fruits and vegetables, giving dishes pleasant sweet and tangy notes. Try the

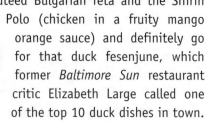

sautéed Bulgarian feta and the Shirin Polo (chicken in a fruity mango orange sauce) and definitely go for that duck fesenjune, which former *Baltimore Sun* restaurant critic Elizabeth Large called one of the top 10 duck dishes in town.

Pappas Restaurant, 1725 Taylor Ave., Parkville, MD 21234; (410) 661-4357; pappascrabcakes.com; Seafood; $$$. Pappas is one of those old-school Baltimore seafood restaurants that are few and far between these days. Many folks might prefer a hipper restaurant with a more chic decor, but Pappas still has its niche. One of many places that claims to have the best crab cake in town, Pappas's is certainly a contender with its large lumps of sweet crab. We like that many seafood options are available fried as well as broiled. Sure, broiled may be marginally healthier, but sometimes food just needs to be fried. There's plenty more than seafood on the menu, including pasta dishes and a slew of sandwiches with fillings like strip steak, pit beef, and shrimp salad. Pappas has another location at 6713 Ritchie Hwy., Glen Burnie, MD 21061; (410) 766-3713.

Szechuan House, 1427 York Rd., Lutherville, MD 21093; (410) 825-8181; szechuanhouse-md.com; Chinese; $$. Every time we've gone to Szechuan House, we've found it packed with diners and people waiting for tables or carryout. We prefer to have our food delivered in order to beat the crowds entirely; despite living several miles away from the restaurant, we're consistently pleased by the fast service and piping-hot food. Even the spring rolls arrive both hot and crispy. If you're lucky enough to snag a table at the restaurant, try the house specialty, Peking duck. Just about everything else from the MSG-free kitchen is uniformly good, and there's an ample selection of sushi and sashimi, but we tend to order from the section labeled Country Side Taste. It features slightly more unusual dishes like aromatic shrimp with ginger and scallions (served with or without head and shell), shredded pork with dry bean curd, and Manila clams with black-bean sauce.

Specialty Stores, Markets & Producers

A. Kirchmayr, 9630 Deereco Rd., Timonium, MD 21093; (410) 561-7705; fineeuropeanchocolate.com. As it's tucked away in an anonymous business park in Timonium, it would be easy to miss this chocolate shop, but you wouldn't want to. Albert Kirchmayr opened his store in 1985 with the mission of introducing Americans to the joy of giving fine chocolates to family and friends. The sales floor is reminiscent of a jewelry store; the delicate chocolates and truffles are displayed in a case that seems quite suited to hold diamond necklaces and fancy watches. And why not? These bon-bons are rare gems. The silky chocolates are subtly enhanced with the flavors of coffee, fruits, and liqueurs, and the truffles feature a pleasant crunchy coating that contrasts nicely with the creamy filling. Kirchmayr also offers special seasonal chocolates during the holidays, plus exquisitely crafted chocolate boxes suitable for any gifting occasion.

Baltimore Coffee & Tea Company, 9 W. Aylesbury Rd., Ste. T, Timonium, MD 21093; (410) 561-1080; baltcoffee.com. This is a serious coffee shop. Talking to one of the baristas at

Baltimore Coffee & Tea is like talking to a sommelier about wine. They're happy to expound on varietals from various countries, each of which possess a distinctive flavor, and the still other coffees that are created by blending these varietals in the perfect combination. If tea is more your speed, they have a vast selection of both international brands and those that are locally blended. Not just a shop, Baltimore Coffee & Tea is also a fine breakfast destination. They offer a selection of bagels, croissants, and other goodies along with 8 coffees brewed daily. Soups, salads, and sandwiches are available for lunch, and the bright and airy space (not to mention the heavenly smell of coffee beans) makes you want to spend time there.

Fenwick Bakery, 7219 Harford Rd., Parkville, MD 21234; (410) 444-6410; thefenwickbakery.com. This bakery is old-fashioned in the best sense of the term. Established by Ernest and Alvena Uebersax in 1927, Fenwick Bakery has been in its current location since 1971 and still uses many of the same family recipes. The storefront on Harford Road looks like a quaint shop from the 1950s, and the interior feels every bit like a mom-and-pop establishment. Of course, nothing stays completely the same, and head baker Michael Meckel has added a few modern cake flavors to their repertoire like amaretto, lemon, orange, and carrot. Although the bakery makes wedding and specialty cakes, it's also a great place to go when you have a craving for the some great pastries. The mini pies are a perfect treat for 2, and we recommend the flaky triangles filled with cheese or fruit. The prices are so inexpensive, you can give yourself serious sugar shock for only a few dollars.

Mastellone's Deli and Wine, 7212 Harford Rd., Parkville, Baltimore, MD 21234; (410) 444-5433. This small shop is packed full of Italian groceries and has a decent selection of wine at the front. We like to visit to pick up a little of this and a little of that, but our favorite part of this shop is the deli case. The display of olives and house-made sausages is always quite tempting, but most of the time we're there to grab a sub or 3 to go. The meatball sub is a real thing of beauty—a half-loaf of Italian bread is gutted and stuffed with tender, flavorful meatballs, tomato sauce, and, if you like, cheese. The Old World Italian sandwich is also a winner, with what we consider to be the perfect Italian cold-cut-to-bread ratio, plus a judicious application of savory olive salad.

Prigel Family Creamery, 4851 Long Green Rd., Glen Arm, MD 21057; (410) 510-7488; prigelfamilycreamery.com. The Prigels have been dairy farming in the Long Green Valley for more than five generations. Their Bellevale Farm was certified organic in 2008, and their cows feast on grass, as all ruminants should. There have been studies that show grass-fed cows produce an unsaturated fat called CLA that might protect the heart and fight cancer. See what we've done? We've just given you a convenient excuse to eat ice cream—you can thank us later. Prigel Family

Creamery sells the good-tasting and potentially healthy stuff in half gallons, quarts, cups, cones, sandwiches, and milkshakes, in flavors like apple strudel, dulce de leche, and good ol' vanilla. In addition to ice cream, Prigel sells milk, eggs, and beef too. Even soaps made from their own milk.

Stone Mill Bakery, 10751 Falls Rd., #123, Timonium, MD 21093; (410) 821-1358. We can remember when Stone Mill Bakery was just that: a bakery that supplied their fantastic fresh-baked artisan breads to restaurants all over town. They still have a fabulous selection of breads and other baked goods for sale at the cafe, but they also have a full menu of soups, sandwiches, salads, and pizzas. At breakfast time there's a selection of eggy things, waffles, and the like, but our favorite thing to order is brioche toast with raspberry preserves and butter and a mug of smooth Brooklyn-based-by-way-of-Switzerland Cafe la Semeuse coffee.

Western Baltimore County

The western side of Baltimore County is a densely populated residential area. Owings Mills, for example, is probably best known nationally because it is the location for the Baltimore Ravens football training facility, but the area has seen tremendous growth during the last quarter century. With major companies like T. Rowe Price establishing corporate campuses in the picturesque community, the inevitable population of stores and restaurants has followed.

Older communities like Reisterstown and Pikesville once catered to the needs of travelers heading into Baltimore City from the west. In later years, however, these towns became home to a large Jewish community. Catonsville was also once an area filled with hotels and taverns, but then became a prime location for wealthy Baltimoreans seeking to build summer homes in the cooler countryside. Many large, Victorian-style homes still dot the landscape.

The communities along the US Route 40 corridor (i.e., Catonsville, Woodlawn, Arbutus, Ilchester) have seen a recent growth in their Asian populations, allowing for the proliferation of Asian restaurants and stores. National supermarket chains like H-Mart and Lotte-Assi-Plaza have built branches in the area, but several mom-and-pop Asian markets are also worth a visit.

Foodie Faves

Artful Gourmet Bistro, 9433 Common Brook Rd., Owings Mills, MD 21117; (410) 356-0363; artfulgourmet.com; Eclectic; $$$. The "artful" part of this restaurant's name is literal. Not only are the walls decorated with replicas of famous works of art, but the menu is also peppered with references to artists and art movements. It's kind of fun trying to figure out why some things are named the way they are. For instance, is the salmon with cherry tomatoes in a rose cream sauce as enigmatic as the Mona Lisa? How is shrimp salad on toasted sourdough related to Georgia O'Keeffe? Would the Al Fresco signature salad be better enjoyed outdoors? Actually, it all tastes just fine indoors. Lunch can be a quick thing, like a veggie panini (the Velasquez), ordered at the counter, or a more leisurely meal at the bar. Dinner is full-service, with a primarily Mediterranean-influenced menu of salads, pastas, and entrees.

Catonsville Gourmet, 829 Frederick Rd., Catonsville, MD 21228; (410) 788-0005; catonsvillegourmet.com; Seafood; $$$. Housed in what used to be a hardware store on Catonsville's main drag, this charming bistro specializes in seafood. Not just the usual Maryland-influenced festival of crab (though there are some very nice crab cakes on the menu) but a variety of interesting choices. For instance, any fresh fish of the day can be prepared in several ways, including broiled, pan fried, or pistachio crusted, with one of many sauces, like a simple lemon butter or a bright mango-and-avocado salsa. And if you want crab imperial on your fish, you can certainly have that too. There are also steaks, a handful of pastas, and lots of sandwiches, including one with shrimp salad on cheese toast called "the Hutzler," an ode to a department store once beloved by Baltimoreans. Most desserts come from Catonsville's own **SugarBakers** (p. 261), including servings of Maryland's official state dessert, the Smith Island Cake. If you can't stay for dinner, stop by the market area of the restaurant and pick up some fresh seafood or meat to prepare at home.

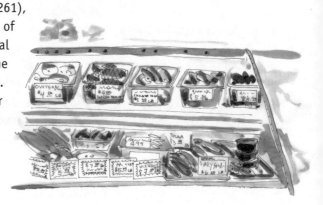

Gianni's Italian Bistro, 3720 Washington Blvd., Arbutus, MD 21227; (410) 242-4555; giannisitalianbistro.com; Italian; $$. Chef-Owner Greg Orendorff and his wife, Colleen, once owned Little

Italy's popular Luigi Petti, and many of that restaurant's favorites can now be found at Gianni's. Pasta dishes like the spaghetti puttanesca and the penne rosa come in large portions and are a good value. Neapolitan-style pizza and subs are also on the menu. Not only that, but there's also a whole separate seafood-centric area of the restaurant with its own menu. Called the Angry Mallet, there you can get steamed crabs all year long, plus ginormous, tennis-ball-size, 10-ounce crab cakes made with lump crab. And when you're finished with your pasta, steak, or crabs, wander over to the Fractured Prune donut franchise on-premises and pick up something for dessert or the next day's breakfast treat.

Grilled Cheese & Co., 500 Edmondson Ave., Catonsville, MD 21228; ilovegrilledcheese.com; (410) 747-2610; Sandwich Shop; $. Grilled Cheese & Co. started out as a dream. Literally. One of the owners dreamt he was selling grilled cheese sandwiches out of an Airstream trailer. Instead, Vic Corbi and partner Matt Lancelotta sold their sandwiches at festivals before opening their first brick-and-mortar restaurant in Catonsville. A handful of years later, they have three locations, and during Ravens home games, they set up on Ravens Walk between M&T Bank Stadium and Oriole Park at Camden Yards. Why grilled cheese? Because who doesn't like them, especially when the bread is light and crisp and the cheese is copious and oozy? We enjoy the Fresco, with fresh mozz and provolone, a hint of pesto and roasted red peppers, and a wee bit of balsamic glaze, to cut the richness. The sandwiches are slightly oversize, so they're perfect for sharing, especially if you get a side of soup, salad, or fries.

BALTIMORE RAVENS FAN FOOD— TASTY TEMPTATIONS AT M&T BANK STADIUM

For the first two seasons that the Baltimore Ravens football team played in the city, they had to make do with the hopelessly outdated Memorial Stadium on 33rd Street. It was a far cry from the gleaming Oriole Park at Camden Yards, but in 1998 the Ravens got their own spanking-new home next door to Oriole Park and fans have been selling the place out ever since. Officially called M&T Bank Stadium, many fans refer to it as the Russell Street Coliseum due to its location. With so many rabid fans flocking to the stadium every fall, the food offerings have to satisfy their hunger.

Since tailgating is limited due to the dearth of parking lots in this downtown location, a special walkway known as **AAA Ravens Walk** is set up between Oriole Park and the stadium. Opening 3 hours before each home game, the walk features stalls set up by some of Baltimore's most famous restaurants, including **Attman's** (attmansdeli.com) and the **Oregon Grille** (theoregongrille.com). Fans can fill up on chicken wings, sliders, crab cakes, cheesesteaks, and all manner of beers and spirits. The sheer crush of purple-clad fans is overwhelming.

Inside the stadium more sports food awaits at the 44 food stands on the lower and upper levels and another 11 stands on the club level. This isn't just hot dogs and peanuts, however. To satisfy varying diets and tastes, the stadium offers items like black-bean burgers, gluten-free pretzels, and sushi. For those willing to shell out the extra bucks for club-level tickets, they can enjoy a climate-controlled concourse with seated service and large TV screens to enjoy the game while they nosh. But why miss out on being in the stands? Ravens fans are some of the most enthusiastic and entertaining around. A beer and a hot dog tastes so much better when 70,000 people are screaming "De-fense!"

There's another Baltimore location at 1036 Light St., Baltimore, MD 21230; (410) 244-6333. A third location is in Carroll County: 577 Johnsville Rd., Ste. 1, Sykesville, MD 21784; (443) 920-3238.

Hunan Taste, 718 N. Rolling Rd., Catonsville, MD 21228; (410) 788-8988; hunantastemd.com; Chinese; $. Out of the many Asian restaurants on the west side of Baltimore County, Hunan Taste stands out because of its expansive selection of authentic specialties originating in China's Hunan province. They have a menu of American-style Chinese dishes, but do yourself a favor, put it aside, and concentrate on the good stuff. Many of the offerings lean toward exotica like soft-shell turtle, Hunan-style frog hot pot, and stir-fried pig kidney. There's also something called bullwhack, which our waitress advised us against, mysteriously describing it as a "part." Ahem. There's plenty else on the menu to try, like the "country bumpkin" chicken, chunks of chicken on the bone in a rich, savory sauce. There's also Hunan-born Chairman Mao's favorite dish, red-braised pork belly, seasoned with star anise and whole garlic cloves. A more unusual but no less delicious dish is the casserole featuring pork and snappy-textured tea tree mushrooms imported from China especially for Hunan Taste. And do try the "beef on toothpicks" which is exactly as described, lovely bits of cumin-flavored crisp fried beef skewered on toothpicks.

Maiwand Kabob, 839 Elkridge Landing Rd., Ste. 110, Linthicum Heights, MD 21090; (410) 850-0273; maiwandkabob.com; Central Asian; $. Don't be distracted by the word "kabob" in the name. Sure, Maiwand Kabob has skewered lamb, chicken, and beef, but they also have traditional Afghan dishes, and to our minds, they are must-tries. Like the *aushak,* ravioli filled with scallions and topped with a mint yogurt sauce and ground beef. Mmm! The pan-fried pumpkin with garlicky yogurt, aka *kaddo borawni,* is seriously good. Try it. OK, now you may proceed to the kabob portion of your meal. All varieties are served in huge portions with heavenly soft tandoori bread, basmati rice, salad, and cilantro yogurt sauce. Everything is cooked to order, so be prepared to wait a while for your food, especially if the joint is jumping. It's worth the wait. There's another location at 7690 Dorchester Blvd., Hanover, MD 21076, (443) 755-0461, plus one in Columbia, Harford County.

Mari Luna Latin Grille, 1010 Reisterstown Rd., Pikesville, MD 21208; (410) 653-5151; mariluna.com; Latin; $$$. Latin Grille is a larger and more ambitious sibling to the original restaurant in the Mari Luna family, **Mexican Grill** (see below), down the road. The menu here includes dishes from Central and South America and the Caribbean as well as some Mexican favorites. (On Mexican Monday there is an extended Mexican menu available, which is great, since Mexican Grill is closed that day.) A good way to start out your meal is with the Luna Sampler, which offers a taste of various appetizers like coconut shrimp and a tortilla-crusted crab cake. Go on to the *Bistec a la Criolla,* a mesquite-grilled skirt steak in a red wine sauce, or order the paella, which comes with a bounty of seafood, including a lobster tail. Folks who like to dine early (as in 4 to 6 p.m.) should take advantage of their 3-course "early-bird special," which comes in under $30 per person and offers a nice selection of dishes. And don't forget to order a caipirinha or margarita with your meal; Latin Grille has a full bar.

Mari Luna Mexican Grill, 102 Reisterstown Rd., Pikesville, MD 21208; (410) 486-9910; mariluna.com; Mexican; $$. This charming little restaurant, with bright-yellow walls and blue ceiling meant to evoke the sky, is often crowded with happy diners. With good reason: The service is attentive, the food is delicious, and the prices are right. One of the things we really love about Mari Luna is that there are tons of a la carte options, so if you want one *taco de barbacoa* (lamb) and one of the chicken and cheese-stuffed chile rellenos, you can get just those items (which do come with pico de gallo, sour cream, and guacamole) and avoid the ubiquitous side dishes of Mexican rice and charro beans. If, however, you love beans and rice, there are all manner of DIY combination platters too. And make sure to try a bowl of the black-bean or chicken tortilla soup. Mari Luna is BYOC (bring your own cerveza). There's another Mari Luna serving Mexican food, Mexican Bistro, in downtown Baltimore City: 1225 Cathedral St., Baltimore, MD 21201; (410) 637-8013. It has a slightly different but no less delicious menu.

SMITH ISLAND CAKE—
OFFICIAL DESSERT OF MARYLAND

Smith Island is only a little over 9 square miles in size and is home to about 400 residents. It's the only populated island in the Chesapeake Bay, but that's not why so many Marylanders are familiar with it. Most know the tiny island for the dessert named after it: the Smith Island Cake.

No one knows exactly when it was created or how, but the recipe is pretty consistent. Typically, the Smith Island Cake is 6 to 12 layers of extremely thin yellow cake glued together with loads of rich chocolate fudge icing. Some believe the cake is a variation of the English tortes made by the Welsh settlers who came to the island in the 1600s. Others claim that the cake was invented by the wives of the island's crabbers and oystermen who were looking to create a dessert that would keep well at sea. Regardless, the cake was officially named the State Dessert of Maryland in 2008.

Several places on the Eastern Shore make Smith Island Cake, such as the **Original Smith Island Cake Co.** (originalsmithislandcakeco.com), which sells the standard version and variations like carrot cake and red velvet. The **Smith Island Sweet Shoppe** (smithislandcakes.net) in Crisfield, Maryland, and **Smith Island Baking Co.** (smithislandbakingco.com) on Smith Island also sell their cakes online so everyone can try this Maryland original. In the Baltimore area Smith Island Cakes can be purchased at **SugarBakers Cakes** in Catonsville, Maryland (see their listing on p. 261).

Pho #1, 5764 Baltimore National Pike, Catonsville, MD 21228; (410) 719-7500; pho1md.com; Vietnamese; $. Pho #1 is prettier than the average strip-mall restaurant, with dark wood and lots of floral arrangements. They might also have tastier food than the average strip-mall restaurant. As the name suggests, the restaurant specializes in pho, the famous noodle soup of Vietnam, but there are all manner of other noodle dishes on the menu. For example, there are 17 varieties of *bun,* chilled noodles with warm toppings like spicy charbroiled pork and crisp slices of egg roll. There's also *hu tieu,* a soup featuring glass noodles, and 21 types of *com,* or rice dishes, topped with yummies like shrimp on sugarcane, stir-fried squid, and pork chops. Beverages include delicious Vietnamese coffee and Thai iced tea, but bubble tea (flavored iced teas with large chewy pearls of tapioca) do a nice double-duty of drink and dessert all in one.

Regions, 805 Frederick Rd., Catonsville, MD 21228; (410) 788-0075; regionsrestaurant.com; American; $$$. **Catonsville Gourmet** (p. 247) owners Sean T. Dunworth and Rob Rehmert have teamed up with Ed and Kathleen Geil to create Regions, located just down the road from their other restaurant. The dining room has a rustic-chic feel, with dark walls, darker trim, and exposed ceiling beams. Grazers—people who like to taste several different things during the course of a meal—will love the menu, which is divided into small and "big" plates. The food at Regions is the kind we're seeing more and more of these days, a veritable melting pot of comfort food and elevated pub grub that borrows heavily from several global influences. Take, for example, the tempura-battered ahi tuna roll, or the French Quarter pasta with blackened shellfish and andouille sausage. Weekends at Regions bring a brunch with some pretty creative dishes like the cereal-crusted French toast and the "scrapple-apple sandwich" with cheddar and a mini-omelette on a brioche roll. But the restaurant is BYOB, so if you want mimosas, you'll have to bring your own champagne.

Reter's Crab House & Grille, 509 Main St., Reisterstown, MD 21136; (410) 526-3300; reterscrabhouse.com; Crab House; $$. Though the restaurant is 30 or so miles away from any salt water, the peachy-pink walls, surfboards, and replicas of Ocean City beach signs make Reter's feel like it's a lot closer. So do the piles of hot steamed crabs, smothered in the restaurant's own blend of spices, being enjoyed by tables full of mallet-wielding locals. Other beachy favorites include a variety of raw oysters, steamed shrimp, and even funnel cake for dessert. Tried-and-true landlubbers might prefer a Western shore–style meal, like the tender baby back ribs, the generous cuts of prime rib, or any of several different burgers. If you prefer to take your feast off-premises, Reter's also has a seafood market where you can buy live lobsters, oysters, shrimp, crab soup, and steamed crabs by the dozen, bushel, or half bushel.

Silk Road Bistro, 607 Reisterstown Rd., Pikesville, MD 21208; (410) 878-2929; Central Asian; $$. When we see a restaurant filled with people from the homeland eating and having what looks to be a pretty good time, it bodes well for the authenticity of the cuisine. Silk Road Bistro serves the food of Uzbekistan, the most populous country in Central Asia and neighbor to Afghanistan. Lamb and yogurt are staples of the region and feature prominently on the menu. We love the *suzma,* a simple salad of radishes and cucumbers in yogurt seasoned with dill, and both fried and steamed version of the fist-size dumplings called *manti.* There are several varieties of kebabs available, the best of which are the juicy lamb ribs and the "delicatessen," which is, er, lamb's testicle. Don't say "ewww," try it; they're fluffy and have a delicate flavor. Everything is plated on beautifully patterned Uzbek pottery and served on tables covered with colorful ikat-like tablecloths, and sometimes there looks to be an Uzbek soap opera playing on the TV at the back of the restaurant.

Landmarks

Double T Diner, 6300 Baltimore National Pike, Catonsville, MD 21228; (410) 744-4151; doubletdiner.com; Diner; $$. This location, the original, was opened in 1959 by Thomas and Tony Doxanas, hence the "double T" moniker. Later, in the 1980s, the business was sold to the three Korologos brothers (only one has a name starting with a *T*), who now own and manage eight Double Ts around Maryland. Like any classic Greek diner worth its salt, the

Catonsville branch is open 24 hours and serves breakfast round the clock. The huge menu has literally something for everyone. We like their Florentine omelette (spinach and feta) with a side of scrapple, the patty melt (served with soup, fries, coleslaw, and a pickle), and when we're feeling especially piggy, the "triple-stuffed combo" (a fillet of flounder, a shrimp, and a mushroom, each stuffed with crabmeat) with soup, salad, starch, and a veg. While the huge pastry case is always tempting, we prefer a cup of classic, diner-style rice pudding for dessert. Not that there's ever any room. There are 2 other Double Ts in the Baltimore area: 10741 Pulaski Hwy., White Marsh, MD 21162, (410) 344-1020; and 4140 E. Joppa Rd., Baltimore, MD 21236, (410) 248-0160.

The Grill at Harryman House, 340 Main St., Reisterstown, MD 21136; (410) 833-8850; harrymanhouse.com; American; $$$. There's just something . . . American . . . about eating in a log cabin that was built over 200 years ago. It's that whole Abraham Lincoln thing. So when we eat at Harryman House, we try to dine in the room that shows the exposed logs of the original house, built circa 1791. (But we like dining on the porches too!) While the building has history, the Grill's menu is built for the 21st century and offers something for all tastes. You can get a full 3-course dinner, starting with something from the raw bar and ending with a decadent dessert, or just grab a burger. The burger, made from Kobe beef and served on a brioche bun, comes with sautéed onions and mushrooms and a side of fries, which you can swap out for the duck fat fries with basil aioli. The burger is also available during weekend brunch, along with several other savory and sweet options.

Gunning's Seafood, 7304 Parkway Dr., Hanover, MD 21076; (410) 712-9404; gunningsonline.com; Crab House; $$$. Over the years, Gunning's morphed from a South Baltimore bar to a crab house to a bonafide seafood restaurant, earning a reputation for being one of the best in Baltimore. Today, the third generation of Gunnings runs the restaurant, which has been relocated to Baltimore County. There's no water view in Hanover, but you don't need one to enjoy bashing a couple dozen fat and meaty steamed crabs, which are available year-round. With the crabs, try an order of the "world famous" fried bell pepper rings, which are battered, fried, and dusted in powdered sugar. Another fried specialty is the "crab fluff," a jumbo lump crab cake, dipped in batter and deep-fried. Hard crabs, topped with a mound of crabmeat and, you guessed it, battered and fried, are also on the menu. It's a bit of a messy challenge to eat, but if you're game, it's worth the effort.

Linwood's, 25 Crossroads Dr., Owings Mills, MD 21117; (410) 356-3030; linwoods.com; American; $$$$. Now in its third decade, Linwood and Ellen Dame's stylish restaurant continues its tradition as one of the best special-occasion restaurants in Baltimore County. It's expensive, but the food is often exquisite, and the service is top-notch. If you can, grab a seat at the grill line to watch the chefs do their thing in the open kitchen. Try the sea bass with lemon crab salad, or the caramelized sea scallops with grilled duck salad and oranges. But even if the occasion isn't particularly special, if you just want a juicy, well-made burger for dinner, or maybe a pizza from the wood-burning oven, those are also excellent choices. Linwood's wine list is fairly extensive, and there are a number of interesting specialty cocktails to enjoy with your meal.

Suburban House, 1700 Reisterstown Rd., Pikesville, MD 21208; (410) 484-7775; suburbanhousedeli.com; Deli; $. Suburban House was devastated by a fire back in 2009, and regulars worried that the best matzoh ball soup in town was gone forever. But like the phoenix, Suburban House emerged from the ashes a couple blocks down the road. As one of the last remaining old-world Jewish delis in Baltimore, Suburban House has been responsible for providing food for many a bris, mitzvah, and shiva over the past 50 or so years, something they continue to this day. They also still serve their famous "chicken in the pot" (half a stewed chicken, soup, noodles, carrots, peas, and a matzoh ball), and several interesting twists on a club sandwich, including "the Mayven," with corned beef and chopped liver, and "The Chutzpah," with chicken salad and bacon. (So not kosher!) Breakfast is available all day, including their famous "gezunta" (big) omelettes.

Specialty Stores, Markets & Producers

Patel Brothers, 6402 Baltimore National Pike, Catonsville, MD 21228; (410) 719-2822. If you're like us, you enjoy cooking as much as eating. Sometimes, tracking down exotic ingredients for a favorite dish can be difficult, so it's always a thrill to find Indian or Asian grocers in the area that carry those hard-to-find items. Patel Brothers has a wide selection of Indian spices, sauce mixes, and chutneys, along with numerous varieties of lentils and rice. Their extensive inventory is neatly organized on shelves that are easy to search through and the store is clean and bright. They also carry hard-to-find fruits, vegetables, and herbs like bitter gourd and curry leaves.

SugarBakers Cakes, 752 Frederick Rd., Catonsville, MD 21228; (410) 788-9478; sugarbakerscakes.com. In a quaint brick building on Frederick Road in Catonsville is a nationally recognized purveyor of elaborate wedding and specialty cakes. Their work has been featured in wedding magazines and on NBC's *Today* show, but you can sample their wares just by walking through the front door. Their retail store is open 6 days a week and offers delicacies like tarts, éclairs, coffee cake, cannolis, 6-inch cakes, and cakes by the slice. It's one of the few bakeries in the area that sells Smith Island Cake, the official dessert of Maryland. Thick, fudgy icing cradles numerous layers of moist yellow cake for a decadent chocolate fix. We also recommend the Classic Ivory Cake with silky French buttercream. Oh, just about anything would be great with that buttercream on it. . . .

Worth the Drive

Baltimore City and Baltimore County are home to many terrific restaurants, but there are tons more throughout the rest of Maryland. It would take a whole other book to chronicle them all, particularly those in the counties closer to Washington, DC, but we thought we'd include some of our favorite restaurants located in the counties adjacent to Baltimore County: Carroll, Harford, Howard, and Anne Arundel. All of the restaurants included in this section are, we think, worth the drive.

Aida Bistro & Wine Bar, 6741 Columbia Gateway Dr., Columbia, MD 21046; (410) 953-0500; aidabistro.com; Wine Bar; $$$. Joe and Mary Barbera have always had a passion for food and wine. What better way to celebrate both than by opening a restaurant? Aida Bistro, named after Joe's mom (who is often in the restaurant on the weekends), celebrates Italian-influenced cuisine with a variety of small plates and entrees that use seasonal, locally sourced products as much as possible. A 3-course prix-fixe dinner is a bargain at $40; there's also a special Chef's Table dinner of 6 to 8 courses for 2 to 4 diners available by request. The food is fine, but don't neglect libations. After all, it is a wine bar, and there's a large selection of wines on tap. Yes, you read that correctly—wines on tap. Like draught beer, wines on tap tend to be fresher and retain consistent flavor from the first glass to the last. Currently, there are 30 available, from both local and international producers, available by the glass, half and full carafes, even by the taste.

Antrim 1844, 30 Trevanion Rd., Taneytown, MD 21787; (410) 756-6812; antrim1844.com; American; $$$$. Antrim was once a thriving plantation, established in 1844. Currently, the property houses an inn with 40 luxuriously appointed rooms, a pub, wine cellar, and the Smokehouse Restaurant. A perennial fixture on Maryland media "best of" lists, including top 10 status from *Baltimore* magazine for several years running, the romantic restaurant features the French-American cuisine of Executive Chef Michael Gettier. Gettier has cooked in some of the best restaurants in Baltimore, including the posh Conservatory at the Peabody Court Hotel, and his eponymous M. Gettier in Fells Point, both of which we remember fondly. At Antrim he and his staff orchestrate a rich 6-course prix-fixe dinner which includes passed hors d'oeuvres, an amuse, a salad, a choice of appetizers and main course, and a "panache" of desserts. There is usually an app involving *foie gras,* and there's always fish, fowl, and fillet on the menu of mains. The food is often spectacular, and so is the wine list, which spans about 80 pages and has been called by *Wine Spectator* "one of the most outstanding in the world."

Asian Court, 9180 Baltimore National Pike, Ellicott City, MD 21042; (410) 461-8388; Chinese; $$. We love dim sum, and Asian Court is one of our favorite places to eat that often lavish selection of dumplings, noodles, and fried goodies. On weekends the restaurant is packed with families enjoying slippery *cheung fun* (steamed crepes filled with shrimp and topped with a sweet soy), *hom sui gok* (football-shaped dumplings made from sweet rice flour filled with pork), and chicken feet. If we don't see it on the carts, we like to order either soy sauce noodles or spicy Singapore noodles from the kitchen, plus Chinese broccoli with oyster sauce, and salt-and-pepper head-on shrimp. Dinner is pretty great too. The Peking duck comes with super-crispy skin, fat-free meat, and plenty of delicate pancakes for wrapping. There's an "authentic cuisine" section of the menu that offers items not found on the typical American-style Chinese restaurant. Be adventurous and try the duck tongues with chive flowers, and the crisp, bright-green *yu choi* sautéed with garlic.

Baldwin's Station, 7618 Main St., Sykesville, MD 21784; (410) 795-1041; baldwinstation.com; American; $$$. History buffs, railroad fans, and foodies alike will enjoy a trip out to Baldwin's Station, set in the sleepy burg of Sykesville, in Carroll County. The Restaurant Association of Maryland's 2012 Favorite Restaurant is set within the town's original 1883 railroad station, now on the National Register of Historic Places. The Queen Anne–style building has original stained-glass windows, exposed brick, and 20-foot ceilings. The building might be an antique, but the menu is completely modern. Special attention is paid to certified organic and local ingredients, and there are gluten-free and vegetarian items on the menu, like the ravioli filled with wild mushrooms and garbanzo ragout tossed in a walnut brown butter sauce. We also love the lunch menu's bison burger, seared in duck fat to add flavor and moisture to the lean, locally produced meat, and topped with baby greens, juicy tomato, and a yummy apricot, fig, and date relish.

Bistro Blanc, 3800 Ten Oaks Rd., Glenelg, MD 21737; (410) 489-7907; bistroblancmd.com; Wine Bar; $$$. Bistro Blanc has this nifty self-serve wine bar that's perfect for experimental people who aren't afraid of trying new things. Like us. We put a special card into the machine, select a wine, choose the size pour we'd like (a taste, 2 ounces, or a full serving), and voilà! Vino. There are also 300 or so bottles available for purchase, and another 40 or so wines by the glass. While there's always a really nice selection of cheeses on the cheese plate, which of course goes perfectly with just about any wine, we prefer to try something more inventive from Chef Marc Dixon's menu of small plates and larger entrees. The chef's not afraid of working with unusual flavor combinations and modernist techniques, so there might be seared tuna with a white miso pistachio puree and lemongrass-infused rhubarb foam, or grilled scallops with apricot pink peppercorn chutney and a yuzu soy "pudding" on the menu. There are a few dessert options for afterward, but we usually prefer to have another glass of wine.

Elkridge Furnace Inn, 5745 Furnace Ave., Elkridge, MD 21075; (410) 379-9336; elkridgefurnaceinn.com; American; $$$$. This elegant and historical restaurant earned its less-than-glamorous name back in 1750 when an iron-smelting furnace was added to the premises of the original 1744 tavern building. Much of the existing interior woodwork and stairways date back to the 18th and 19th centuries, and the longleaf pine floors are original. Executive Chef-Owner Daniel Wecker's food is far more modern, with some very 21st-century small plates, and a multinational selection of entrees that might include chicken and waffles, Greek-style lamb chops, and grilled Mediterranean-style tofu. Diners can order a la carte or choose either the 3- or 4-course prix fixe. While the inn is a lovely place for a romantic date or a special-occasion dinner, there are also some fun special events offered, like a traditional afternoon tea with scones and clotted cream, murder mystery dinners, and wine tastings.

G&M Restaurant & Lounge, 804 N. Hammonds Ferry Rd., Linthicum Heights, MD 21090; (410) 636-1777; gandmcrabcakes .com; Seafood; $$$. In an unofficial and unscientific survey of friends, foes, and complete strangers, G&M was most frequently mentioned as having the best crab cakes in the area. The cakes are pretty glorious; the large mountains of lump crab and little filler are broiled until a crispy golden brown. You can get them in a platter, with 2 sides, or as a sandwich. But you might want to get them to go from the carryout, because the lines of folks waiting for a table at peak noshing times can be a little ridiculous. If you do catch a break and get a table (and a parking space!), there's also a terrific crab imperial, and the jumbo stuffed shrimp are sorta like the crab cakes, but with a bonus shrimp inside. There are chicken entrees and a whole slew of pastas, but really, you waited in line for chicken? At least order the chicken Chesapeake, which comes topped with jumbo lump crabmeat and imperial sauce.

Grace Garden, 1690 Annapolis Rd., Odenton, MD 21113; (410) 672-3581; gracegardenchinese.com; Chinese; $. Located on a dull stretch of road near Fort Meade, this gem was hidden for a good handful of years until local foodie chatboards started to light up with well-deserved praise. Hong Kong–born Chef-Owner Keung Li is a master of Chinese cuisine, specializing in the dishes from Sichuan province that possess the quality of *ma-la,* which is both spicy and numbing. We like to go with a group and order a ridiculous number of dishes. Something with *ma-la,* like the Sichuan fish fillets, is a must, plus the fish noodles (noodles actually made from fish!) or the whole tea-smoked duck. And we always order a couple of family favorites: the chewy, bacon-like Sichuan pork belly stir-fried with leeks, and the vermicelli stir-fried with ground pork and chiles. For the less-adventurous, Grace Garden also does a fine job with more familiar Chinese-American dishes like kung pao chicken, but if you're going to drive all the way to Odenton, why not try something more surprising, like the outrageously delicious

Sichuan Triple Treasures (chilled spicy tripe, tongue, and tendon, with peanuts)?

Great Sage, 5809 Clarksville Square Dr., Clarksville, MD 21029; (443) 535-9400; great-sage.com; Vegetarian/Vegan; $$. There aren't too many vegan restaurants around, so when Great Sage opened in 2004, there was a bit of buzz. We know what you're thinking: Vegan restaurants serve lots of sprouts and weird meat substitutes. While there's some truth in that, vegan restaurants can also be modern, romantic, sophisticated, and upscale. Like Great Sage. The *Baltimore Sun* named it one of the best 100 restaurants for a date night, and *Baltimore* magazine considered it the best vegan restaurant for 2011. With dishes like "adult" mac and cheese made with cauliflower, beans, and white truffle in a vegan Mornay sauce, we can see why. A recent brunch special of pumpkin-and-black-bean enchiladas smothered in a rich mole with a side of Mexican quinoa was outstanding. And if the "crab" cake made with hearts of palm is available, don't miss out. We're also fans of the raw beet ravioli. Desserts are also quite nice at Great Sage, particularly the coconut cake layered with coconut frosting and topped with chocolate ganache and toasted almonds. See Great Sage's recipe for **Raw Beet Ravioli** on p. 323.

Honey Pig Gooldaegee, 10045 Baltimore National Pike, Ellicott City, MD 21042; (410) 696-2426; eathoneypig.com; Korean; $$.

There was a lot of excitement in the foodie community when Honey Pig opened its Ellicott City location—no more would Baltimore-area lovers of Korean barbecue have to drive into northern Virginia (always a bit of a pain) in order to gorge themselves on first-rate bulgogi or galbi at any hour of the day or night. That's right, Honey Pig is open 24 hours a day, 6 days a week (and closed from 2 to 11 a.m. on Mon). The restaurant has an industrial feel, with lots of shiny stainless steel decorated with signs advertising specials. What to order? Well, the pork belly is a good choice; it cooks up brown and crispy, with a satisfying bit of chew, and you can't go wrong with the galbi (beef ribs). The more adventurous might want to brave the beef "viscera" (intestines), but we think everyone should order the crispy seafood pancake in addition to something meaty for the tabletop grill.

Iron Bridge Wine Company, 10435 Rte. 108, Columbia, MD 21044; (410) 997-3456; ironbridgewines.com; Wine Bar; $$$. With an emphasis on small-vineyard and small-production wines, Iron Bridge offers more than 30 vinos by the glass from their selection of 300 or so bottles. You can, of course, buy a bottle or two to drink on the premises while you enjoy the company of your friends in this cozy, convivial restaurant. Stay for a full lunch or dinner, or just nibble on one or more of the small plates, like house-made charcuterie, or the luxuriously pillowy burrata with tomato-fennel jam and grilled baguette. If you're not sure what to order—in the wine

Ocean City Faves

Every resort has loyal visitors who come every year to experience the same fun activities and relive the same fond memories. Some of those fun activities involve food, and Ocean City, Maryland, has a couple of classics most Marylanders have to have whenever they are visiting the peninsula resort: **Thrasher's French Fries** and **Fisher's Popcorn.**

Since 1929 when J. T. Thrasher came up from Georgia with his special recipe for french fries, vacationers have been lining up for hours in the hot sun to buy a bucket-full. The hand-cut fries are sold in three sizes: small (a mere 1 pound!), medium (32 ounces), and the 53-ounce large, which resembles a bucket from a fried chicken joint. The available condiments are salt and malt vinegar but absolutely no ketchup as it would ruin the natural flavor of the fries. The exact recipe is a closely guarded secret, but the potatoes are always freshly peeled and sliced before they are put into the oil. Along with its location by the Ocean City Amusement Pier, Thrasher's Fries can be purchased farther up the Boardwalk at 8th Street, and in Bethany Beach, Delaware. Some people might say, "Why wait in line for french fries?" Those people have probably not tried Thrasher's.

or food categories—the staff at Iron Bridge is happy to point you in a delicious direction. Daily specials are pretty special, particularly Thursday, when corkage fees (normally $10 per bottle) are waived.

The King's Contrivance, 10150 Shaker Dr., Columbia, MD 21046; (410) 995-0500; thekingscontrivance.com; American; $$$. The

If Thrasher's Fries is the salty snack addiction in Ocean City, Fisher's Popcorn is the sweet one. A family-run business since 1937, Fisher's Popcorn is tossed in large drums as sweet caramel is drizzled over it until every piece is lightly coated. You can also get it with peanuts for that Cracker Jack (but better) effect. Located on the Boardwalk at the corner of Talbot Street, Fisher's sells their popcorn in reusable plastic tubs from the half-gallon size to 1½ gallons. You can also buy the popcorn in decorative tins for gifts or for the holidays. While the popcorn does come in flavors like white cheddar, butter, and Old Bay, it's the caramel corn that keeps the tourists coming back each year. Some people would not think of visiting Ocean City without a stop at Fisher's.

Of course, if you can't visit Ocean City, you can order this addictive treat online at fisherspopcorn.com. Along with the familiar tubs, you can buy quart tins in packs of 12 or giant 6½-gallon cans. Fisher's will even double the order at no charge for any shipment going to military personnel.

King's Contrivance is located in a stately old home built just before the turn of the last century on what used to be a large tract of farmland. Sadly much of that farmland is now suburbia, but the King's Contrivance is still a lovely setting for a special occasion, like a birthday or a wedding. The menu seems a little old-fashioned, what with shellfish bisque and escargots Bourguignonne among the appetizers. But look closer: There's house-made mozzarella and seared tuna with pickled ginger too. While not in Baltimore, this restaurant is still firmly in Maryland, so there are several seafood options available at both lunch and dinner. Brunch too. If soft-shell crabs are on offer, try them, particularly if they are part of the tasty "surf and surf" combo that also includes a crab cake.

Kloby's Smokehouse, 7500 Montpelier Rd., Laurel, MD 20723; (301) 362-1510; klobysbbq.com; Barbecue; $$. Real, long-smoked 'que is rare in these parts, but you'll find it at Steve and Michele Klobosits' restaurant, along with 32 beers on tap, including several from local producer **Heavy Seas** (p. 294), and an impressive selection of bourbons. Seriously, it's like a carnivore's paradise there. The Carolina-style pulled-pork sandwich is delicious, and the barbecued brisket cheesesteak is inspired. Folks avoiding red meat can get their smoke on via the sandwich with smoked chicken thighs and portobello mushrooms mingled with melted provolone and barbecue sauce, or the whole smoked chicken wings in any of 11 delicious flavors (we like 'em "dirty and old," double fried, double dipped in Buffalo barbecue sauce, and dusted with Old Bay—crunchy, spicy, and messy as heck.) But don't skip the inventive appetizers, like the pulled-pork-stuffed jalapeño poppers or the fried pickled green tomatoes, served with Kloby's mayo-based Bama Pearl sauce. Meat is also available by the pound to take home, along with bottles of sauce.

Laurrapin Grille, 209 N. Washington St., Havre de Grace, MD 21078; (410) 939-4956; laurrapin.com; American; $$. The charming town of Havre de Grace, near the mouth of the Susquehanna River and the head of the Chesapeake Bay, is home to the Laurrapin Grille. Set on Antique Row about a block from the waterfront (a great place to walk off dinner), the Laurrapin is one of the thankfully increasing number of restaurants that strives to use as many organic, sustainable, and locally produced meats and veggies that they can get their hands on. Many items on Executive Chef-Owner Bruce Clarke's menu include products from farms right there in Harford County: Deer Meadow Farm ham and Havre de Grace's Keyes Creamery cheese is used in their luscious mac-and-cheese appetizer; the beef in their slow-braised short ribs comes from Level Farms; and both duck and wine from Mount Felix are used in their Mon Cheri duck. Check the website for details on weekly specials, including Thursday's steamer bargains and sushi Sunday. There's also live music on Friday and Saturday and great happy-hour deals during the week.

Level, A Small Plates Lounge, 69 West St., Annapolis, MD 21401; (410) 268-0003; levelsmallplateslounge.com; Small Plates; $. This lively restaurant has been racking up the kudos ever since it opened—it was named one of the area's best restaurants by *Baltimore* magazine in 2012. Level is serious about locally sourced products, which is obvious from the impressive list of farms on their menu. Most items are inventive small plates, like a lamb osso bucco with roasted figs, or a radish risotto. There are also larger group plates, like a savory dip made from chorizo and roasted red peppers.

Group drinks too, like the West Street Punch Bowl, which serves 4 to 6. After all, the restaurant's motto is "eat, drink, socialize." Definitely check out Level during happy hour, when many of their cocktails (like the pomegranate caipirinha) and small plates are a tiny $6. Level also offers a late-night menu (until 1 a.m.) with yummy pizzas, cheeses, and desserts.

Lewnes' Steakhouse, 401 4th St., Annapolis, MD 21401; (410) 263-1617; lewnessteakhouse.com; Steakhouse; $$$$. The Lewnes family has been serving food at this location since the 1920s, so it's no wonder that the ambience is old-school—wall paneling, black leather booths, white tablecloths—and the food is classic steakhouse. Start your meal with the shrimp cocktail or the clams casino, then loosen your belt and prepare yourself for the main course. The rib eye, for example: an inches-thick slab of butter-drenched, wet-aged, USDA Prime beef cooked for a short period of time under an extremely hot broiler until crusty on the outside and to your liking on the inside. Don't pass on ordering one or more of the classic side dishes, like Lyonnaise, mashed, or french fried potatoes, creamed spinach, and fried onion rings that are more than adequate for sharing. Food like this insists on an indulgence from the wine list, which includes everything from modest double-digit selections to break-the-bank four-figure wines.

Mango Grove/Mirchi Wok, 8865 Stanford Blvd., Columbia, MD 21045; (410) 884-3426 and (401) 730-4689; themangogrove.net; Indian; $$. Mango Grove is vegetarian. Mirchi Wok specializes in

Indo-Chinese dishes. Together they make quite a tasty combination. The vegetarian restaurant specializes in the perhaps less-familiar south Indian dishes, like the large crepes known as *dosa* and the rice and lentil pancakes called *oothappam,* both of which are served with the traditional accompaniments of *sambar* (a spicy vegetable stew) and chutney. They also have the more usual *malai kofta* and *palak paneer.* But Mirchi Wok serves up an Indian version of Szechuan chicken and interesting lamb dishes like *nargissi kofta,* lamb meatballs in a curry flavored with rosewater and *kewra* (also called *pandan,* it has a somewhat fruity, rosy flavor). How on earth are we supposed to choose between the two? We don't have to. Both restaurants occupy the same space; only the kitchens are separate, so feel free to order from either—or each—menu.

Pairings Bistro, 2105 Laurel Bush Rd., Ste. 108, Bel Air, MD 21015; (410) 569-5006; pairingsbistro.com; Wine Bar; $$$. We're not going to mince words here: Bel Air is generally a restaurant wasteland. Sure, there are lots of fast casual chains, but fine dining is few and far between. And that's why Pairings Bistro is such a hidden gem. Certainly one wouldn't expect to find a wine bar in an office park. The restaurant is pretty small, but we like to think of it as being cozy. Chef-Owner Jon Kohler's kitchen puts out some fine modern American cuisine, with touches of the Mediterranean and . . . Belgium (Kohler's wife is from Brussels.) That influence can definitely be seen in a dish like moules frites (mussels with fries). For the version made with Belgian ale, the menu conveniently pairs it with the Belgian pale ale Duvel. Other items on the a la carte menu of small plates also have wine or beer pairings. After all, the marriage of food and libations is what this place is all about.

Ranazul, 8171 Maple Lawn Blvd., Fulton, MD 20759; (301) 498-9666; ranazul.us; Small Plates; $$. For the past few years, Howard County residents and visitors alike have had their tummies pleasantly tickled by the inventive small plates at Ranazul. So much so, the restaurant has come out on top in the tapas category of *Howard* magazine's readers' poll for three years running (so far!). The *Baltimore Sun* also counts Ranazul as one of the 50 best county restaurants in the state. While Ranazul likes to call their food "tapas," the dishes they serve go far beyond the expected *patatas bravas* and mixed olives. Some items, like the *arepas* topped with seafood, have a more Mexican flair. Others, as in the Gorgonzola risotto and bruschetta, lean toward Italian cuisine. A grilled rib eye and rack of lamb are also on the menu for those diners who are less fond of grazing than their tablemates. Wine, sangria (of course), and fun cocktails are the perfect way to round out the meal.

R&R Taqueria, 7894 Washington Blvd., Elkridge, MD 21075; (410) 799-0001; rrtaqueria.com; Mexican; $. "Wait," you say, as you pull up to 7894 Washington Blvd., "that's a Shell station." "Yes, yes it is," is our answer. R&R Taqueria is in the convenience mart, just eight stools at a counter. Despite the oddball location,

owner Rodrigo Albarran-Torres is committed
to serving authentic and delicious Mexican
food. The menu changes seasonally, or at
whim, and includes huaraches (yes, like
the shoe), oblongs of fried masa, with
your choice of toppings. Tacos come with all kinds of fillings, like
lamb, pork shoulder, steak, pork belly, chorizo, and tongue, and
are a ridiculously cheap $2 each. There's a second R&R location in
Baltimore County, in the White Marsh Mall food court, 8200 Perry
Hall Blvd., #2435; Baltimore, MD 21236; (410) 870-0185.

Shin Chon Garden, 8801 Baltimore National Pike, Ellicott City,
MD 21043; (410) 461-3280; Korean; $$$. Shin Chon Garden gives
diners the option to cook their own food at a table-top grill, or
to sit at a regular table. We're always torn; while we love Korean
barbecue, particularly the beef specialties called galbi and bulgogi,
we're more enamored of the various stews and rice dishes of Korea.
Dolsot bi bim bop, for instance. Rice, meat, veggies, and an egg are
placed in a screaming-hot stone bowl. Mix everything together and
let it rest for a few minutes; the sizzling sound is the rice crisping
up into a yummy treat at the bottom of the bowl. We also enjoy
the seafood-and-scallion pancake known as *pa jeon,* and any of the
delightful array of *panchan* (small portions of vegetable dishes that
will include kimchee and perhaps a Korean version of potato salad)
that come with every meal. The staff at Shin Chon doesn't have a
uniform understanding of English, so if you don't speak Korean,
please be patient. The meal will be delicious either way.

Sushi Sono, 10215 Wincopin Circle, Columbia, MD 21044; (410) 997-6131; sushisonomd.com; Japanese; $$. This restaurant at the edge of Lake Kittamaqundi is always hopping. When we asked friends about their favorite restaurants outside of Baltimore, a good 75 percent of them insisted we include Sushi Sono in this book. The restaurant has received many professional accolades as well, including best sushi 2000–09 in Howard County by *Howard* magazine. Who are we to argue? And we can't, really. Sushi Sono does have some of the best sushi around, always extremely fresh.

So fresh that some nights you can get live scallops presented in their shells. And for a small charge, you can get real grated wasabi instead of the typical green-colored horseradish paste found everywhere else. In addition to gorging ourselves on *o-toro* when they have it, we like the rolls, especially the Bridal Veil (spicy lobster salad, tempura flakes, wrapped with rice paper, topped with tuna) and the unusual *Yasai-maki* (seaweed salad, shiitake mushroom, avocado, Japanese squash, tempura sweet potato, wrapped with soy paper).

Tersiguel's, 8293 Main St., Ellicott City, MD 21043; (410) 465-4004; tersiguels.com; French; $$$. Tersiguel's has consistently made Baltimore's Best lists year after year. Technically not located in Baltimore but in nearby Howard County, it's close enough to count. In any case it's well worth the drive. The restaurant is set in a 19th-century home that has 6 dining rooms, so a lunch or dinner experience can be quiet and intimate. Chef-Owner Michel Tersiguel describes his food as having a French soul but designed for an American palate. He uses many of his mother's classic recipes, like the one for her delicious country pâté, but there are several decidedly modern touches. The tuna carpaccio appetizer, for instance, is given a French twist with a drizzle of tapenade-flavored oil. Much of the produce served at Tersiguel's is grown on their own small farm, which is a nice touch that guarantees freshness.

Trattoria Alberto, 1660 Crain Hwy. S., Glen Burnie, MD 21061; (410) 761-0922; trattoriaalberto.com; Italian; $$$$. We're going to be honest here: Glen Burnie is not the first place we think of when we're in the mood for a meal of fine Italian cuisine. After all, Baltimore has Little Italy, which is chock-full of Italian masterpieces. But this strip-mall restaurant produces really good food—astonishingly good food. Why else would it have made Zagat's survey of the World's Top Restaurants for 2009–10? And of course it's consistently on *Baltimore* magazine's Best Restaurants list too. Perhaps it's for the house-made pasta dishes, like the spaghetti tutto mare with shrimp, scallops, and clams in a marinara sauce, or the meltingly tender veal saltimbocca, or the gorgeous Angus fillet served with Gorgonzola, chives, and crispy pancetta—the colors of the Italian flag. It could also be the handsome interior and the congenial, helpful staff. Personally, we think it's for the lemon-kissed grilled calamari and their silky and rich fettuccine Alfredo.

Victoria Gastro Pub, 8201 Snowden River Pkwy., Columbia, MD 21045; (410) 750-1880; victoriagastropub.com; Gastropub; $$$. Before Randy Marriner opened his place in Columbia, he took a tour of New York gastropubs to get a feel for these new tavern-style restaurants that offer food that is a bit more upscale than the normal pub grub. Named after his daughter, Victoria Gastro Pub is a handsome place, with a grand walnut bar, reclaimed wood, and velvet drapes. The menu, as expected, is full of elevated pub-style favorites like fish-and-chips, here served with a crab remoulade, and a Kobe beef burger that can be had with truffle cheese and hand-cut fries dusted with smoked paprika. Or have the fries cooked in duck fat instead. Those tasty fries can also be had in an appetizer modeled after the Quebecois snack called poutine: duck fat fries, duck confit, gruyère, and duck gravy. As befitting a pub, there's an ample selection of beverages. There's even a beer club that meets every Monday, plus beer-tasting dinners every month (check the website for more information).

Food Trucks

Baltimore's food truck scene is relatively new, and while there aren't that many trucks on the road just yet, there seems to be one or two new ones popping up every month. Their offerings run the gamut from cupcakes to grilled cheese to pulled pork. Most of them hang out in downtown Baltimore City, in order to feed the scores of hungry office workers, but once in a while a truck or two will park in a county location. It's best to follow your favorite truck on Twitter or Facebook in order to get location and menu updates. The *Baltimore Sun* also has a "Food Truck Finder" online at data .baltimoresun.com/food-truck-finder. If you don't happen to be downtown at lunchtime, there's also a fairly regular monthly event called the Gathering during which time most of the food trucks congregate in one place. Check the Baltimore Food Truck website for more details: bmorefoodtrucks.com.

Cazbar on the Go, (410) 528-1222; $. Popular downtown Baltimore restaurant **Cazbar** (p. 131), known for their delicious Turkish fare, has hit the road with their food truck. Appropriately named Cazbar on the Go, the truck offers reasonably priced lunch items like salads and tacos filled with char-grilled chicken, doner meat (a beef and lamb mixture), or falafel. Side dishes like baba ghanoush and desserts, including baklava, are also on the menu.

Chicken 'n' Waffles, @chicknwaffle; (202) 437-1228; chicken waffle.net; $. We always thought chicken and waffles seemed like an odd combination until we tried it and discovered a daring duo of deliciousness. That's especially true of the chicken and waffles available on this truck. The waffles come as large, fluffy disks drenched in butter, with pancake syrup on the side. Chicken is plainly seasoned and plainly delicious. If you're lucky to get some that's straight out of the fryer, it'll be piping hot and almost painfully crisp. Dunk your wings in the little cup of barbecue sauce included with your order, or drench it in hot sauce. We like it as-is. Fish sandwiches and dinners can also be had, with your choice of fish (whiting or tilapia) and 2 sides.

Chowhound Burger Wagon, @brgrwagon; kooperschowhound .com; $. Kooper's Tavern got a head start on the food truck business in town; they started the Chowhound Burger Wagon way back in 2009. The truck serves burgers and more burgers with your choice of Angus beef, Kobe beef, free-range turkey, veggie, or Maryland's own Gunpowder bison patties, topped with your choice of cheese, sauce, and stuff like grilled onions and roasted red peppers. Or you could choose one of their specialty burgers, like the hefty 1-pound Charlie Brown, or Elvis Got the Blues with bacon and Maytag blue cheese. Class things up with an order of truffle fries or, even better, the very tasty sweet-potato fries.

Cupcake Runners, @cupcake_runners; cupcakerunners.com; $. This truck offers some of the sweetest treats on wheels, namely, cupcakes—the perfect dessert, snack, or pick-me-up, especially when that sweet tooth demands to be satisfied. Cupcake Runners sells a variety of classic, specialty, and seasonal flavors, but not all are available every day. We're partial to the Pumpkin Spice (pumpkin spice cake with cinnamon maple cream cheese frosting) and the Candy Cane (peppermint vanilla cake with candy cane baked inside with a candy cane buttercream frosting), and the Cookies & Cream (vanilla cake with crushed vanilla cream-filled chocolate cookies mixed in, topped with a buttercream frosting flavored with more cookies) is yet another fine choice. They all are.

Dangerously Delicious Pies, @baltopietruck; dangerouspies .com; $. Rodney Henry not only has a popular pie shop in Canton, he also sells both sweet and savory pies from his food truck. This truck isn't around every day, but if you can't find the pie mobile on the street, it's usually at the monthly Food Truck Gathering event.

GrrChe, @grrche; grrche.com; $. Don't ask us how to pronounce it—we just call it the "grilled cheese truck." What's a more perfect lunch than a grilled cheese sandwich? It's griddled to a crispness that's almost as good as being deep fried, and it's filled with cheese. Like we said: perfect. GrrChe has your basic grilled cheese sammies on your choice of wheat, white, or sourdough, but they also have fancy-pants grilled cheeses with lobster, or macaroni and cheese, or lobster and mac and cheese. They also have the perfect accompaniment for a grilled cheese sandwich, especially when the winter winds are blowing: tomato basil soup.

Gypsy Queen Cafe, @thegypsytruck; (443) 717-2957; gypsy queencafe.com; $. Chefs Tom Looney and Annemarie Langton, who once ran the popular Helen's Garden restaurant in Canton, have taken their sassy attitude and eclectic cuisine to the streets. Both the Gypsy Queen and their smaller truck, Lil' Gypsy, offer a variety of tacos, pitas, "chubbies" (burgers), and cones. As in waffle cones, filled with all manner of stuff. Most (in)famous is the mac-and-cheese cone, topped with an onion-and-bacon jam. That not weird enough? Then try the crab cake cone with chipotle mayo and fries. Personally, we prefer the crab cake stuffed into a griddled corn tortilla, taco-style. Another favorite is the Baltimore po' boy, which is really a fried fish sandwich on Texas toast. Portions are large, so you may not need to make dinner plans for afterward. See Annemarie Langton's recipe for **Crab Cake Tacos** on p. 312.

IcedGems Cupcakes, @icedgemsbaking; (443) 690-7056; iced gemsbaking.com/truck.html; $. This popular food truck offers only one thing: cupcakes, made by IcedGems Creations, a bakery in Western Baltimore County. On weekdays more than a dozen varieties of cupcakes are peddled all over Baltimore City and County in a refrigerated van festooned with pink polka dots. We've never spotted the truck without a considerable line, and by early afternoon many of the dozen or so daily flavors sell out. Our favorite is the French Toast, with a lightly cinnamon-flavored cake and mapley frosting. Also recommended are any of the chocolate varieties, and the vanilla-flavored, confetti-sprinkled Birthday Cake.

The Jolly Pig, @thejollypig; (410) 984-5789; thejollypig.com; $. This jolly pink truck is usually found in Baltimore County, somewhere in Towson or Owings Mills. The pork-centric menu changes regularly, but barbecue is always on board. There are mix-and-match pork tacos to be had, and tangy Carolina barbecue sliders, but burgers, salads, and soups are also available.

Karlita's, @karlitaxf; (443) 324-5107; $. Karlita's little red wagon serves Latin-inspired goodies like shrimp tacos, tostadas, taquitos, and fried plantains at supercheap prices. Hot and cheesy wedges of quesadilla stuffed with beef and dipped in a bit of sour cream makes a very satisfying lunch, and is a real deal at $5. Big burritos with your choice of chicken or steak are also a fine choice, especially at 6 bucks. Add a cup of freshly squeezed lemonade and you've got a tasty belly-full.

Miss Shirley's, @missshirleys; missshirleys.com/foodtruck.php; $. This mobile companion to the popular Miss Shirley's restaurants lets Baltimore's lunchtime crowd eat blueberry pancakes without leaving the office. Well, they do have to leave the office to get the food from the truck, but they don't have to go all the way to the restaurant. You know what we mean. Besides pancakes, one can also get chicken and white cheddar-green onion waffles or a simple bacon, egg, and cheese on ciabatta. If you'd prefer more lunchy food, there are sandwiches with Carolina pulled pork and coleslaw, cups of gumbo, and yummy fried green tomatoes with a lemon-herb mayo.

Miss Twist, misstwisticecream.com; $. We remember begging our parents for money whenever we heard the siren song of the ice cream truck. Chocolate or vanilla twist, or both, we liked our soft serve on a cake cone. Tammy Radtke's old-fashioned ice cream truck specializes in childhood goodies like sundaes and shakes, floats and malts, and of course, cups and cones, for not all that much more money than we remember paying in our youth.

Noodlerolla, facebook.com/noodlerolla; $. Korea meets Japan on this food truck that serves both bibimbap and sushi. The easily portable burrito comes with beef or chicken and kimchee fried rice, but if you aren't eating on the run, there are bento boxes that include rice, dumplings, pickles, and 4 pieces of California roll with your choice of entree. Portions are generous and flavors have that customary Korean sweet heat thing going on. It's nice to be able to get fresh sushi without visiting a restaurant too.

Silver Platter, @silverplattbalt; (410) 274-2619; $. The Silver Platter is the odd truck with a semipermanent address, but that, of course, makes it easier to find. Warm weather has found the truck near Harbor East on Central Avenue, but in cooler weather it was spending time some miles away in Timonium, in Baltimore County. The truck's menu includes lobster rolls, pit beef, crab tostadas, and other upscale-for-a-truck treats.

Souper Freak, @souperfreaky; souperfreaks.com; $. Before opening her full-service restaurant, **Woman's Industrial Kitchen** (p. 144), Irene Smith spent much of her day running her Souper Freak truck, feeding Baltimore's hungry lunchtime crowds. Now her friendly team takes care of dishing up the Freak's healthy and delicious soups and sandwiches. Many of the truck's offer- ings are vegetarian, and we think they are some of the tastiest options. Our hands-down favorite is the grilled asparagus wrap with creamy goat cheese, grilled onion, arugula, and a balsamic vinaigrette; we even get a little (a lot) depressed when it's not on offer. But there is always something else to satisfy, be it a grilled cheese sandwich with plums and Gouda, a smooth shrimp-and-corn bisque, or the chunky and spicy gazpacho.

South Carolina BBQ, @ScCaterers; (410) 227-4808; sccaterers .com; $. The South Carolina BBQ truck sells pit beef and turkey sandwiches, plus pulled pork, chicken gyros, ribs, and more. There's some real wood-smoked flavor in those meats, particularly the pit beef, which we like to order smothered in horseradish. The sandwiches are sizable, full of juicy meat, but we're also fond of the slow-smoked ribs, which come 4 to an order, topped with their own, authentic South Carolina sauce recipe. And then there's the signature sandwich, the Chicken Carolina, that combines chicken, bacon, ranch dressing and mayo, cheese, lettuce and tomato, and more of that delish barbecue sauce.

The Wild Dog Cart, @thewilddogcart; thewilddogcart.com; $. Hot-dog carts are probably the original food truck. At least the original food trailer. The Wild Dog serves yummy Nathan's all-beef

dogs, gussied up with a variety of toppings from the traditional sauerkraut and chili to coleslaw and Old Bay seasoning. We like the Mexicana dog, a messy creation with salsa, green chiles, onions, cheese, and crushed tortilla chips. The Wild Dog can usually (Mon through Fri) be found in the parking lot of the Cockeysville Lowes, and at Hess Auctions, 11101 Pulaski Hwy., on Mon nights.

Breweries & Wineries

Not too long ago, buying a beer meant purchasing one of a handful of national-brand lagers that all tasted about the same. Baltimoreans favored their locally brewed National Bohemian, but even Natty Boh moved to North Carolina. In the 1980s preppies and yuppies sought more sophisticated beers from overseas, and a new brew consciousness arose. Some intrepid entrepreneurs decided to bring back brewing techniques from places like Germany and Belgium and make their own versions of porters, stouts, and India pale ales (IPAs). When the Maryland legislature legalized brewpubs in the late '80s, the microbrew movement was on. Baltimore is now awash in locally made, handcrafted beers that can be purchased at your local spirits store or sampled in numerous brewpubs in the area. While national brands still command the most market share, microbrews are rapidly growing in popularity.

Winemaking in Maryland has a much longer tradition. Many European immigrants brought their winemaking techniques to

Maryland and began making wine for private use. By the mid–20th century, commercial wineries started to pop up along what is known as the Piedmont Wine Trail, which runs through Baltimore and Harford Counties. Within the past decade, with a greater emphasis on locally grown produce, several new wineries have taken root in the region, offering not only wine but great destinations for food, music, and fun.

Breweries & Brewpubs

Baltimore Washington Beer Works, PO Box 9829, Baltimore, MD 21284; (410) 321-1892; ravenbeer.com. Although the Raven was named after Edgar Allan Poe's famous poem, this German-style lager started life in the Black Forest region of Baden-Württemberg, Germany. Stephen Demczuk partnered with beer distributor Wolfgang Stark to produce a beer with an American marketing theme. The beer was brewed in Germany, but the company was registered in Baltimore. Starting in 1998, the Raven Special Lager was produced by the Baltimore Washington Beer Works in Landsdowne, Maryland, but has recently moved to the new Peabody Heights Brewing facility in Waverly, where they plan to introduce three new beers with an Edgar Allan Poe theme.

Bare Bones Grill & Brewery, 9150-22 Baltimore National Pike, Ellicott City, MD 21042; (410) 461-0070; barebonesgrill.com/

maryland/index.php. Back in days of yore, when we first started dating, we went to Bare Bones pretty regularly to indulge in a dose of friendly atmosphere and delicious ribs. While food took precedence over beer for us, we sampled as many of Bare Bones' 8 special brews as possible. (Tiber River Red is a favorite.) From the Hunt Valley Light to the rich Savage Mill Porter, Bare Bones' brews aptly complement the hearty pub grub on the menu.

The Brewer's Art, 1106 N. Charles St.,
Baltimore, MD 21201; (410) 547-6925;
thebrewersart.com. The ornate columns
that frame the entrance to the Mount
Vernon town house where the Brewer's Art
is located suggest a rather formal atmosphere. The interior, however, is casual
and inviting, with a bar that would likely
have made Baltimore journalist, critic, and

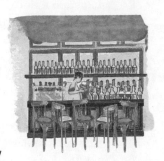

beer lover H. L. Mencken feel at home. Along with their 4 regular beers (Zodiac Ale, Ozzie, Resurrection, and Proletary Ale), there is a rotating array of some 20 seasonal brews, along with wines and spirits. Resurrection is our favorite and it's available in several area restaurants. There's little wonder why *Esquire* magazine named the Brewer's Art the Best Bar in America for 2008.

DuClaw Brewing Company, 7000 Arundel Mills Circle, Ste. R4, Hanover, MD 21076; (410) 799-1166; duclaw.com. With beer names like Bad Ass, Sawtooth, and Venom, DuClaw Brewing Company

Have a Natty Boh, Hon!
National Bohemian Beer

With the large influx of German immigrants to Baltimore, it was inevitable that a number of breweries would spring up in the city. Brewers like Gunther's, Shaefer, and Hamm's were household names once upon a time, but no beer became identified with Baltimore like National Bohemian. Started in 1885, the National Brewing Company made National Bohemian, National Premium, and Colt 45 Malt Liquor in its brewery on O'Donnell and Conkling Streets until 1978. Despite being the cheapest of the three, National Boh was the most popular. At one point, 60 percent of the beer sold in Baltimore was National Boh.

It didn't hurt that the president, Jerold Hoffberger, owned the Baltimore Orioles and National Boh was the beer served at Memorial Stadium. Each player received two cases each during home games. By the late 1960s National Boh was the official beer of Baltimore.

Baby boomers remember fondly the animated TV commercials where the National Troubadour sang the catchy jingle about the beer "from the Land of Pleasant Living," referring to the Chesapeake Bay. The most iconic symbol of National Boh, however, was Mr. Boh. Looking like a barber-shop-quartet singer with his slicked-down hair

cultivates an image of biker-bar rebellion, but don't be fooled: This brewpub's locations are generally large and inviting. The cuisine, which is typical pub-style comfort food, is not really the attraction. Rather, it's the 12 or more uniquely brewed beers that they

and handlebar moustache, Mr. Boh only had one eye. No one knew why. When Gunthers Beer used the slogan "Gunther's got it!" the people at National Brewing Co. replied, "Where is Mr. Boh's eye? Gunther's got it!"

As breweries like Anheuser-Busch dominated the national market in the 1970s and 1980s, the National Brewing Company suffered. First they were sold to Carling, and the brewery in Canton was closed to move operations to Halethorpe, Maryland. The Premium brand was phased out and the National Boh brand was then sold to Stroh's, which closed the Halethorpe plant. National Boh is now brewed in Eden, North Carolina, and distributed by Pabst Brewing Co., but National Boh is still thought of as Baltimore's beer. Several years ago Todd Unger purchased the licensing rights to Mr. Boh and now produces memorabilia featuring the iconic little man with one eye. The old brewery in Canton has been renovated into offices, warehouses, and apartments, and the area is now known as Brewers Hill. A giant neon sign of Mr. Boh sits atop the building, staring down on the city that loves him.

As for the beer itself, National Boh was treated as a novelty for a time, only available in bottles and cans. In February 2011, however, the beer started selling in kegs, so Baltimore bars, pubs, and taverns can now proudly claim that they sell Natty Boh on tap.

always have on draught. They also have locations at 16 A Belair South Pkwy., Belair, MD 21015; 4000 Town Center Blvd., Bowie, MD 20716; and the Southwest Terminal of BWI-Marshall Airport, Baltimore, MD 21240.

Ellicott Mills Brewing Company, 8308 Main St., Ellicott City, MD 21043; (410) 313-8141; ellicottmillsbrewing.com. Home of the Alpenhof line of lagers and ales, Ellicott Mills Brewing Company offers 4 regular beers on tap as well as 4 seasonal beers at all times. They are especially known for their bock beers since they brew a wider variety of bocks than any other brewery in the US. The food menu leans heavily toward seafood, but there are steaks and some German favorites like Bavarian soft pretzel sticks, *Kasseler Rippchen* (smoked pork chops), and a sausage mixed grill.

Heavy Seas, 4615 Hollins Ferry Rd., Halethorpe, MD 21227; (410) 247-7822; hsbeer.com. Hugh Sisson could be considered the founding father of the craft beer movement in Baltimore. Along with Brewmaster Ernesto Igot, Sisson has set out to create several beer lines (or fleets, as they like to call them), each with distinctive flavors and attention to detail. The Clipper Fleet beers are the most accessible, with alcohol content of less than 6 percent. The Pyrate Fleet beers are more robust, and the Mutiny Fleet are finely aged brews made seasonally in small batches. Widely available in Baltimore spirit shops and restaurants, Heavy Seas beers can also be found in many parts of the US. Heavy Seas recently lent their name to a new brewpub, Heavy Seas Ale House, at 1300 Bank St., Baltimore, MD 21202. The pub features a raw bar, steak and seafood entrees, and a late-night happy hour with both beer and food specials.

Pratt Street Ale House, 206 W. Pratt St., Baltimore, MD 21201; (410) 244-8900; prattstreetalehouse.com. The location has had several names over the years, but it's still the home of Oliver Breweries, makers of handcrafted English-style ales. Brewmaster Steve Jones is from Coventry, England, and he takes great pride in producing a wide range of ales that reflect his British heritage. The current incarnation of the restaurant is more American, with familiar favorites like burgers, pizza, and wings. Pratt Street Ale House is within walking distance of most Inner Harbor attractions like Oriole Park and the Convention Center, so it's a popular place to grab a bite and enjoy your favorite draught, smooth pull, or hand-pumped ale before heading off for your entertainment destination.

Red Brick Station, 8149 Honeygo Blvd., White Marsh, MD 21236; (410) 931-7827; redbrickstation.com. Located on the popular Avenue in White Marsh, Red Brick Station is modeled after the pubs of England and offers traditional British favorites like roast beef and Yorkshire pudding and bangers and mash. Their regular lineup of beers numbers five: Avenue Ale, HoneyGo Lite, Daily Crisis IPA, Something Red, and Spooner's Stout. We've tried them all and have not been disappointed. They also slip in the occasional seasonal beer—the wintry Solstice was one of our favorites.

Stillwater Artisanal Ales, stillwaterales.blogspot.com. Brian Strumke and Brooklyn importer Brian Ewing got into business together after Ewing tasted some of Strumke's homebrews. While the duo doesn't own an actual brewery, they borrow space from production brewers in Europe and the US. So far, they've collaborated with Oliver Ales (Pratt Street Ale House), the Voodoo Brewery in Meadville, Pennsylvania, and with a small brewery in Beerzel, Belgium. **Of Love & Regret** (p. 110), a restaurant and bar in the Brewers Hill section of town, is a joint venture between Strumke and **Jack's Bistro** (p. 107) Chef-Co-owner Ted Stelzenmuller and an ideal place to get yourself fixed up with Stillwater's excellent brews.

Wineries & Vineyards

Basignani Winery, 15722 Falls Rd., Sparks, MD 21152; (410) 472-0703; basignani.com. For over 25 years, Bert Basignani has been making wine on his small vineyard near Hunt Valley. The winery produces about 6,500 gallons of wine per year and is sold in area wine shops and restaurants. The wines tend to be on the sweet side, so we favor their smooth Riesling, which is a perfect complement to spicy food. You can visit the winery Wed through Sat from 11:30 a.m. to 5:30 p.m. and on Sun from noon to 6 p.m. Basignani schedules several special events throughout the year like pizza evenings where the family makes homemade pizzas in their brick oven, and outdoor movie viewings on Friday nights during the summer.

Boordy Vineyards, 12820 Long Green Pike, Hydes, MD 21082; (410) 592-5015; boordy.com. A winery since 1945, the 240-acre farm in the Long Green Valley of Baltimore County was taken over by the Deford family in 1980. Their wines are broken out into three series: Landmark, Icons of Maryland, and Just for Fun. The Landmark wines are blended from grapes only grown in Maryland and represent the best of the vintage year. Icons of Maryland are wines developed to pair with different types of food, and the Just for Fun wines are fruity party wines that can be served chilled or warmed. Wine tastings and tours are available, and events like summer concerts, the Gunpowder River Artfest, and the Good Life Thursdays Farmers' Market are held on-site.

DeJon Vineyards, 5300 Hydes Rd., Hydes, MD 21082; (443) 253-9802; dejonvineyard.com. The owners understand if people confuse the name of their vineyard with French mustard, but the name is actually a merging of their own names, John and Denise. DeJon is one of the newer wineries in the Long Green Valley, but their wines are surprisingly pleasant for such a new vintage. Their wine tastings are held in a converted barn that looks out over the picturesque vineyards. In addition to the daily tastings from noon to 5 p.m., John and Denise host concerts on Wed and Sat nights during the summer.

Fiore Winery, 3026 Whiteford Rd., Pylesvilles, MD 21132; (410) 879-4007; fiorewinery.com. Mike Fiore owned a vineyard in Italy before he came to America, but he didn't think about owning one here until 1975 when he and his wife, Rose, purchased a farm in Harford County and created La Felicetta Vineyard. Eleven years later, the Fiore Winery was born. They produce 35,000 gallons of wine per year in numerous varieties of white and red, including sparkling and dessert wines. The tasting room is open 7 days a week and concert events are held throughout the summer.

Galloping Goose Vineyards, 4326 Maple Grove Rd., Hampstead, MD 21074; (410) 374-6596; gallopinggoosevineyards.com. Although the Hale family has worked the land in Carroll County since 1969, they did not start growing grapes until the late 1990s. For many years, their grapes were sold only to other wine producers, but in 2008 they started their own label. Made in small lots of no more than 50 cases, the wines that bear the Galloping Goose label are carefully crafted to bring out the best of the grape.

Harford Vineyard & Winery, 1311 W. Jarrettsville Rd., Forest Hill, MD 21050; (443) 495-1699; harfordvineyard.com. A relative newcomer to the Maryland wine scene, Harford put out its first bottles in 2009. They are primarily a supplier of grapes from all over the country and special equipment for the home winemaker. However, their own line of 11 wines covers a wide range, from sweet wines familiar to the Piedmont Trail to drier, more complex wines. Their tasting room is open Fri and Sun from noon to 5 p.m. and Sat from 10 a.m. to 5 p.m.

Legends Vineyard, 521 Asbury Rd., Churchville, MD 21028; (410) 914-5122; legendsvineyardmd.com. Another new winery to the Piedmont Trail, Ashby and Carrie Everhart did not release their first vintages until 2008. However, they are off to a strong start, earning gold medals from the 2011 Winemasters Choice Awards for their Pinot Gris, Riesling, Meritage, and Cabernet Sauvignon. They just recently added a tasting room, which is open Wed through Sat from Mar through Dec and Thurs through Sat in Jan and Feb.

Mount Felix Vineyard & Winery, 2000 Level Rd., Havre De Grace, MD 21078; (410) 939-0913; mountfelix.com. *Terroir* refers to the soil, weather conditions, and grapes of a particular vineyard, which give personality to a wine. Mary and Peter Ianniello believe that not only is their terroir in the land where grapes are grown but in the history of the families that grow them. Their southeastern-sloping fields receive maximum sunlight and a steady breeze off the Chesapeake Bay, allowing for proper photosynthesis of the grapevines. Peter also attributes much of their winemaking prowess to his grandfathers and the tradition of wine-making in his family. Many of their wines are blends using Chambourcin, a very fruity grape that grows well in the Maryland area. Flavored wines such as their pumpkin wine and cherry and chocolate wine are fun alternatives.

Royal Rabbit Vineyards, 1090 Jordan Sawmill Rd., Parkton, MD 21120; (443) 721-6692; royalrabbitvineyards.com. Roy Albin's vineyard is one of the newest in the Parkton area and perhaps the smallest, with 3 acres of grapes. Despite the size, he has produced 11 different wines, blending a variety of grapes in the tradition of great winemaking regions like Rhone and Burgundy. Because of his small production, availability is limited, so it may be best to visit the vineyard directly to sample his selection of somewhat dry reds and whites. The tasting room is open Fri and Sat from noon to 5 p.m.

Serpent Ridge Vineyard, 2962 Nicodemus Rd., Westminster, MD 21157; (410) 858-6511; serpentridge.com. Greg and Karen Lambrecht are trying to bring a little West Coast sophistication to the East Coast wine scene. For example, they do not add sugar to their wines, and they strive to eliminate the green flavor that so many East Coast white wines tend to have. Greg developed a passion for winemaking while stationed in the Russian Valley region of California serving in the Coast Guard. Since his wife came from a home-winemaking family, the idea of starting a vineyard seemed natural. They combine old traditions with new technology in their winemaking process, such as using old oak barrels for fermentation but the newest Zork corks, which combine the best attributes of screw tops and corks. Although Serpent Ridge is new, they are getting the word out with summer Friday night concerts, and their wines are already offered in numerous restaurants and liquor stores.

Woodhall Wine Cellars, 17912 York Rd., Parkton, MD 21120; (410) 357-8644; woodhallwinecellars.com. Established in 1983, Woodhall offers a full range of table wines and specialty wines. While pretty respectable overall, some of their reserve wines are exceptional. In February Woodhall has barrel tastings where visitors can try samples directly from the barrels to experience how the wines are developing. If a wine interests you, you can pay half down and another half when the wine is bottled. They also have open-mic nights on Friday nights featuring the Baltimore Guitar Group. The tasting room, a rustic place reminiscent of a 19th-century carriage house, is available for parties and special events.

Recipes

Cream of Crab Soup

Cream of crab soup is a Maryland specialty. The ideal soup should be creamy and only lightly thick, with lots of crabby flavor, but many places serve what seems to be seafood-flavored wallpaper paste. At the Rusty Scupper they've perfected cream of crab soup, adding only a whisper of roux to thicken their lusciously creamy concoction, which has a pronounced sherry flavor.

Serves 10–12

5 ounces unsalted butter

5 ounces all-purpose flour

2 ounces crab base (lobster base may be substituted)

2 teaspoons Old Bay seasoning

1 teaspoon ground white pepper

40 ounces crab stock (recipe follows)

14 ounces whole milk

40 ounces heavy cream

5 ounces cream sherry

1 pound lump crabmeat

In a large Dutch oven or stock pot, make a roux by melting butter and whisking in flour. Cook, stirring, until well combined but not brown, approximately 5 minutes. Add crab base and seasonings.

Slowly whisk in crab stock and milk, making sure there are no lumps. Bring to a simmer and add heavy cream. Continue to simmer for 30 minutes. Add sherry, stir well. Remove from heat and stir in crabmeat. Serve immediately.

Crab Stock

3 ounces chopped carrots

3 ounces chopped celery

3 ounces chopped white onion

2 sprigs fresh thyme

5 sprigs parsley, chopped

1 bay leaf

1 crab body

80 ounces water

Place all ingredients in a large pot and bring to a low simmer. Continue to cook until stock is reduced by half. Strain and set aside.

Courtesy of Edward Prutzer Jr., General Manager of Rusty Scupper (p. 44)

Tuna Crab Tartare

Chef Neal Langermann serves this refreshing and flavorful appetizer at his eponymous Canton restaurant. It's as gorgeous on the plate as it is on the palate. If you don't have easy access to the seaweed salad, you can omit it.

Yields 1 serving

- 3 ounces diced sushi-grade tuna
- 2 ounces local Maryland jumbo lump crabmeat
- 1 tablespoon diced ripe mango
- 1 teaspoon chopped fresh cilantro
- 2 ounces creamy avocado dressing (recipe follows)
- 3 ounces seaweed salad
- 2 pink grapefruit sections

In a small salad bowl, combine the diced tuna, crabmeat, mango, cilantro, and avocado dressing. Fold gently as to not to break up the crab lumps.

Use a 3-inch-diameter ring mold to place a perfectly round layer of seaweed salad in the center of a 9-inch plate.

Fill the rest of the mold with the crab and tuna mixture, smoothing the top.

Remove mold, top the "tower" with 1 teaspoon of seaweed salad.

Garnish top of tower with the 2 sections of pink grapefruit.

Serve the dish with a glass of Infamous Goose Sauvignon Blanc . . . a perfect accompaniment!

Creamy Avocado Dressing

2 pounds avocado

2 ounces lemon juice

2 ounces cider vinegar

2 cups sour cream

3 ounces Sriracha chili sauce

2 ounces sugar

1 tablespoon salt

Place all ingredients in a food processor and puree. Refrigerate until ready to use.

Courtesy of Neal Langermann, Chef and Owner of Langermann's (p. 108)

Kooper's Gonzo Sliders

Sliders are the perfect three- or four-bite snack, and so much neater to eat than a full-size burger, especially when hanging out with a group of friends (they're happily shareable too). Kooper's is famous for their burgers, and their Gonzo Sliders are some of the tastiest we've ever had. We think it's the secret bacon-and-veg mixture.

Makes 3 sliders

2 slices applewood-smoked bacon, cut into small strips

1 tablespoon diced onion

1 tablespoon diced celery

2 tablespoons diced fresh shiitake mushrooms

1½ tablespoons Flying Dog Gonzo Porter beer

9 ounces ground beef, preferably Black Angus

Shredded cheddar cheese

3 slider buns

Jalapeño ranch dressing (recipe follows)

Lettuce

3 slices plum (Roma) tomato

3 ounces caramelized onion

Heat a sauté pan over medium heat and render bacon until crispy. Add onion, celery, and mushrooms and sauté until golden brown. Deglaze the pan with Flying Dog Gonzo Porter, scraping up any brown bits on the bottom, and cook until the beer has evaporated. Set aside to cool.

When cooked ingredients have cooled, mix them thoroughly into the ground beef. Form 3 square patties, approximately 3 ounces each. Cook the burgers on a grill or in a hot skillet until they are done to your liking. In the last few minutes of cooking, top with shredded cheddar so it melts.

Toast the slider buns and smear both halves with a bit of jalapeño ranch dressing. Top bottom bun with lettuce, slice of tomato, hamburger patty, caramelized onions, and top bun.

Jalapeño Ranch Dressing

1 jalapeño   **1 cup ranch dressing**
1 lime

In a food processor, puree the jalapeño with the juice of one lime. Add the ranch dressing and pulse to combine.

Courtesy of Kooper's Tavern (p. 82)

Tuna & Beet Tartare

The menu at B&O American Brasserie has a raw-bar section that offers a bit more than the usual oysters and clams on the half shell. The tuna and beet tartare shows off how delicious a "surf and turf" dish can be. Beets, their sweet earthiness making them the ultimate in "turf," match surprisingly well with cubes of raw tuna. The two, when combined with an avocado and wasabi puree, make a dish that is as visually stunning as it is flavorful.

Serves 2–4 as an appetizer

2 large golden beets
1 pound sushi-grade ahi tuna
Zest and juice of 1 lime
1 tablespoon minced shallots
1 teaspoon finely grated ginger
1½ tablespoons olive oil
½ tablespoon minced chives
½ teaspoon finely chopped
  serrano chili
Salt, white pepper, and black
  pepper to taste

1 avocado
1 tablespoon wasabi powder
¼ cup sour cream
2 tablespoons lime juice
Tabasco sauce to taste
1 teaspoon American sturgeon
  caviar
1 tablespoon olive oil
Micro greens for garnish

Preheat oven to 325°F. Place beets in a baking dish, drizzle with 1½ tablespoons olive oil, and season with salt and pepper. Cover dish and bake for 2 to 3 hours, or until beets are tender. Remove beets from oven and allow to cool. Once cool, peel beets and dice them into ½-inch squares.

Dice tuna into ½-inch squares and place into a bowl with the beets. Dress the tuna and beets with 1 teaspoon of the lime zest, the lime juice, shallots, ginger, olive oil, chives, and serranos. Season with salt and black pepper to taste.

Slice avocado in half, remove pit, and scoop flesh into a blender. Add wasabi powder, sour cream, and lime juice and puree the mixture until smooth. Season with salt, white pepper, and Tabasco.

To plate, place avocado-wasabi mousse on the plate and top with tuna and beet mixture. Combine caviar and 1 tablespoon olive oil and drizzle over the tuna and around the plate; top with micro greens.

Courtesy of Executive Chef Thomas Dunklin of B&O American Brasserie (p. 129)

Woody's Fish Tacos

Woody's Rum Bar's version of the fish taco is so fresh tasting, it will take you straight to Baja California. The recipe below calls for removing the seeds and ribs from the jalapeños (the source of capsaicin, the compound that makes peppers hot); if you'd prefer a spicier dish, leave in some of the seeds in either or both the sauce and the pico de gallo.

Serves 2–4

1 teaspoon ground cumin
½ teaspoon ground paprika
1 teaspoon chopped garlic
1 pound fish fillets, cut into finger-size pieces (we recommend mahimahi or tilapia)

1 tablespoon cooking oil
Salt and pepper
Small flour tortillas
Shredded cheese
Woody's sauce (recipe follows)
Pico de gallo (recipe follows)
Taco slaw (recipe follows)

Combine spices, garlic, and fish fingers in a large bowl, mixing well to coat fish. Cover and refrigerate for 1 hour.

Heat the oil in a skillet. Fry the fish until browned and crisp. Season with salt and pepper.

Assemble tacos by placing a couple pieces of fish in a warmed flour tortilla. Top with cheese, Woody's sauce, pico de gallo, and slaw. Enjoy!

Woody's Sauce

½ cup mayonnaise
½ cup sour cream
½ bunch cilantro
2 green onions

1 small jalapeño, seeds and ribs removed
Juice of 2 small limes
Salt and pepper

In a blender, puree all ingredients together until smooth. Season to taste.

Pico de Gallo

6 plum (Roma) tomatoes, diced
1 small red onion, diced fine
1 small jalapeño, seeds and ribs removed, diced fine

Juice of 1 lime
½ bunch of cilantro, chopped fine
Salt and pepper to taste

In a medium bowl combine all ingredients.

Taco Slaw

4 cups shredded cabbage
½ cup diced red onion
½ bunch cilantro, chopped

¼ cup lime juice
Salt and pepper to taste

In a large bowl combine all ingredients.

Courtesy of Woody's Rum Bar (p. 90)

Crab Cake Tacos

Crab cakes are an unconventional filling for tacos, to say the least, but somehow the Gypsy Queen Food Truck makes it work. The red chile aioli, with its touch of sweet heat, is so delicious, we find ourselves slathering it on burgers, turkey sandwiches, and as a dip for vegetables.

Serves 4–6

- 2 eggs
- ½ cup homemade or store-bought mayo
- White bread, cut into small cubes, to fill 1 cup
- 2 tablespoons Worcestershire sauce
- 1 tablespoon Old Bay

- 2 pounds jumbo lump crabmeat
- 2 tablespoons butter
- Taco-size corn tortillas
- Shredded cabbage
- Red chile aioli (recipe follows)
- Chopped cilantro

Beat eggs and mayonnaise together until well combined and stir in bread cubes. Add Worcestershire and Old Bay. Carefully fold in crabmeat. Form mixture into 10 patties and refrigerate for at least 1 hour.

In a cast-iron skillet, melt butter over medium heat. Add crab cakes in 2 batches and cook until golden brown on both sides, about 3 minutes per side.

To serve, warm a corn tortilla on a hot griddle or toast over an open flame. Fill with a large pinch of shredded cabbage, top with a crab cake, drizzle with red chile aioli, and sprinkle with fresh cilantro.

Red Chile Aioli

1 cup homemade or store-
bought mayonnaise

2 cloves chopped garlic

1 tablespoon of chipotle in
adobo, minced

¼ cup cilantro, finely chopped

2 tablespoons of brown sugar

Pinch of Old Bay

Combine all ingredients. Refrigerate until ready to use.

Courtesy of Annemarie Langton, Chef and Owner of the Gypsy Queen Food Truck (p. 284)

Spaghettoni all' Amatriciana

Traditionally, this dish is made with bucatini, a thick spaghetti-like pasta with a hole running down the length of it. At Chazz they use a thick, hole-less spaghetti called spaghettoni that they make in-house. You can use any sort of long, thick tubular or cylindrical pasta. Guanciale is a bacon made from pork jowl or cheek; if you can't find that, pancetta makes a fine substitute. Either way, the dish will be spicy and delicious.

Serves 4

- 1 pound spaghettoni (or your favorite pasta shape)
- ½ pound guanciale, thinly sliced (by hand), then diced into ¼-inch squares
- 1 teaspoon extra virgin olive oil (to cook guanciale)
- 1–2 tablespoons extra-virgin olive oil
- 3 cloves garlic, thinly sliced
- 1 small red onion, cut into very thin julienne slices
- 1½ teaspoons red pepper flakes
- 2 cups basic fresh tomato sauce
- Salt and pepper to taste
- Grated pecorino cheese to taste
- Chopped Italian parsley as garnish

Bring salted water to a boil and cook the pasta according to the package directions until al dente, about 12 minutes, while preparing the sauce.

Place the guanciale (or pancetta) in one layer in a large sauté pan along with a teaspoon of the olive oil, and cook over medium heat until most of the fat has been rendered, about 4

minutes. *Discard all but 1 tablespoon of the rendered fat from the pan. Add the remaining olive oil, garlic, onion, and pepper flakes and cook over medium heat until the vegetables are a light golden brown. Add the tomato sauce and season lightly with salt and pepper to taste. Reduce the heat and allow to simmer for 8 minutes.*

Drain and do not rinse the pasta. Add it to the pan with the sauce. Increase the heat to high and toss to coat the pasta well, about 1 minute. Add chopped parsley and pecorino cheese, toss well, and portion the pasta into 4 plates. Serve immediately.

Courtesy of Sergio Vitale, Owner of Chazz: A Bronx Original (p. 47)

Ropa Vieja

While the recipe for Chef Marta Ines Quintana's delectable ropa vieja, served at her restaurant, Havana Road, seems involved, it's a great dish to tackle on a weekend afternoon. The dish can be prepared in advance, which will enhance the flavors, and it's easy to reheat for a quick weeknight supper. In Cuba this dish is traditionally served with black beans and rice (congri), yucca with mojo, and sweet plantains.

Serves 4–6

- **2 quarts water or enough to cover the brisket**
- **3 pounds flat/first cut brisket, trimmed of excess fat**
- **1 teaspoon whole black peppercorns**
- **3 dried bay leaves**
- **1 teaspoon sea salt**
- **4 cloves peeled garlic**
- **1 teaspoon extra-virgin olive oil**

Use a Dutch oven or roasting pan with a tight-fitting lid into which the brisket will fit snugly. Put 2 quarts of water into the pan and bring to a boil. Add the brisket. The water should just cover the meat; if there is too much or too little, remove or add as needed.

Add the remaining ingredients. Reduce heat and cover the pan, keeping the liquid at a rapid simmer. Cook for 2 to 2½ hours, until meat is fork tender, checking from time to time to make sure the water hasn't evaporated by more than half.

When brisket is done, turn off the heat, remove the lid, and allow meat to sit in the cooking liquid for 30 minutes. While meat is resting, make the sauce.

Sauce

¼ cup extra-virgin olive oil

1 cup finely diced green pepper

1 cup finely diced yellow onion

1 tablespoon finely minced
garlic

1 tablespoon Kosher salt

1 cup dry white wine (divided
use)

1 teaspoon ground black pepper

1 teaspoon sweet paprika

1 teaspoon ground cumin

1 tablespoon onion powder

1 tablespoon garlic powder

1 teaspoon dried oregano

1 teaspoon dried basil

¾ cup tomato paste

1 cup tomato sauce

Juice of 2 limes

Heat a large 4- or 5-quart saucepan over medium high heat. To it, add the ¼ cup of extra-virgin olive oil, the green peppers, onions, garlic, and Kosher salt. Stir for about 2 minutes, then add ½ cup of the white wine. Cook until the onions become translucent. At this point stir in the ground black pepper, sweet paprika, cumin, onion powder, and garlic powder. Rub the dried oregano and basil between the palms of your hands before adding to the pot. Stir, then add the tomato paste and remaining white wine. Continue stirring for 5 to 8 minutes, making sure ingredients are well blended before adding the tomato sauce.

Simmer sauce for an additional 6 to 8 minutes. Sauce will be thick; if you want to thin the sauce, add a bit more white wine.

Assembly:

Remove brisket from cooking liquid and place on a cutting board.

Strain cooking liquid. In the Dutch oven used to cook the meat, combine 2 cups of strained cooking liquid with the finished sauce and the juice of 2 limes. Reserve any leftover cooking liquid (leftovers can be frozen).

With 2 forks, shred the still-hot meat into long strings. Once all of the meat has been shredded, add to the prepared sauce. Simmer meat and sauce over low heat for 20 to 30 minutes. If the sauce starts to get too thick, thin with a bit of the reserved cooking liquid.

Courtesy of Marta Ines Quintana, Chef and Owner of Havana Road (p. 223)

Wild Boar Ragu

Aldo's wild boar ragu, an aromatic sauce thick with shredded meat, became a signature for the restaurant shortly after its introduction nearly 10 years ago. The wild boar used at Aldo's is raised on a Texas ranch; ask your favorite butcher for availability. If you can't find it in your area, then substitute a nice piece of pork shoulder. Serve it Aldo's-style, over fresh pappardelle, a wide flat noodle a bit broader than fettuccine, or any other fresh pasta.

Serves 6–8

3½ pounds wild boar shoulder or butt
Salt and pepper
½ cup extra-virgin olive oil
2 onions, finely diced
2 carrots, finely diced
5 stalks celery, finely diced
3 bay leaves

6 cloves garlic, smashed
1 teaspoon minced fresh rosemary leaves
3 tablespoons tomato paste
2 bottles dry red wine
½ can peeled plum tomatoes
8 cups chicken stock
Pappardelle

Season the meat with salt and pepper. Cut the meat into large pieces about the size of a hamburger. Heat half of the olive oil in a large casserole over high heat and add the meat. Cook the meat, turning frequently, until it is browned on all sides, about 15 minutes.

At the same time in a separate large casserole over high heat, sauté the onions in the remaining olive oil and cook until golden. Add the carrots, celery, bay leaves, garlic cloves, and rosemary. Season well with salt and pepper. Stir in the tomato paste. Add the wine *and simmer for 30 minutes. Add the tomatoes, the browned meat, and the stock, stir them in thoroughly, then simmer for about 1 hour, or until the meat is very tender.*

Remove the meat and set aside. Once it's cool enough to handle, shred the meat with a fork. Return the meat to the pot and simmer for another 15 to 30 minutes, until it is a nice thick ragu consistency.

Cook the pasta to al dente, according to the package directions. Drain and do not rinse. Sauté the pasta and add enough ragu to coat—but not overwhelm—over medium heat for a few minutes. Serve with Parmigiana Reggiano.

Courtesy of Sergio Vitale, Owner of Aldo's (p. 62)

Imperial Crab

Typically, crab imperial is made with a mayonnaise-based sauce. Not so at the Prime Rib, where their over-the-top delicious crab imperial is made with a decadent, mustard-flavored béchamel. It's gorgeous on its own, served in ramekins, with some crusty slices of baguette on the side, but it becomes a completely evil indulgence when served atop a juicy steak, broiled fish, or even chicken.

Serves 6–8

2 quarts half-and-half
12 ounces chicken stock
2½ ounces dry sherry
2 ounces Gulden's mustard
⅛ teaspoon Old Bay seasoning
½ cup of butter
½ cup of flour

1 pound of jumbo lump crab
3 tablespoons clarified butter, melted
3 teaspoons finely minced parsley
Lemon wedges

In a 3-quart saucepan, whisk together half-and-half, chicken stock, dry sherry, Gulden's mustard, and Old Bay seasoning. Cook on low heat for 1 hour, until reduced by about one-quarter.

While the half-and-half mixture is cooking, make the roux. In separate saucepan melt the butter and whisk in flour. Cook until golden brown, stirring nearly constantly.

Gradually whisk in the reduced half-and-half mixture. The sauce should be thickened to a medium cream consistency.

Allow sauce to cool. Once cool, gently fold in the crabmeat, taking care not to break the lumps. Spoon mixture into 6 to 8 small ceramic cooking shells or ramekins.

Preheat oven to 350°F. Bake filled ramekins for 15 to 20 minutes, until heated through.

Remove from oven, drizzle with clarified butter and sprinkle with parsley. Serve with lemon wedges.

Wine pairing suggestions: 2010 Pine Ridge Winery Chenin Blanc/Viognier; 2008 Grgich Hills "Estate Grown" Fume Blanc; 2009 Duckhorn Sauvignon Blanc.

Courtesy of David J. Derewicz, General Manager of The Prime Rib (p. 148)

Raw Beet Ravioli

Proponents of the raw-food movement favor uncooked and unprocessed plant foods that have not been heated above 104°F. Great Sage, in Howard County, offers several dishes that please the raw foodie's palate, including this savory concoction of raw beets filled with a nut "cheese." It's so delicious, you won't care that it's completely raw, and you definitely won't miss the dairy.

Serves 6–8

For the sunflower cheese:

1 cup sunflower seeds
½ cup cashews
¼ cup pecans
3 tablespoons fresh rosemary, chopped
3 tablespoons fresh thyme, chopped

3 tablespoons fresh oregano, chopped
1 cup water
4 tablespoons lemon juice
Salt and pepper to taste

For the beet slices:

4 red or golden beets
2 cups rice wine vinegar
2 tablespoons ground coriander
2 cups olive oil

4 tablespoons lemon juice
1 tablespoon salt
1 teaspoon black pepper

For the basil pesto:

1 cup olive oil
⅓ cup cashews
2 cups fresh basil
1 tablespoon lemon juice

Salt and pepper to taste
Salad greens for garnish

Soak the sunflower seeds and nuts in water for at least 2 hours or overnight. Drain when ready to use.

Peel the beets and slice with a mandolin so that slices are very thin and round.

Make the beet marinade by combining the rice wine vinegar, ground coriander, olive oil, lemon juice, and salt and pepper with a whisk.

Place beets into the marinade and let sit at least 2 hours or until slices are tender.

After the sunflower seeds and nuts are drained, place them into a food processor with the rest of the ingredients for the cheese and blend until smooth. If the cheese is too thick and will not smooth out, add water a tablespoon at a time while blending.

When beet slices are tender, remove them from the marinade and lay slices out on a flat work surface.

Place a spoonful of cheese (a melon scoop or small ice cream scoop works great for this) on each beet slice and cover cheese with another beet slice to form each ravioli.

Make the basil pesto by placing all ingredients in a high-powered blender and blending until smooth.

Place 3 beet raviolis in the center of a plate, place a small amount of salad greens on top and garnish with basil pesto.

Courtesy of Holly Kaufman, Managing Partner of Great Sage (p. 268)

Cape Fear River Scallops

One of the most popular dishes at Langermann's is the Cape Fear River Scallops, which are served over a pile of decadently creamy grits. This dish is quite rich, but worth every calorie.

Serves 4

- **16 ounces clam juice**
- **1 ounce heavy cream**
- **8 ounces softened butter**
- **1 ounce diced tomatoes**
- **1 teaspoon chopped scallions**
- **3 strips bacon, cooked and chopped**
- **1 tablespoon cooking oil**

- **12 10/20-per-pound drypack sea scallops (if you can't find drypack scallops, make sure to blot the shellfish dry with paper towels)**
- **Salt and pepper to taste**
- **12 ounces of cooked creamy grits (recipe follows)**
- **Parsley for garnish**

In a small saucepan over low heat, reduce the clam juice to 2 ounces. Add cream and allow to reduce until large bubbles appear in mixture. Whisk in butter.

Stir in tomatoes, scallions, and bacon. Remove from heat and set aside in a warm area.

Heat a large sauté pan over medium-high heat and add a tablespoonful of oil. When the oil shimmers and barely begins to smoke, add the scallops and cook them until golden brown on the bottom, about 2 minutes. Using tongs, flip scallops and brown on the other side. Season with salt and pepper and remove from heat.

For each serving, place three ounces of grits in a mound at the bottom of a bowl. Arrange three scallops over grits in a triangular shape. Pour sauce over scallops. Garnish with a sprig of parsley.

Creamy Grits

8 ounces unsalted butter	2 tablespoons Kosher salt
2 quarts milk	16 ounces stone ground grits

In a sauce pot bring butter, milk, and salt to a boil. Slowly whisk in grits. Return to a boil, then turn the heat down so the grits are at a simmer. Cook for about 25 minutes, or until the grits are cooked to your liking, stirring occasionally so they don't stick or form a skin.

Courtesy of Neal Langermann, Chef and Owner of Langermann's (p. 108)

Sláinte's Shepherd's Pie

While soccer is religion at Sláinte, the food and beverages certainly don't come in second place. It's more like a three-way tie for first. Their shepherd's pie is a pretty traditional version of the mashed-potato-topped ground-beef pie. To make it even more traditional, substitute ground lamb for the ground beef.

Serves 6

- **2 pounds ground beef**
- **1 onion, finely diced**
- **1 carrot, small, diced**
- **½ tablespoon chopped garlic**
- **1 teaspoon salt**
- **1 teaspoon black pepper**
- **½ tablespoon fresh chopped thyme**
- **½ tablespoon fresh chopped rosemary**
- **1 tablespoon melted butter**
- **1 tablespoon flour**
- **2 cups beef broth**
- **Green peas**
- **Mashed potatoes**

In a large skillet add the beef, breaking up with a wooden spoon. Cook the meat about halfway, then add the onion, carrot, garlic, salt, pepper, and herbs. Continue to cook until all of the liquid that comes out of the meat and vegetables has evaporated and the beef is fully cooked. Strain off any excess fat.

Melt the butter in a sauce pot and whisk in the flour to make a roux. Cook for about 3 minutes, stirring constantly, then slowly whisk in the beef broth. Cook for an additional 5 minutes or so until the broth has thickened. Add the thickened broth to the cooked ground beef and vegetable mixture.

Preheat oven to 400°F.

In an oven-safe bowl, add beef mixture and a small handful of green peas. Top with mashed potatoes (we recommend using a piping bag) and bake for about 15 minutes or until the potatoes start to slightly brown and the meat mixture is heated through.

Courtesy of Sláinte (p. 85)

Donna's Bread Pudding

This recipe is deceptively simple. The result of all those eggs and milk is a moist pudding with a custardy bottom. While the recipe says any sort of white bread works fine, we prefer to make it with bits and pieces of leftover baguettes, brioche, and even walnut raisin bread.

Serves 10

1 cup sugar
10 eggs
6 cups milk
1 tablespoon cinnamon
1 tablespoon vanilla

1 loaf white bread (inexpensive, noncrusty bread works well), cut into 1-inch cubes (about 6 cups)
1 cup raisins

Preheat oven to 300°F.

In a large bowl combine sugar, eggs, milk, cinnamon, and vanilla; mix well.

Add bread and raisins. Allow to sit until bread is soaked through.

Pour into greased 9 x 12-inch baking dish. Bake for 1 hour, rotating dish halfway through baking time.

Serve warm or cold.

Courtesy of Alan Hirsch, Co-Owner of Donna's (p. 171)

Lemon Basil Sorbetto

This light and refreshing treat from Sotto Sopra makes an ideal palate cleanser between rich courses. It also makes a nice light dessert when served with a simple sugar cookie.

Serves 6–12

2 cups sugar
1½ cups water

2 cups fresh lemon juice
2–3 cups fresh basil leaves

Make a simple syrup by combining the sugar and water in a pot and bringing to a boil. Stir occasionally, to make sure the sugar has dissolved. Remove from heat and allow to cool.

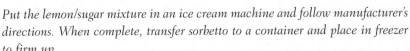

In a blender jar combine the basil and lemon juice. Blend until the basil has been broken down into small pieces.

Strain the lemon-basil mixture through a fine sieve. Place the liquid into a large bowl and discard the solids. Stir in the cooled simple syrup.

Put the lemon/sugar mixture in an ice cream machine and follow manufacturer's directions. When complete, transfer sorbetto to a container and place in freezer to firm up.

Courtesy of Sotto Sopra (p. 141)

Appendix A: Eateries by Cuisine

Maiwand Kabob, 252
Silk Road Bistro, 256

Chinese
Asian Court, 264
Chopstix Gourmet, 203
Grace Garden, 267
Hunan Taste, 251
Orient Restaurant, The, 239
Szechuan House, 241
Zhongshan Restaurant, 145

Coffeehouse
Daily Grind, 96
Lamill Coffee, 50
Spro, 162

Crab House
Bo Brooks, 102
Captain James Crabhouse &
    Restaurant, 103
Gunning's Seafood, 259
Mr. Bill's Terrace Inn, 195, 207
Reter's Crab House & Grille, 256
Riptide by the Bay, 85
Schultz's Crab House, 210

Deli
Attman's, 69, 250
Krakus Deli, 97
Lenny's Deli of Lombard Street, 67
Luigi's Italian Deli, 160
Mastellone's Deli and Wine, 244
Suburban House, 260
Weiss Deli, 68

Diner
Boulevard Diner, 201
Broadway Diner, 201
Double T Diner, 257
Jimmy's, 92
Nautilus Diner, 227
Pete's Grille, 179
Sip & Bite, 114

Eclectic
Alonso's, 167
Annabel Lee Tavern, 101
Artful Gourmet Bistro, 247
Club Charles, 146
Golden West Cafe, 159
Jack's Bistro, 107
Meet 27, 161
Rocket to Venus, 161

Edo Sushi, 36
Joss Cafe, 136
Kyodai Rotating Sushi Bar, 224
Matsuri, 24
Minato , 138
Pabu, 52
RA Sushi, 53
San Sushi Too, 231
Sushi Hana, 181
Sushi Sono, 278
Umi Sake, 234
Yamato Sushi, 236

Korean
Honey Pig Gooldaegee, 268
Jong Kak, 176
Nak Won, 177
Nam Kang, 178
Noodlerolla, 286
Shin Chon Garden, 277

Latin
Chicken Rico, 117
Fogo de Chão, 36
Havana Road, 223, 320
Mari Luna Latin Grille, 252
Max's Empanadas, 67

Talara, 54

Mediterranean
Baba's Mediterranean Kitchen, 21
Donna's, 171
Kali's Court, 79
Kali's Mezze, 79
7 West Bistro Grille, 232

Mexican
Blue Agave, 21
El Salto, 218
Fiesta Mexicana, 204
Holy Frijoles, 164
Loco Hombre, 177
Mari Luna Mexican Grill, 253
Miguel's Cocina y Cantina, 24
Nacho Mama's, 109
No Way Jose Cafe, 25
R&R Taqueria, 276
Tortilleria Sinaloa, 88

Middle Eastern
Cazbar, 131
Egyptian Pizza, 172
Lebanese Taverna, 50
Orchard Market & Cafe, 240

Appendix B: Dishes, Specialties & Specialty Food

Index